Women in Ritual
and Symbolic Roles

Women in Ritual and Symbolic Roles

Edited by
JUDITH HOCH-SMITH
Florida International University, Miami

and
ANITA SPRING
University of Florida, Gainesville

PLENUM PRESS · NEW YORK AND LONDON

Library of Congress Cataloging in Publication Data

Main entry under title:

Women in ritual and symbolic roles.

Includes bibliographies and index.
1. Women and religion—Addresses, essays, lectures. 2. Women (in religion, folk-lore, etc.)—Addresses, essays, lectures. 3. Sex role— Addresses, essays, lectures. I. Hoch-Smith, Judith. II. Spring, Anita.

BL458.W65   301.41'2   77-17448
ISBN 0-306-31067-8

© 1978 Plenum Press, New York
A Division of Plenum Publishing Corporation
227 West 17th Street, New York, N.Y. 10011

Printed in the United States of America

Preface

This volume of essays grew out of a symposium organized by Judith Hoch-Smith and Anita Spring for the 1974 American Anthropological Association meetings in Mexico City. The two-part symposium was entitled "Women in Ritual and Symbolic Systems: I. Midwives, Madonnas, and Mediums; II. Prostitutes, Witches, and Androgynes." The symposium participants were asked to explore theological, ritual, and symbolic aspects—both positive and negative—of the feminine cultural domain, using ethnographic materials with which they were familiar. The resulting papers have been revised, edited, and gathered together in *Women in Ritual and Symbolic Roles*.

The theoretical importance of these papers for the study of women's participation in culture and society rests on the assumption that religious ideas are paramount forces in social life, that relationships between the sexes, the nature of female sexuality, and the social and cultural roles of women are in large part defined by religious ideas. That this proposition remains valid long after religion itself has ceased to be a living truth in the lives of many people can be seen from the tenaciousness of Judeo-Christian ideas about women in the contemporary Western world. Both the expansion of life options for women and the creation of more positive cultural images of the female are intimately related to changes in the mytho-symbolic portraits that people carry around in their heads. These portraits are almost exclusively constructed from mythological and religious conceptions inherent in all facets of culture.

We feel that the focus of this collection on female religious representation and participation is unique to anthropological literature, which has for the most part considered only images and roles of men in religious expression. *Women in Ritual and Symbolic Roles* provides a cross-cultural perspective on women and religion, and some feeling for how these roles and images shape and determine the participation of women in social life.

We would like to thank Bernd Lambert, James Fernandez, Frances Henry, and Lucille Newman for offering valuable comments and criticisms of the papers when they were first read in Mexico City. We would like to thank Randy Kandel and Patricia Schmidt for reading and commenting on the introduction. Hyla Bassel Carey and Paulette Cohen at Plenum Publishing Corporation offered excellent critique and guidance throughout the preparation of the volume, and for their assistance we are grateful.

Judith Hoch-Smith

Miami

Anita Spring

Gainesville

Contributors

LORNA RHODES AMARASINGHAM received her Ph.D. in anthropology from Cornell University. She has taught anthropology at the University of Kentucky and Brandeis University, and has lectured at the Harvard Medical School. She has done field research in Sri Lanka and at the Laboratory in Social Psychiatry, Harvard Medical School. Her major areas of interest are symbolic anthropology, medical and psychological anthropology, oriental religion and philosophy, and South Asian ethnography. She has authored several articles on Sinhalese society. Among these is "Kuveni's Revenge: Images of Women in a Sinhalese Myth" in *Modern Ceylon Studies.* She is currently conducting follow-up research in Sri Lanka.

MARIGENE ARNOLD received her Ph.D. in anthropology from the University of Florida. She is Assistant Professor of Anthropology at Kalamazoo College, Michigan, and serves on the Women's Studies Advisory Board of the Great Lakes College Association. Past field work includes research on the status and role of women in the Mexican village of Cajititlán. She is involved in interdisciplinary teaching and a major area of interest is anthropology and education.

RUTH ANN BORKER received her Ph.D. in anthropology from the University of California, Berkeley. She is Assistant Professor of Anthropology and Women's Studies at Cornell University. She did field research in Edinburgh, Scotland, on religious communication and expressive strategies in three evangelical churches. Her main areas of interest are religion and symbolism, the anthropology of women, the ethnography of communication, and the study of complex societies. Publications include "Performing with Words," a review of *Explorations in the Ethnography of Speaking,* edited by Bauman and Sherzer, in *Reviews in Anthropology.*

PATRICIA JANE CLECKNER received her Ph.D. in anthropology from Cornell University, after having conducted research on heroin addicts and rehabilitation programs in New York City. She continued research among polydrug users in Florida as Director of Ethnography at the Center for Theoretical Social Research on Drug Abuse at the University of Miami. Currently, as Director of Research at Up Front, Inc., a drug information center in Miami, she is studying drug information dissemination and the social basis of functional drug use. She has published numberous articles on the cultural aspects of drug use in the U.S., which include "Blowing Some Lines: Intracultural Variation among Miami Cocaine Users" in *Journal of Psychedelic Drugs*, and "Cognitive and Ritual Aspects of Drug Use among Black Urban Males" in *Drugs, Ritual and Altered States of Consciousness*, edited by B. du Toit.

MOLLY C. DOUGHERTY received her Ph.D. in anthropology and a Master's degree in Nursing from the University of Florida, where she is now Associate Professor of Nursing. She is the author of *Becoming a Woman in Rural Black Culture* and several articles on health in rural communities. Her major areas of interest are health of minorities, health behaviors in community settings, women's health care, and population.

JUDITH HOCH-SMITH received her Ph.D. in anthropology from McGill University. She is Assistant Professor of Anthropology at Florida International University in Miami. She has carried out field research among the Mistassini Cree of north–central Quebec and the Yoruba of southwestern Nigeria. While in Nigeria her topic of research was modern, vernacular Yoruba folk theater and its relationship to social change. She has written articles on the folk theater, on Yoruba women, and on the Yoruba trickster. Her interests include images of women in religion and literature, African religion, meditation, self-healing, and natural diets.

DANIEL NATHAN MALTZ is a Ph.D. candidate in anthropology at the University of California at Berkeley. His field research was on religious speech and religious meaning in the pentecostal churches in Edinburgh, Scotland. His publications include "Primitive Time Reckoning as a Symbolic System" in the *Cornell Journal of Social Relations*, and "Introduction: Processual Analysis of American Kinship" in *Kroeber Anthropological Society Papers*. Current research interests include variation in world religions, anthropological perspectives on religious history, and anthropological approaches to American and British society.

SUSAN MIDDLETON-KEIRN received her Ph.D. in anthropology from the University of Florida. She is Associate Professor of Sociology and Anthropology at Jacksonville State University, Alabama. She spent more than two years doing field research in two apartheid-created urban black ghettos in the Republic of South Africa. She is the author of articles and papers on black South African urban living and women's studies, including "Voluntary Associations among Urban African Women" in *Communications from the African Studies Center*. Her major areas of interest are urban anthropology, applied anthropology, social structures and theory, and network analysis.

BARBARA G. MYERHOFF received her Ph.D. in anthropology from the University of California at Los Angeles. She is Professor of Anthropology at the University of Southern California. She has authored numerous books and articles, which include *Peyote Hunt: The Sacred Journey of the Huichol Indians*, a nominee for the National Book Award. She is the coeditor of *Symbol and Politics in Communal Ideology*, *Secular Ritual: Forms and Meanings*, and *Lifes' Careers: Cross-Cultural Studies of Growing Old*. Her film, *Number Our Days*, on Jewish octogenarians in Southern California, won the Special Jury Award for Outstanding Achievement in the Twentieth International San Francisco Film Festival, and the Public Broadcasting Corporation Special Interest Award in 1976 as well as an Academy Award for outstanding documentaries. She has done field research among the Huichol Indians of Mexico and among adolescents and the elderly in southern California. Her interests are wide-ranging and include religion, symbolism, gerontology, youth problems, and women's studies.

LOIS PAUL studied social science and psychiatric social work at the University of Chicago. She was a Research Associate in Anthropology at Stanford University and has taught anthropology in a program of nurses' training at Massachusetts General Hospital. She did field research in Guatemala on child development and the role of women in the Maya community of San Pedro la Laguna, and on various mental health projects in the Greater Boston area. She is the author of "The Mastery of Work and the Mystery of Sex in a Guatemalan Village" in M. Rosaldo and L. Lamphere, editors, *Woman, Culture and Society* and the coauthor of several papers on the life cycle in Middle America and changing marriage patterns. Ms. Paul died December 21, 1975.

RIV-ELLEN PRELL-FOLDES received her Ph.D. in anthropology from the University of Chicago. She is an instructor of anthropology at the University of Minnesota. She has conducted research in an urban American Jewish prayer community and has authored several papers on the subject, including "The Service of the Heart: The Self in Jewish Prayer." Her major areas of interest are religion, urban anthropology, ritual, myth and symbolism, and women in American culture.

ANITA SPRING received her Ph.D. in anthropology from Cornell University. She has taught in the Women's Studies Program at Cornell and at San Francisco State College. Currently, she is Assistant Professor of Behavioral Studies and Anthropology at the University of Florida. Her field work includes research among black families in San Francisco, the Washo Indians of Nevada, and the Luvale of Zambia. Her main interests are African studies, human sex roles, medical anthropology, and population. She is the author of "An Indigenous Therapeutic Style and Its Consequences for Natality" in J. Marshall and S. Polgar, editors, *Culture, Natality and Family Planning,* as well as other articles on ritual, women, and family life.

Contents

PART II

DUAL ASPECTS OF WOMEN: ARCHETYPIC NURTURANCE

Part III
Dual Aspects of Women: Archetypic Destruction

JUDITH HOCH-SMITH AND ANITA SPRING

Introduction

Female religious participation, female religious metaphors, and beliefs concerning female sexuality have similarities cross-culturally and historically. *Women in Ritual and Symbolic Roles* brings together a group of articles discussing the relationship of dominant female metaphors and ritual roles to ideas and practices concerning female reproductive and sexual energies in a variety of cultures and religious systems. The articles include discussions of Christian, Jewish, and Buddhist representations of women in sacred scriptures and ritual roles for women within those religions; feminine ritual participation in midwifery and possession cults in South Africa, Zambia, the southeastern United States, and Latin America; and negative feminine metaphors such as the witch and the prostitute from Ceylon, Africa, North America, and Europe. Most of these negative metaphors are based on ideas derived from mythology concerning female sexuality.

Women draw sacred attention primarily in connection with their reproductive statuses: as virgins and brides women may serve as pure, untainted symbolic vessels who can be "filled" with divine energy or who can approach the divine in public ceremonies. Sexually mature women receive the most attention in symbol, myth, and ritual, for society sees their "reproductive potential" as both highly positive and highly negative and in need of much control. Women who spend their sexually active years in childbearing channel their reproductive potential into positive cultural ends and their ritual roles are domestic rather than public. They care for household and lineage shrines, consecrate food, and ritually purify themselves before or after menstruation, intercourse, and childbirth. Those women whose reproductive capacities are limited

JUDITH HOCH-SMITH · Assistant Professor of Anthropology, Florida International University, Miami, Florida.   ANITA SPRING · Assistant Professor of Behavioral Studies and Anthropology, University of Florida, Gainesville, Florida.

through barrenness, illness, celibacy, infant and child mortality, or menopause often symbolically rechannel their reproductive energies into helping other women bear children by becoming midwives or healers. Divine calls and possession legitimate these ritual roles.

In no religious system do women's dominant metaphors derive from characteristics other than their sexual and reproductive status, while for men sexual status has little to do with religious representation and participation. Whether men are virgins or not does not determine their participation in ritual. Women are strikingly one-dimensional characters in mythology and ritual action. Images of women are reduced to their sexual function, women are excluded from leadership roles in most public rituals, and images of the divine are usually male. An exception to this occurs in some matrilineal societies where female ancestors constitute the most important aspect of the relationship between the divine and living people. However, in both unilineal and nonunilineal societies, women find ritual roles related to childbirth, rearing, and nurturing. Female healers can be seen as extending this female nurturing role to many afflicted members of society.

In most traditions, religion and its mythologies are the ultimate synthesizers of female metaphor from which many other forms of symbolic expression derive and find legitimation. At the heart of woman's exclusion from most public ritual roles and representations of the divine is what Hayes (1972) has called "the myth of feminine evil." This myth includes beliefs that female sexuality is polluting and contaminating to all things male, that women are more lustful and animal-like than men, weaker, less intelligent, and responsible for many of the ills of male society. We will begin this introduction by considering the dual modes, negative and positive, through which many cultures conceptualize the female image, and will further discuss the myth of feminine evil.

1. Chaotic Female Sexuality

Among the mythological ideas that both shape and reflect belief systems exists the notion that if woman is not the embodiment of evil she at least has long-standing ties with it. It is possible to see two thousand years of Western female history condensed in the story of Adam and Eve. Eve was caught by the Lord with the half-eaten fruit of knowledge and Adam claimed that even if he were guilty, nevertheless Eve had sinned first. The angry God of Israel—a strong male character—saw some merit in the excuse, for he then promptly made all womanhood subject to mankind. "I will greatly multiply your pain in childbearing," the Lord God is declared to have announced, "in pain you shall bring forth children, yet your desire shall be for your husband, and he shall rule over you" (Campbell 1970:322; Genesis 3:16). As Campbell ironically notes, "For nearly two thousand years [this myth] was accepted throughout the Western World as the absolutely dependable account of an event supposed to have taken place about a fortnight after the creation of the universe . . ." (1970:322–323). Campbell further suggests that this myth has had enormous influence on "the structure of human beliefs and the consequent course of civilization" for more than two millenia (1970:333). For this reason, it is impossible to understand contemporary images of women without first understanding the influence of the feminine archetype generated by the Judeo-Christian creation myth. As Ardener, following Jung, indicates, unconscious or general ideas (archetypes) are historically realized in specific guises (1975:xiv). It is possible to see that while general ideas of carnal female sexuality have existed for centuries, their specific cultural forms have included the witch, the prostitute, the evil seductress, the nagging wife, the overpowering mother, and the movie queen. The evolution of this carnal feminine image can be traced at a glance through the lineage of female seducers, one-dimensional women who bring about the downfall of men. Thus Eve begat Delilah, who begat Pandora, who begat Lady Macbeth, who begat Hedda Gabler, who begat Dietrich in *The Blue Angel*. As Janeway remarks, "In the process of art, a theme, often a mythic theme, is taken out of the dark and placed in a context that jibes with the world as it is seen and understood by both artist and audience. The theme is tested as a scientific hypothesis is tested: by confronting it with reality" (1971:31).

The idea of female evil is transformed into specific cultural expression through the manifestation of that culture's ideological content in art. (Thus Western authors continue Eve's geneology in literature and the theater.)All that woman is today is brought forward through thousands of years of history, changing in specific cultural form but generated by the same basic archetypes.

Many cultures outside the West reflect a similar view of women. Female sexuality is seen as a disruptive, chaotic force that must be controlled or coopted by men, periodically purified, and at times destroyed. Nowhere is this more true than in the creation myths of Hindu India, where originally the godhead was a unity containing both male and female principles. At the moment of creation the "feminine" leaps forward, spontaneously separating herself from the masculine, which results in the dualistic world. This feminine principle is personified by the goddess Kali, also called *Mahamaya*, Vast Illusion, or Mother of the World.

As Watts explains, "[Kali] is the embodiment of the Terrible Mother, the Spider Woman, the all devouring maw of the abyss, image of everything of which the human soul seems ultimately to be afraid. On the other hand . . . she is eternal womanhood, cherishing mother of the world . . ." (1969:84). According to Hindu mythology, the godhead Brahma evoked this "infinitely wily mother" for the beguiling of Shiva. She was brought up through her childhood in the practice of loving devotion to Shiva, who, when he first looked on Kali, allowed his heart to skip a beat, just enough time for an arrow of love to reach its mark. From then on Shiva left his yogic austerities alone while he and Kali lived together for 3600 years absorbed in sexual union or "world-illusion." Shiva's sexual entanglement with Kali lost him favor with the other gods, who thought Shiva was mired in "female illusion." In Hindu mythology women came to symbolize the eternal struggle that men must wage between materiality and spirit. Kali symbolizes the womb, connected with rebirth and consequent illusion and entanglement in the world. Creation myths like this, blaming women for the appearance of evil, for the disappearance of the gods from the earth, or for all the troubles of the present world are extremely common in many male-dominated cultures (Bamberger 1974).

The social causes behind this historical emphasis on the more carnal aspects of female sexuality have stimulated a considerable number of scholarly hypotheses. Douglas (1966) suggests an explanation for this "contamination" of female sexuality. When society strongly enforces male dominance as the primary principle of social organization, even by violence if need be, beliefs in sexual pollution are not highly developed. But, if other social rights of women—their economic, ritual, or political freedom, their sexual independence, or their right to be protected from male violence—interfere with the consistent application of the principles of male dominance, then beliefs concerning sexual pollution flourish. Gluckman (1965a, 1965b) believes that mystical beliefs in feminine evil mask basic conflicts in women's social position in all tribal societies. Douglas and Gluckman, drawing on data from the Lele, Zulu, Nupe, and Mae-Enga societies, among others, both agree that anxiety about female sexuality is attributed to the real disruptive role of women in the social system.

For example, men among the matrilineal Lele of Zaire (Douglas 1966) use women as a kind of currency with which to claim and settle disputes with one another. Men fight with each other over women, but they do not harm women physically. Women challenge total male rule by coquettish games in which they play off one man against the other. Among the Lele there exists considerable pollution concerning sex and blood.* Women are especially dangerous to male activities and male ritual participation calls for abstinence from sexual intercourse.

In the patrilineal culture of ancient Greece, contamination was avoided by limiting the "freedom" of Athenian women. Pomeroy (1976) records how Solon, the homosexual Athenian lawgiver of the sixth century B.C., solved the contradictions in male dominance which the independence of Athenian women implied. In order to stop his "cultured" male citizens from fighting among themselves over women and strengthen his "democracy," he regulated the walks, feasts, mourning, trousseaux, food, and drink of Athenian citizen women, who worked indoors and could not even go to the market. This distinction between good women and whores was instituted legally in that he abolished all forms of slavery and sale except one, the right of a male guardian to sell a woman who had lost her virginity. Female debasement and control of women by men was incipient in the mythic depiction of Greek goddesses who were once powerful but who later were dethroned by male gods. The divine progression from female-dominated generations to the superior and rational monarchy of Olympian Zeus, in which Athenian goddesses were denied sexual activity and became single-dimensional sexual women, finds documentation by Hesiod in the seventh century B.C. As Pomeroy observes,

> . . . three of the five Olympian goddesses are virgins. Athena is warrior, judge, and giver of wisdom, but she is masculinized and denied sexual activity and motherhood. Artemis is huntress and warrior, but also a virgin. Hestia is respected as an old maid. The two non-virginal goddesses come off no better: Aphrodite is pure sexual love, exercised with a pronounced irresponsibility. Hera is wife, mother and powerful queen, but she must remain faithful and suffer the promiscuity of her husband (1976:8).

The reduction of women to their function was stressed by Demosthenes, who said in the fourth century B.C., "We have mistresses for our enjoyment, concubines to serve our person, and wives for the bearing of legitimate offspring" (quoted in Pomeroy 1976:8). Coming close to agreeing with Douglas, Pomeroy, summarizing the Greek experience, states that a fully realized female engenders anxiety in the insecure male (1976:9).

---

*By contrast, the Pygmies, who share work between the sexes, and among whom women have much autonomy, do not view sex and menstrual blood as harmful. They do not have a male-dominated social organization either (Friedl 1975:29–31: Sacks 1974).

Fatima Mernissi (1975) describes how Moroccan Muslims solve the contradictions in male supremacy which female sexuality and independence pose for their society: they veil their sexually mature women and banish them to the indoors. Women are veiled to protect society from *fitna* (which means both chaos and beautiful woman). Muslim women are thought to have *qaid* power, the power to deceive and defeat men, not by force, but by cunning and intrigues; *qaid* is seen by several male Islamic scholars as the most disruptive force in Muslim society. Sexually mature, married women are thought to be insatiable, and the folk culture tells of a repugnant female demon called *Aicha Kandisha*, libidinous and with pendulous lips and breasts, who assaults men in dark places and penetrates their bodies. The Prophet, who no doubt would have been in sympathy with Solon and the inventors of Genesis, said, "After my disappearance there will be no greater source of chaos and disorder for my nation than women"(quoted in Mernissi 1975:13).

In their classic pamphlet, *Witches, Midwives and Nurses,* Ehrenreich and English (n.d.) describe how church fathers in the European Middle Ages sought to reduce contradictions in their dominance. Female folk specialists, revered as wisewomen, healers, and priestesses, were accused of lasciviousness and witchcraft. The church's conceptualization of female carnality included the fear that witches could castrate men, steal their genital organs, or make them impotent during their sleep. In the fifteenth century, two Dominican priests wrote the *Malleus Maleficarum,* a manual describing how to recognize, torture, and execute witches. This grotesque book depicts women as weak, light-headed, impressionable, whimsical, and evilly consumed by rage. The book elucidates that for these reasons the Devil easily seduces women and fills a woman's body during her sleep, thus setting in motion her witchly enterprises. As depicted by the two Friars, the witch was the mirror image of the wisewoman or midwife. She received a call from the Devil rather than from God, she killed babies rather than helping them live, she caused illness rather than curing it, she ruined crops rather than helping them to grow, she castrated men rather than nurturing them with love. Witches were gradually eliminated during three centuries of history. Estimates vary as to how many women were executed, but it is certain that when witch trials ended, medicine was completely in the hands of university-trained male physicians, and the "old religion" of the wisewoman had almost totally disappeared.

Unlike the social contradictions in male-dominance theories, psychological explanations regarding female carnality derive from the ambivilance of the mother–child relationship (Klein 1932; Janeway 1971; Campbell 1970). At birth, the child and its mother constitute one being;

the child feeds from the mother and the mother omnipotently fulfills the infant's desires. However, the mother cannot anticipate every desire and sometimes the child is left alone or is hungry or experiences fear and pain. Eventually, the mother must break the link with her child, at which time the two no longer are one and the child is left alone. With such experiences the child begins to associate the Holy Mother image with danger and a fear of loss, separation, and destruction, which are deeply imprinted on its psyche. Thus the carnal female image is combined with that of the loving woman. The Hansel and Gretel story may be cited as a story synthesizing these elements: children are attracted to a beautiful house in the forest, a house made of sweets—analogous to the nourishment that the mother offers the child with her own body— but instead a witch lives there who will try to devour the children. However one wishes to interpret the dual faces of the Mother, as Campbell says, "In mythology and rite, as well as in the psychology of the infant, we find the imagery of the mother associated almost equally with beatitude and danger, birth and death, the inexhaustible nourishing beast and the tearing claws of the ogress"(1970:71). When the boy becomes an adult, this model in part defines the man's intimate relationships with all other women. Thus while a woman offers intense pleasure to a man in intercourse, her sexuality unconsciously may be feared by him as exposing him to loss and destruction, that is, castration. When the girl becomes an adult, this model defines in part her own actions as a mother and her relationships to other females.

These theories try to explain the cultural notions of the mystical and evil nature of woman. Rooted as these are in female sexuality, we note the amazing predominance of male thinking about female sexuality. For example, it is certainly remarkable that things as *periodic* as female monthly and reproductive cycles are understood as intrusions of chaos into an otherwise orderly universe. One of the greatest problems facing the liberation of women is the tenacity with which this negative and single-dimensional imagery regarding female sexuality persists in ritual and myth.

2. Positive Female Images

When we examine the mythological records of many cultures we find that an age of "matriarchy" precedes the present paternalistic order. This was an age in which women served as priestesses and political leaders, in which the divine was imbued with feminine attributes, and in which female sexuality was not considered evil. An interest in myths about feminine divinity is current once again among some poets and members of the counterculture, who link the present ecological crises to the forgetting of our Mother the Earth, who shows people the laws of the natural order. Robert Graves, expressing this view, remarks that the longer we postpone the revitalizing hour of the return to the Goddess, "the more exhausted by man's irreligious improvidence the natural resources of the soil and sea become" (1971:486). Graves and others believe that the "true Matrilineal religion" was spread through Europe, the Near East, and perhaps Africa, and was corrupted in late Minoan times by patrilineal Asian invaders with aggressive male gods who subordinated the Great Goddess. The revival of the Goddess hypothesis rests on historically speculative data, and Grave's own adoration of "the Goddess Muse" is subject to criticism as a myth that puts woman on a pedestal from which she must not stir and from which she intuitively directs the activities of the male universe, a role not unfamiliar to contemporary women. Bamberger notes that in many "rule of women" myths, women eventually lose control of power or do not know how to handle it correctly (1974:279). The myth of Lilith's banishment from the Garden of Eden and Adam's subsequent domination of Eve fits the model (Goldenberg 1974).* Bamberger fears that the myth of matriarchy thus reiterates the justification for male dominance and female inferiority and "instead of heralding a promising future harks back to a past darkened by repeated failures" (1974:280). Webster (1975), on the other hand, sees in the myth a model for the feminist future.

Perhaps the poet Adrienne Rich (1976) has appreciated the spiritual difference between the Great Goddess and, say, the Virgin Mother, the image that the pedestal represents, more than any other author. According to Rich, the question "was there ever a true matriarchy" obscures the more important point that there was most certainly a time when Woman was revered in several aspects, when worship of the Goddess prevailed, and when myths depicted strong and sacred feminine figures. Speaking of the Venus figures that have been found from Western Europe into Siberia, Rich asks us to consider their image:

> . . . they express an attitude toward the female charged with the awareness of her intrinsic importance, her depth of meaning, her existence at the very center of what is necessary and sacred. She is beautiful in ways we have almost forgotten, or which have become defined as ugliness. Her body pos-

---

*Lilith was the first woman created by the Lord, who formed her from the ground just as he formed Adam. She was equal to Adam in all ways and refused to do his bidding. Adam accused her of many crimes and she was later banished.

sesses mass, interior depth, inner rest, and balance. She is not smiling; her expression is inward looking or ecstatic, and sometimes her eyeballs seem to burn through the air. If, as very often, there is a child at her breast, or on her lap, she is not absorbed in contemplation of him (the adoration of the Virgin with the Son as the Center of the world will come later). She is not particularly young, or rather, she is absolutely without age. She is *for-herself* even when suckling an infant, even when, like the image of the Ephesian Diana, she appears as a cone of many breasts. Sometimes she is fanged, wielding a club, sometimes she is girdled by serpents; but even in her most benign aspect the ancient Goddess is not beckoning to her worshippers, she exists, not to cajole or reassure man, but to assert herself (1976:93–94).

This prepatriarchal religion saw the female presence in all parts of the universe, but especially in the cycles of the moon. Rich refers to this as "gynomorphized" thought.* Lucius, in Apuleius's *Golden Ass*, addresses this feminine periodic influence while invoking the Lunar goddess:

Then I thought with myself that this was the most secret time, when that goddess had most puissance and force, considering that all human things be governed by her providence; and that not only all beasts private and tame, wild and savage, be made strong by the governance of her light and godhead, but also things inanimate and without life; and I considered that all bodies in the heavens, the earth, and the seas be by her increasing motions increased and by her diminishing motions diminished. . . (quoted in Graves 1971:70)

Lucius, in this speech to the Great Lunar Goddess, poetically acknowledges the intimate correspondence between lunar and human cycles. Campbell finds that goddess figures are associated with the agricultural cycle and the weather; the protection of children, adults, and all animals; sea journeys; illness and health; and hunting (1970:138–139).

Certainly the connection of the moon with the female cycle finds recognition by nearly every culture, but it is only recently that we are beginning to understand the intimate correspondence of the cycles of the moon to other human life cycles in terms of conception, birth, and bleeding. Recent scientific studies suggest the interdependence of natural, human, and cosmic cycles. The moon controls tidal rhythms, which all marine animals that have both a daily and a monthly lunar cycle share; heavy rains occur most often on days after the full and the new moon; all life has metabolic rhythms corresponding to the lunar period. Called the "great midwife" by some cultures, the moon is corre-

---

*Some feel that the ideas and practices associated with prehistoric gynomorphized religion were retained in the mystery cults of Eleusis (centered on mother and daughter), Corinth, and Samothrace; in the mystery schools of Ireland and Wales; and in the witch covens of western Europe (Graves 1971; Pomeroy 1976; Rich 1976; Ehrenreich and English 1973).

lated with human birth times and menstrual cycles; the ability of a mature woman to conceive may be found to correlate with the phase of the moon on her own day of birth. The moon's phases coincide with bleeding crises in hospitals, violent episodes in mental patients, crimes of psychotic motivation, and fluctuations in the human life field. The sun's activities also correlate with a diverse number of human and terrestrial phenomena (Watson 1973:21–31, 47–51, 59–70; Blair 1976). The goddess-cult religions may have had knowledge of these relationships, which we are just beginning to admit are inextricably tied. Such correlations would have been established through careful, concentrated observation of one's own body and agricultural fields in nature over time and would have been synthesized in the symbolic expression of the Great Goddess cult.

Many non-Western peoples' rituals associated with agriculture connect with the goddess and the gynomorphization of the earth. Among the Hopi (Waters 1963) the Corn Mother is central to every ceremonial and represents the nourishing functions of the Earth in relationship to the people. The Hopi recognize that corn, their staple crop, will be built into their flesh, and thus they are mystically and physically united with the Mother. Many Hopi ceremonials focus on the growing of corn; the crop is foremost in the minds and hearts of the people while its growth and ritual cycle unfold in close relationship to the movements of celestial bodies.

Symbolic correspondences between human, earth, and lunar cycles appear to be celebrated within the enormous Neolithic conical chalk structure near Avebury, England, called Silbury Hill. Michael Dames (1976) recently linked this structure to a prehistoric cult of gynomorphic theology in Europe. He discovered through careful observation, measurements, and aerial photography that the hill and the moat enclosing it may be a portrayal of the Great Goddess in the pregnant squatting position; Silbury Hill is her womb and the rest of her body forms the moat around her. At Silbury, reflections of the full moon on the subterranean water at the time of the annual first fruits ceremony display the birth of the Divine Harvest Child. The hill synthesizes meanings from the cult of the Goddess: the dynamic processes of the fattening of the moon, the transformation of corn from green to gold, and the stirrings of the unborn child, which are linked together in universal cosmic rhythm. Megalithic religion survived into Celtic Britain through the Druids, whom the Romans later brutally persecuted. Some postulate the presence of many women among the Druid priests, and women may well have been in charge of the cult. These very women may have been preservers of the knowledge of natural birth, healing, and agriculture, passing it from woman to woman throughout the centuries until their descendants were later prosecuted as witches during the European Middle Ages when the male monopolization of religion and healing was taking place (Ehrenreich and English n.d.). It is worthwhile to reiterate that far from being "superstitious primitive" cultists of Moon Worship, Great Goddess cult members may have understood, and been capable of working with, simple natural laws of the universe. If women were in charge of such cults, if their beings metaphorically suggested the unity of the universe and the continuity between natural laws and human generations, we can well imagine, as Rich has said, the "sense of herself" that prehistoric woman may have had.

Although positive attributes of the female nurturant metaphor continue to exist in the Western world, they are reserved for only those women who literally fulfill that function, i.e., those who actually become good wives and mothers. Women outside the middle-class Western world retain power in some ritual domains—midwifery, possession cults, curing rituals—but women within the West for the most part have lost these gynomorphic alternatives to their procreative role. Even the childbirth process itself has been taken out of female hands and mystified by male medicine (Ehrenreigh and English n.d., 1973). It is significant that an important part of the women's liberation movement in the United States has been occupied with returning childbirth to females and "renaturalizing" and spiritualizing the process. With the publication of books like May's *Spiritual Midwifery* (1975) childbirth among Western white women is again becoming known as an ecstatic time during which a woman may even experience the divine.

Some of the new images of women also may come from the documentation of the similarities between male and female sexual response. Scientific research dispels many negative themes in the representation of female sexuality: carnality, insatiability, passivity, frigidity (Masters and Johnson 1966, 1970). Female sexuality is no longer passive; orgasm is a woman's birthright, and sex is undertaken more often for enjoyment than for procreation. The comparability of female with male sexuality may alter the negative or unidimensional images of women's sexuality as intrinsically different from man's. Research overturns the remnants of female sexual duality that focused on different types of orgasm (vaginal and clitoral). Female sexuality, now a unified whole, is fast becoming devoid of male-created myths, which mystified the female sexual process. In the modern world, science often proves to be the great leveler. Perhaps it is in fact from science, the *de facto* religion of the twentieth century, and not traditional religions and sacred scriptures, that new metaphors for women will arise.

3. Women in Ritual and Symbolic Roles

The authors of the papers in this volume examine the theoretical and ethnographic relationship between feminine metaphor in religious and symbolic systems, female ritual and social roles, and beliefs about female sexuality. The first group of articles in this collection focuses on femininity and divinity as it exists in sacred scripture and as people act on the texts, predominantly within the hierarchic model. Daniel Maltz in "The Bride of Christ Is Filled with His Spirit" considers "the bride of Christ" as a dominant metaphor, which members of pentecostal churches of Edinburgh, Scotland, understand and use to express their relationship to the Christian church. The metaphoric usage rests directly on the nature of the sexual and marital relationship between men and women. The "bride" represents femaleness, which is defined as seductive and enticing—forces that draw and attract. "Christ" represents maleness, which is defined as overpowering and filling—forces that enter and penetrate. The hierarchical metaphor represents church members to Christ, Christ to God, humanity to divinity. Biological sexuality and social gender roles provide a set of structural metaphors for the relationship between nature and culture and receiver and giver. "Femaleness" is subservient to "maleness" at each level.

Marigene Arnold's paper, "Célibes, Mothers, and Church Cockroaches: Religious Participation of Women in a Mexican Village," generally follows the orientation of Maltz in that she finds that in Jalisco, Mexico, a woman's sexual and marital relationships correspond to her symbolic and ritual roles in the church. In contrast to the Scots, the mestizo Catholics attribute different meanings to the limiting cases of female sexual expression: thus the virgin rather than the bride plays a significant part in public religious rituals. Virginal, nonmarried women (adolescents and spinsters) and nonsexual widows carry out public rituals. Married, sexually active women center their religious participation around the household rather than the public arena. Thus "virginal" women provide a link between the communal ritual participation of men and the familial ritual participation of fertile women. These women are not religious experts or sacred professionals (cf. the chapters by Paul, Spring, Middleton-Keirn, and Dougherty); rather they are ordinary women who act out the hierarchical metaphors by virtue of their sexual experience.

Two papers discuss how women react to and utilize the metaphor and images about them through their participation in religious organizations. Ruth Borker in "To Honor Her Head" demonstrates that the multivocality of symbols (Turner 1967, 1974) permits men and women a variety of "symbolic strategies." This chapter examines a key symbol (Turner 1967) of women's position, the wearing of hats, in terms of their Biblical core meanings and situational meanings among Scottish Evangelical Christians. The Biblical symbolic repertoire shows the use of head coverings as representing subordination, dignity and modesty, and formality. The situational meanings vary and relate to the participation of women vis-à-vis men in various churches: the more equal the participation, the fewer hats worn by women. Pastors and women are part of the same social arena and manipulate hat wearing in terms of different strategies for women's participation.

Riv-Ellen Prell-Foldes in "Coming of Age in Kelton: The Constraints on Gender Symbolism in Jewish Ritual" analyzes a contemporary urban group of women who are trying to create new ritual roles for women within *halakhic* (law-centered) Judaism. Through her description, she questions the elasticity, flexibility, and accommodating nature of the ritual symbol. The Minyan, a communal prayer group of men and women, allows women ritual participation. Consequently, a creative "Sabbath Ritual" is rewritten by some of the women members to alter the notion of Jewish women in ritual by expanding a dominant, referential symbol, the Torah. Women in the Minyan begin to see their exclusion from ritual not as individual problems but rather as problems of their sex and culture. Further, women feel that it is not their lack of training and knowledge or their exclusion from this small prayer group that make them feel ritually alienated, but rather the fact that the experience of worship, the language of prayer, and the culture out of which the prayer was produced are alien to women. The Minyan women discover that ritual cannot change belief, but it can be used to present "female consciousness" of the present age. Rituals provide precise boundaries of tradition that allow people to dare great feats with safety, because the form itself suppresses any denial of tradition. Furthermore, the author argues that the male imagery and metaphors contained in liturgy, which the Minyan women found "exclusionary," cannot be changed without changing wider meanings. Symbols do have limits beyond which new meanings cannot be incorporated.

In Lorna AmaraSingham's chapter, "The Misery of the Embodied: Representations of Women in Sinhalese Myth," people view a non Western woman's domain of metaphor as a vehicle for the impermanence and sorrow of worldly pleasure. Sinhalese Buddhism, both doctrinal and operational, uses assumptions about physiological processes to contribute to negative symbolic images of women. The orientation of Buddhism is toward eventual release from the world of birth and death through salvation. Women's involvement with the physical birth process implicates them irrevocably in the ensnarements of the world; thus women and femaleness become the metaphors for suffering and worldly attachment, which are so devalued in ritual and spiritual life. The chapter examines various myths that detail the aggression and desire surrounding women as an *a priori* condition of their existence. These characteristics, which inhere in women's nature and bodies, innately give "birth" to fierce demons, who in turn prey upon and seek to destroy those on the path toward salvation, namely men. Demons are born to women who seek inappropriate unions or have "unnatural" pregnancy cravings. Often, however, women are passive recipients, or simply vessels, of men's "misplaced, unnatural" desires. Here the demonic is seen as anything that is excessive, and through mythology women find symbolic representation as this inevitable excess.

Another dimension of the construction of public and symbolic feminine metaphors is women's participation in ritual. One set of ritual roles that women perform is a direct result of their fertility and procreation, and concerns the culturally ascribed roles of nurturing. Here we find the midwife, healer, nurse, doctor, and medium, who are for the most part seen in positive images, as healers of people and society. One significant and positive generalization that emerges from the discussions on these women is that women who play nurturant roles themselves come to form close and expressive personal bonds with other women. They thereby create a horizontally affective association, which crosscuts otherwise hierarchic social orders. The importance of this "community of sisters," to use the rhetoric of the women's movement, may or may not be recognized by the men of the society, and usually it is neither documented nor appreciated by male researchers. We suggest that such female communities provide an alternative, essential, and basic mode of human relatedness for the entire society.

When women become ritual specialists they join their male counterparts as sacred professionals; license and privilege accrue to these roles, which are of high status and publicly valued. Through ritual roles women may become autonomous persons, no longer embedded in the lives of others, no longer the recipients of "reflected glory." Two features of these women's lives stand out in the chapters by Paul, Middleton-Keirn, Dougherty, and Spring. First, to become sacred professionals, women must become nonfeminine in their use of power and follow nonstandard feminine-gender tasks. Second women who undertake these positive nurturant roles are often those whose own fertility is either reduced or attenuated. Judith Brown (1970) submits that fertile, reproductively active women with children can take up only those jobs that are compatible with child care; i.e., they can be interrupted easily, are not far from home, and do not place the children in danger. Attending at births and curing the sick do not meet these criteria, hence only women with reduced numbers of children are ready and able to take up new roles that intrigue them intellectually and bring them power and autonomy.

The positive ritual roles of women require that women learn much esoteric knowledge to become ritually competent. Since women have much domestic competency, it is not difficult for them to transfer this competency and mastery to the ritual realm (Paul 1974). To learn ritual esoterica involves an intellectual commitment, an emotive relationship between ritual expert and novice, and a mystical individual experience or calling. Years of arduous apprenticeship and training may be required for the woman novice to become a medium, midwife, shaman, or priest. During this apprenticeship a transformation occurs, turning an ordinary woman into a sacred professional (Paul and Paul 1975). Only some women learn the entire system and become ritual experts, but many women learn a little and will participate as patients, clients, and aides. This transference of ritual knowledge and its accompanying power, in passing from woman to woman, forms the basis of a "charismatic sisterhood," which crosscuts the dominant male political structure or, in some matrilineal societies, supports the alliance of female ancestors that Spring discusses.

In many societies female physiological processes require that women come together for treatment, consultation, and education (Raphael 1975). The job of the ritual expert is to control and channel this suffering; ritual experts create a "community of sisters" by acting upon female psysiology. The midwife, the medium, and the healer are the archetype of nurturance *in relation to* their patients. This is quite different from nonpersonal, "masculinizing" modern medicine, in which male doctors obsfuscate the nurturing role. Relationships built on the healer–patient tie and the ritual expert-to-novice tie crosscut ties based on kinship, friendship, and residence. Ritual validates bonds between women.

To communicate with divinity, or the supernatural, a person must direct her life toward this pursuit. For a woman to devote her attention to spiritual concerns, she must not be hindered by physical fertility but comes to develop instead the potential of symbolic motherhood. In focusing on spiritual systems, a woman puts domestic, child care, and wifely tasks aside during communication with divinity and in her role as sacred professional. The supernatural provides the legitimacy that enables women to leave the domestic sphere. Furthermore, this legitimacy is not amenable to human intervention. The woman's husband and/or family who protest are liable to find they have little or no control—she becomes a ritual expert, or sickens and dies. Women who are able to obtain supernatural legitimacy through ritual often have much power. When women's ritual expertise is valued and when ritual participation opens the way for the flow of power, women become important in the religious well-being of society.

The careers of Guatemalan midwives provide an interesting example of these points. Lois Paul in "Careers of Midwives in a Mayan Community" shows that midwives along with shamans are supernaturally mandated ritual specialists. Midwives are not selected randomly but must come from families of other sacred professionals, who may be male or female. Divine election comes by birth signs or through dreams. To become a midwife requires a combination of deep commitment and much training. Only women in their prime become midwives and this may cause problems with their families. Unlike other women, the midwife must neglect economic tasks, abstain from sexual intercourse (to her husband's dismay), and act aggressively and authoritatively in unfamiliar settings. Midwives gain high status and material reward, but they are often in conflict over appropriate female behavior. Yet failure to take up the calling can be ruinous. Interestingly, persons with a variety of backgrounds and personalities can become midwives. Two cases are presented. In one, a classically "good" woman who demonstrates all the socially approved female behaviors, attitudes, and values becomes a midwife by putting these behaviors aside. By contrast, another woman becomes a midwife because of her aggressiveness. Women incorporate "good" (positive) and "bad" (negative) features. One either needs to become aggressive to play the role or takes on the role because one displays aggressive traits. A fascinating characteristic of both types is that women with reduced fertility of their own take up the calling and, as such, midwifery becomes an alternate to the procreative role in this society.

Black lay midwives in North Florida follow similar careers, as Molly Dougherty details in "Southern Lay Midwives as Ritual Specialists." A woman who has a calling to be a midwife may experience inner conflict but must take up the calling and receive supernatural validation. The apprenticeship is long, esoteric, and interwoven with licensing from public health officials. Midwifery is, in this sense, a substitute for and a continuation of procreation.

Among the matrilineal Luvale, women who have difficulty having children participate in a series of possession cults described in Anita Spring's chapter, "Epidemiology of Spirit Possession among the Luvale of Zambia." Women's difficulties, which these rituals attempt to remedy, are real illnesses, not manifestations of social tensions as so many other interpretations claim. Participation in these rituals occurs among women who have low natality and whose children sicken and die. Through these rituals, however, women learn a vast repertoire of ritual knowledge. The rituals integrate dispersed matrilineal women as well as nonrelated females into a community of "suffering sisters." Women who become midwives, spirit possession doctors, and herbalists gain high status and material rewards. Often these women have low fertility—which has entitled them to go through the rituals, and which has given them the time to learn the esoterica. They translate their reproductive potential, so to speak, into alternative healing roles.

Middleton-Keirn's chapter, Convivial Sisterhood: Spirit Medium-ship and Client-Core Network among Black South African Women," considers spirit mediumship as practiced by urban South African black women. These women occupy a position of structural inferiority in relation to their men as well as in relation to all other color-castes in white-minority-dominated South Africa. However, through spirit medium-ship, powerful feelings of communion, equality, euphoria, and empathy emerge. The medium, who is at the center of a core group of long-standing clients, offers a place of symbolic retreat and safety. Together-ness characterizes the core's interaction, offering respite from the participant's structural inferiority. This feeling of community provides the desire to become a ritual expert and the path consists of a calling, illness, and recovery followed by a long apprenticeship. These highly intelligent and educated women often must overcome the resistance of their husbands and families to take up their calling.

Women's roles may change with age and may in fact result in a reversal of the roles of youth. Older women may become autonomous. Myerhoff writes: "Before she was decorous, modest, ashamed, restrained. Now she is ribald, loud and bold. She may be profane where before she was chaste. And whereas before she polluted because of her identity with non-cultural forces, now she may bend them to the purposes of the group" (1974:5). In the sensitively written "Bobbes and Zeydes: Old and New Roles for Elderly Jews" Barbara Myerhoff observes that women can cope better than men with old age and that during this time men finally acknowledge that women are as intelligent and important as they themselves are. Men and women reciprocally nourish one another at religious observances that re-create a time when they were both young and vital. Men nourish women with ritual at these sacred celebrations and women in turn nourish men with food. Women, however, become autonomous, powerful, and self-directed social leaders in old age because androgynous behavior of the women was prefigured, not in the sexually stereotyped behavior of wife and mother, but in women's contingent roles as custodians of everyday life. Roles based on nurturant functions are expandable for a lifetime. Women have always been *bricoleurs,* "creating structures by means of events," making do, and constructing whole lives out of leftovers. Retirement is a time when sociability and full-time nurturing come to the fore; in this women are experts. In contrast, men do not take pleasure in caring for themselves or others. The loss of work is a serious blow and they cannot maintain their autonomous leadership except in the traditional male ritual prerogatives.

A final dimension of the book focuses on themes of the negatively ascribed attributes of women's public and symbolic selves—being dangerous and bringing death. The chapters provide case studies of the negative symbolic roles of witch and prostitute which are threatening to the community of men. The theme of woman as the personification of evil is addressed by Judith Hoch-Smith in "Radical Yoruba Female Sexuality: The Witch and the Prostitute." Among the Yoruba of Nigeria, women are socially and economically independent of men. This is a patrilineal society whose existence depends on the incorporation of women. But feminine independence leads to the negative stereotyping of the female image dealing with nurturing and sexuality. Thus the witch and the prostitute store or enlarge sexual energies, not for the nurturing or creation of the universe, but rather for the destruction of it. An analysis of several theater plays in Ibadan, whose audiences are composed of male urban workers, reveals stereotyped modes of male–female relationships, which reflect male views of the destructive nature of women. An immoral prostitute ruins an older, traditional man; a senior wife manipulates her husband to give her preferential treatment over co-wives; old witches manipulate young men's desires for monetary success; a transvestite posing as a wife takes advantage of an impotent man's desire for children. All the relationships have disastrous consequences for men; all are related to men's carnal image of women. Further, women are seen as forming conspiratorial links with each other and repeatedly mulcting men. These figures all relate to a carnal witch who has many faces, and who embodies real and perceived transgressions against the order of patrilineal society. Thus the image of the Yoruba witch resembles other European and African ones in that she uses feminine reproductive processes toward the destruction of life-forms rather than for their creation.

In the final chapter, "Jive Dope Fiend Whoes: In the Street and in Rehabilitation," Patricia Cleckner examines black women and men drug addicts in an urban area. Therapeutic communities for drug offenders treat women not only for drug addiction but also for sexual offenses, i.e., prostitution. The female drug addict's existence as a sexual offender pollutes society. The therapeutic community strives to control, purify, and remodel women's sexuality to emulate the sexual behavior of traditional middle-class women.

4. Conclusion

Three themes predominate in this volume: the relationship of women to divinity, women's ritual roles as midwives, healers and nurturers, and negative, stereotyped images of women as witches and prostitutes. These three themes combine to create the image of women in sacred scripture, a dualist image that includes both the nurturing mother and the destructive witch. We see that the symbolic image of woman usually is reduced to her function: She traditionally is equated with "female sexuality," which acts on and through a predominantly male-controlled world composed of individualized male characters who are often seduced, betrayed, enraged, or motivated by feminine sexuality. Or she heals, makes things well, aids the birth of a child, or cooks nourishing food for her men. These dualistic metaphors and roles exist today in symbolic expression perpetuated mainly by males, but females also perpetuate them, having long ago internalized the image of themselves held by men.

4.1. Women and Divinity

Western and some Eastern sacred scriptures limit the divine by imbuing divinity only with male qualities. When female qualities are part of divinity they are lesser and subordinate. Ruether argues that in the "dilemma of women's liberation . . . religion has been not only a contributing factor [but] undoubtedly the single most important shaper and enforcer of the image and role of women in culture and society" (1974:9). Doyle calls the "debate on women and religion . . . the single most important and radical question for our time and the foreseeable future . . . because . . . religion concerns the deepest and most ultimate aspects of human life, individually and collectively" (1974:15). Yet one wonders if it is possible even to reach a nonhierarchic model in contemporary religions. Hierarchic models saturate today's world religions so that to change them could destroy the faith. Although women in contemporary Western societies gradually are entering religion in roles as priests, in the year 1977 papal decree forbids women to enter the

Catholic priesthood because women do not resemble Christ (that is, they are not men). In any case, it will take more than women becoming celibate priests to free the "feminine metaphor" and eliminate hierarchy based on sexual distinctions from theology.

A horizontal, or complementary, model of social organization—a situation that levels hierarchy—depends on a basic restructuring of religious metaphor. Despite the urban Minyan's attempt to feminize the Torah, as discussed by Prell-Foldes, it seems unlikely that women can share religious domains equally with men until discrimination based on sexual distinctions is eliminated entirely from scripture. The question sometimes asked is "Why cannot God be a woman?" but this misses the point. The real question is rather "Why does the Infinite have finite or cultural attributes at all?" To conceive of God only in the feminine is to limit Divinity just as much as to conceive of God only in the masculine. And most importantly, to conceive of God in either gender will have significant social and cultural consequences for people of both sexes.

One of the obstacles to redefining feminine imagery is that women ordinarily do not undertake a variety of roles simultaneously; a woman who becomes a mother often de-emphasizes her career for a period of time and may return to it only later. Many religions demand this sequential channeling of the creative function, by mystifying the Mother image, and retaining divine calls only for those women who have forgone or completed childbirth. The only exception to this has traditionally been where women inherited political and ritual offices that demand multiple functions for successful tenure. The image of the Divine Queen includes childbearing, ritual authority, political control, and grace. Queen Victoria is an excellent example of such a woman in the Western world; Lovedu queens in South Africa hold positions that demand these multiple functions (Krige 1943). The image of the Queen, related symbolically to the Divine Mother, is a female image as fully realized as the gynomorphic images from Neolithic Europe or from Hopi culture.

4.2. Women and Healing

No matter how we may wish to interpret a prehistoric gynomorphic world and women's ritual roles in it, it is clear that feminine ritual domains and roles today usually center on midwifery, participation in possession cults, and healing. Women participate in rituals of healing nearly everywhere, for in most cultures such ritual roles are both achieved and ascribed. Therefore even if men inherit certain ritual offices, women can gain access to ritual through spontaneous divine calls or through possession cults where patients become healers. Recently, in the women's movement, women are helping one another find ways to achieve their full potentials. Women's groups in the Western world are analogous in function to the charismatic sisterhoods spoken of earlier, which provide the society with an alternative model of interrelatedness different from the vertical patriarchal structure. Such groups may be recreating images and roles that will contribute to the gynomorphization of the modern world.

4.3. Women as Witches

Despite their association with healing and nurturing, women are potentially the creators of illness. These women are the witches spoken of above onto whose persons many of the tensions of their society are scapegoated. The accusations are that women witches harm babies, exacerbate illnesses of all types, cause crop failures and weather disasters—all a perversion of the gynomorphized universe. Women still are very powerful through their mystical ties to nature, but men believe that on account of female envy, greed, or sheer evil these powers are turned to world destruction and cataclysm. The seductress and the prostitute are symbolically identical with the witch in that they use their sexual energies either outside, or to thwart the control of, male-dominated society. Women who are prostitutes are not channeling their reproductive potentials into the continuance of the patriarchal structure, and women who are seductresses bring about the downfall of man by separating him from God or from the rest of the male universe.

References

Ardener, Shirley. 1975. Introduction. In *Perceiving Women*. New York: Halstead Press. vii–xiii.

Bamberger, Joan. 1974. The myth of matriarchy: Why men rule in primitive society. In M. Z. Rosaldo and L. Lamphere (eds.), *Woman, Culture and Society*. Stanford: Stanford University Press. 263–280.

Blair, Lawrence. 1976. *Rhythms of Vision: The Changing Patterns of Belief*. London: Croom Helm.

Brown, Judith. 1970. A note on the division of labor. *American Anthropologist* 77:1037–1968.

Campbell, Joseph. 1970. *The Masks of God: Primitive Mythology*. New York: Viking Press.

Dames, Michael. 1976. *The Silbury Treasure: The Great Goddess Rediscovered*. London: Thames and Hudson.

Douglas, Mary. 1966. *Purity and Danger*. London: Routledge and Kegan Paul.

Doyle, Patricia. 1974. Women and religion: Psychological and cultural implications. In R. Ruether (ed.), *Religion and Sexism*. New York: Simon & Schuster. 15–41.

Ehrenreich, Barbara and Deirdre English. n.d. *Witches, Midwives, and Nurses: A History of Women Healers*. Westbury, New York: Feminist Press.

Ehrenreich, Barbara and Deirdre English. 1973. *Complaints and Disorders: The Sexual Politics of Sickness*. Westbury, New York: Feminist Press.

Friedl, Ernestine. 1975. *Women and Men: An Anthropologist's View*. New York: Holt, Rinehart & Winston.

Gluckman, Max. 1965a. *Custom and Conflict in Africa*. Oxford: Basil Blackwell.

Gluckman, Max. 1965b. *Politics, Law and Ritual in Tribal Society*. Oxford: Basil Blackwell.

Goldenberg, Judith. 1974. Epilogue: The coming of Lilith: In R. Ruether (ed.), *Religion and Sexism*. New York: Simon & Schuster. 341–343.

Graves, Robert. 1971. *The White Goddess*. London: Faber and Faber.

Hayes, H. R. 1972. *The Dangerous Sex: The Myth of Feminine Evil*. New York: Pocket Books.

Janeway, Elizabeth. 1971. *Man's World, Woman's Place: A Study in Social Mythology*. New York: Delta Books.

Klein, Melanie. 1932. *The Psychoanalysis of Children*. London: Hogarth Press.

Krige, Eileen and J. D. Krige. 1943. *The Realm of the Rain Queen*. London: Oxford University Press.

Masters, William and Virginia Johnson. 1966. *Human Sexual Response*. Boston: Little, Brown.

Masters, William and Virginia Johnson. 1970. *Human Sexual Inadequacy*. Boston: Little, Brown.

May, Ana. 1975. *Spiritual Midwifery*. Seattle: Book Publishing.

Mernissi, Fatima. 1975. *Beyond the Veil: Male–Female Dynamics in a Modern Muslim Society*. Cambridge, Mass.: Schenkman.

Myerhoff, Barbara. 1974. The older woman as androgyne. Paper presented at the annual meeting of the American Anthropological Association, November 23.

Paul, Lois, 1974. The mastery of work and the mystery of sex in a Guatemalan village. In M. Z. Rosaldo and L. Lamphere (eds.), *Woman, Culture and Society*. Stanford: Stanford University Press. 281–339.

Paul, Lois. 1975. Recruitment to a ritual role: The midwife in a Maya community. *Ethos* 3(3):449–467.

Paul, Lois and Benjamin Paul. 1975. The Maya midwife as sacred professional. *American Ethnologist* 2(4):707–726.

Pomeroy, Sarah B. 1976. *Goddesses, Whores, Wives and Slaves*. New York: Schocken Books.

Raphael, Dana (ed.). 1975. *Being Female: Reproduction, Power, and Change*. The Hague: Mouton.

Rich, Adrienne. 1976. *Of Woman Born: Motherhood as Experience and Institution*. New York: W. W. Norton.

Ruether, Rosemary (ed.). 1974. *Religion and Sexism: Images of Women in Jewish and Christian Traditions*. New York: Simon & Schuster.

Sacks, Karen. 1974. Engles revisited: Women, the organization of production and private property. In M. Z. Rosaldo and L. Lamphere (eds.), *Woman, Culture and Society*. Stanford: Stanford University Press. 207–222.

Summers, Montague (trans.). 1971. *The Malleus Maleficarum of Heinrich Kramer and James Sprenger*. New York: Dover Publications.

Turner, Victor W. 1967. *The Forest of Symbols: Aspects of Ndembu Ritual*. Ithaca and London: Cornell University Press.

Turner, Victor W. 1968. *The Drums of Affiliation*. Oxford: Clarendon Press.

Turner, Victor W. 1969. *The Ritual Process: Structure and Anti-Structure*. Chicago: Aldine.

Turner, Victor W. 1974. *Dramas, Fields, and Metaphors: Symbolic Action in Human Society*. Ithaca: Cornell University Press.

Waters, Frank. 1963. *Book of the Hopi*. New York: Viking Press.

Watson, Lyall. 1973. *Supernature*. London: Hodder and Stroughton.

Watts, Alan. 1969. *The Two Hands of God: The Myths of Polarity*. Toronto: Collier Books.

Webster, Paula. 1975. Matriarchy: A vision of power. In R. Reiter (ed.), *Toward an Anthropology of Women*. New York: Monthly Review Press. 141–156.

Part I
Women and Divinity

2

DANIEL N. MALTZ

The Bride of Christ Is Filled With His Spirit

1. Introduction

The purpose of this chapter is to examine female imagery as it is interpreted in a particular Bible-centered Protestant tradition, the pentecostal
churches of Edinburgh, Scotland.* My intention is to throw light on
some general characteristics of female imagery, some particular aspects
of Christian female imagery, and a specific case of pentecostal female
imagery which de-emphasizes motherhood and virginity.

Religious texts can and often do define the nature of acceptable
female behavior in three different ways. First, they may contain explicit
statements of proper behavior for women and in relation to women.
Second, they may contain depictions of female characters who serve as
potential models for desirable or undesirable female behavior. Third,
they may contain female imagery, metaphors that use terms such as
mother, sister, wife, or *mistress* to describe by analogy some other domain
of reality such as "mother nature," the "motherland," or the "whore of
Babylon." Such metaphors, based upon cultural *models of* femininity,
may in turn be read in reverse as *models for* correct female behavior, so
that one may conclude that a proper mother should be like the land or
like nature. Christianity and the Christian Bible provide examples of all
three of these mechanisms for defining female behavior. First, there are

---

*Sociological discussions of some of the same pentecostal denominations in other British
localities may be found in Allen and Wallis (1976), Hollenweger (1969:191–217), Walker
and Atherton (1971), and Wilson (1959, 1961).

DANIEL N. MALTZ · Department of Anthropology, University of California, Berkeley,
California.

explicit New Testament texts defining the proper position of women. These Pauline teachings tend to present two somewhat complementary themes: restrictions of women's rights to authority (such as I Timothy 2:9–14 and I Corinthians 1:5–16, 14:34–35) and statements that in Christ "there is neither male nor female" (as in Galatians 3:28). Second, the Bible includes a number of female personages of whom some, such as the Virgin Mary, have been used as models of female virtue and others, such as Eve, have been used to support arguments of female inferiority and inherent sinfulness. Third, the Bible includes at least one major feminine metaphor: the church as the bride of Christ.

Pentecostalism, with its de-emphasis of human authority in general and emphasis on active participation by all church members, tends to define the position of women less strictly than many other evangelical and fundamentalist religious groups that place greater emphasis on rules and less on spiritual freedom. Thus of the four pentecostal denominations represented in Edinburgh, only the Apostolic Church, with its greater emphasis on human positions of authority, did not allow women to preach in church, and even here women were allowed active roles in prayer, testimony, prophesy, speaking in tongues, and other public displays of verbal participation. As compared to other evangelical denominations in Edinburgh (see Borker, this volume), the roles of women were comparatively unrestricted, at least in theory, and little energy was put into stressing female submission to males as opposed to human submission to Christ.

The image of the Virgin Mary has long been stressed by the Catholic Church and de-emphasized by Protestants. In Scotland, as in neighboring Northern Ireland, where the religious contrast between Irish Catholics and Scottish Calvinist Presbyterians is a major one, the concept of "preaching the Virgin Mary" has become a kind of Protestant key metonym for what is wrong with the Catholic church. The image of a drunken Irishman insisting on the superiority of the Virgin to Christ was sometimes presented in sermons as an example of Christianity gone wrong. In contrast, I cannot remember a single sermon that cited the Virgin Mary as an appropriate model for female behavior. The image of Eve as an example of female inferiority is also rarely used, but for a different reason. In a theology that stresses the equal sinfulness of all unconverted humankind, Eve's sin is no greater than Adam's, or anyone else's for that matter. Sin is not so much an act as it is a state of being "separated from God." Thus, there are no greater or lesser sins, and the specific nature of one's sinfulness is quite irrelevant.

Finally, there is the metaphoric equation between the Christian church and the bride of Christ. This image, utilized in both Catholic and

Protestant churches, varies in its specific interpretation in relation to other aspects of the larger cultural system. It is the meaning of this single metaphor with which this chapter is primarily concerned. To understand the pentecostal interpretation of this metaphor, it is essential to understand certain fundamental aspects of pentecostal belief and practice. First, we must examine the importance of Biblical metaphor in pentecostal thought and the role of metaphoric exegesis in religious practice. Second, we must understand the pentecostal definition of "the church." Then we will be able to consider the specific implications of this metaphor as they are understood within the churches in question.

2. The Nature of Metaphor

The New Testament is a heavily metaphoric text. Characteristically, religious ideas are expressed through analogies with everyday secular objects and activities such as water, fire, kinship, farming, fishing, slavery, and freedom. The significance of metaphor is recognized in pentecostal preaching, and a majority of the sermons I heard preached in the pentecostal churches of Edinburgh were concerned with either attempting to understand the meaning of a particular Biblical metaphor or exploring a specific religious concept through the use of Biblical metaphors.

Analytically useful characterizations of the nature and functions of metaphor have been made by Fernandez (1972, 1973, 1974), Rosaldo (1975; Rosaldo and Atkinson 1975), and Black (1962). Many of their characterizations have been helpful for understanding the role of Biblical metaphor in pentecostal sermons, prayers, and hymns. Others must be modified to adequately deal with the nature of Biblical metaphor in a Bible-based religious context. My present characterization of metaphor is summarized as follows:

1. A metaphor is an analogy between two domains.
2. This analogy may be "structural," an analogy of shape, or "textual," an analogy of feeling (Fernandez 1974:120).
3. A metaphoric statement is as much a statement about the meaning of the second term as it is about the first. Thus "God is our father" is as much a statement about the nature of fathers as it is a statement about the nature of God (Maltz 1974). To paraphrase Black's (1962:38–44) "interactional view" of metaphor, a metaphor directs its audience to think about two distinct domains in terms of one another.
4. The logic of a metaphor is never totally opaque. That is, there is a

reason, a "motivation" based on "apt correspondence" (Fernandez 1973:1366), for choosing a particular metaphoric vehicle. A corollary of this fact is that each metaphor seems to possess a motivating logic of its own. It lends itself to being extended in certain directions as opposed to others and thus leads its users into pursuing specific arguments and making specific further comparisons.

5. Biblical metaphor use within the churches I studied possesses a different dynamic from either the strategic choosing of rhetorical metaphors discussed by Fernandez (1972, 1974) or the building of metaphoric *bricolages* in the magical spells discussed by Rosaldo (1975; Rosaldo and Atkinson 1975). Since a Biblical metaphor is considered to be God-given rather than humanly created, the central issue for metaphor users is the understanding of metaphors rather than the skillful selection of them. The central focus of pentecostal sermons is thus not creativity but exegesis.

6. Biblical metaphors are of extreme "weight" or "emphasis." Black's caution that "we need to know how 'seriously' [the user] treats the metaphorical focus" (Black 1962:29) applies more to literature than to Biblical exegesis in a Bible-centered religious tradition. Since Biblical metaphors are considered to be *absolutely* true, it is not possible to read more into a Biblical metaphor than was intended.

7. A pentecostal analysis of a Biblical metaphor is not concerned with why a particular metaphor appears in the Bible, since God's will is considered unknowable, but rather with how the metaphor functions or what it implies. To guide his exegesis of such a metaphor, a preacher draws upon (a) his personal commonsense experience, (b) Biblical cross-references, which help place the metaphor in context, and (c) analysis of those aspects of the logic of the metaphor itself which are independent of context.

3. The Church

As defined within pentecostalism, "the church" refers not to a formal organization or to a body of religious officials but rather to the totality of all "born-again Christians." A typical expression of this view is the third tenet of the Elim Pentecostal Church: "We believe that the church consists of all persons who have been regenerated by the Holy Ghost and made new creatures in Christ Jesus." Thus when pentecostals use the phrase "the church is the bride of Christ," they are not saying "this organization is the bride of Christ," or "those officials are the bride of Christ," but rather that *our* relation to Christ is like that of a bride to a bridegroom.

The New Testament and much of Christian thought, both Catholic and Protestant, defines the relationship between the Christian church and Christ in a series of images or metaphors (Minear 1960; Dulles 1974:17). At least four of these are frequently expressed and explored in pentecostal sermons, prayers, and hymns. First, the church is to Christ as a building is to its foundation. Second, the church is to Christ as branches are to a vine. Third, the church is to Christ as a body is to its head. Fourth, the church is to Christ as a bride is to her bridegroom. The point being made by all four metaphors is that the relationship with Christ is the *central* and defining characteristic of the Christian church. In the foundation metaphor, the emphasis is on the fact that Christ provides support for the church, that he is the "solid ground" on which a Christian stands, as summarized in the hymn lines "The Lord's our Rock, in Him we hide: A shelter in the time of storm!" In the vine and branches metaphor, the emphasis is on the dependence of the church on Christ for growth and nourishment. In the head and body metaphor, the emphasis is on the fact that Christ provides guidance and leadership for the church. The specific implications of the wedding metaphor constitute the central concern of the rest of this chapter.

4. The Bride of Christ

To uncover the meaning of the bride of Christ metaphor, it is useful to disassemble the concept of "bride" into its constituent elements. In so doing it becomes necessary to consider those characteristics of brides that are universal, those that are pan-Christian, and those that are culturally specific to British or even urban Scottish pentecostals. It is also necessary to stay as close as possible to the specific uses and interpretations of the metaphor which occur within the context of church services.

Since the bride of Christ metaphor is primarily a metaphor of marriage, I find it helpful to begin with a depiction of the pentecostal attitude toward marriage as quoted from a privately published collection of editorials reprinted from the Assemblies of God church magazine, *Redemption Tidings:*

> Spurgeon speaks of a couple on honeymoon as exhausting the honey and leaving nothing but moonshine. Marriage can be full of disillusionment. You wed a vision, she turns out to be a dream: you marry a man, and find him a mouse. The person you felt you could not live without you now find it impossible to live with. . . . The power that will take you through through life is love—true love. The four elements of married love are first *mutual*

> *physical attraction.* This is the basis of the "one-flesh" union that makes a true
> marriage. Understanding and acceptance of this side of marriage is essential
> to keep it afloat. But marriage is more than sex; there is also *mutual respect.* . . .
> Then comes *mutual trust.* . . . A fourth element is *acceptance of the inevitable.*
> We should be prepared to accept our spouses for what they are, not what we
> think they should be. . . . But what of a breakdown. Well, a pilot learns to
> keep his plane in the air if one or even two of his four engines fails. So if some
> aspect of your marriage breaks down, it is better to struggle on under difficul-
> ties than to crash-land in divorce. Divorce is not a solution, it is a catastrophe:
> for Christians it should be an unthinkable impossibility. "For better, for
> worse.". . . If added to all this there is trust in the One in whose Presence our
> vows are made, nothing can untie the bond (Linford n.d.: 37–38, emphasis in
> the original).

This extended quote captures quite effectively many of the characteristics of British pentecostals which are relevant to their interpretations of
the bride of Christ metaphor: a down-to-earth as opposed to a romanticized attitude toward life, an acceptance of the sexual aspect of marriage, a de-emphasis of female subordination, a rejection of divorce,
and an emphasis on the individual's personal relationship with Christ.

My examination of the bride of Christ metaphor has led me to
distinguish five characteristics of a bride in her relationship to her
bridegroom which are exploited in pentecostal sermons, prayers,
hymns, and personal conversations. Being a bride implies possessing a
relationship that (1) unites two individuals into a larger whole, (2) is
sexual and intimate, (3) is pure and legitimate, (4) is expressed from a
female point of view, as opposed to the relationship of a bridegroom to
his bride, and (5) is active in the sense that a bride is *in the process of
becoming* a wife. Each of these characteristics will be explored below.

The first relevant characteristic of a bride is that she is linked to a
bridegroom. To be a bride is to be part of a larger entity, a divinely
sanctioned union. The existence of a marital bond is the very essence of
brideness. This quality most clearly parallels the other metaphors for the
church, that of the building, that of the vine, and that of the body. Thus,
to say that the church is the bride of Christ is to say that the church is
defined by its relationship to Christ and that this relationship is one
of union.

The second characteristic of a bride is that the relationship in
which she is involved is a sexual one. This fact has two metaphoric
implications, one structural, the other textual. Structurally, having a
sexual relationship implies a contrast with not having one. Thus being a
bride implies a contrast with being a virgin. Textually, having a sexual
relationship implies emotion and intimacy. By equating women with
churches and sexual relationships with spiritual ones, the contrast between virgins and nonvirgins (including wives and brides) can be used

to express metaphorically the relationships between churches and Christ. Such an argument need not imply the Freudian notion that religious experience is mere compensation for repressed sexuality but rather that sexuality provides a convenient and useful metaphor for religious experience because of the structural (and emotional) similarity between the two. The "bride of Christ" provides a metaphor for a correct spiritual relationship with Christ, and as such, its sexual component is religiously valued. By reading the metaphor in the reverse direction, one may argue, as I have heard at least one pentecostal pastor do, that it is because the relation between a husband and his wife is like that between Christ and His church that divorce is not permissible in a true Christian church.

A virgin, in contrast,* provides a metaphor for the lack of any spiritual relationship. As such, the image of virginity is not a particularly positive one. The Virgin Mary is de-emphasized, and the spiritual value of celibacy is rejected. Thus the Protestant interpretation of the bride of Christ metaphor forms a contrast with the Catholic one. The intimate emotional quality of the sexuality of a bride, on the other hand, is exploited in both Catholic and Protestant thought. The textual analogy between the physical love expressed in the Song of Songs and the spiritual love between the church and Christ is one of long-standing and widespread acceptance in Christianity. Thus, according to Lloyd Warner (1959:366), this analogy was explicitly recognized in the official annotations of "most Protestant and all Catholic Bibles as well as [by] their sectarian interpreters" in twentieth-century "Yankee City," Massachusetts.

In Catholic thought, the intimacy of a bride is combined with the apparently contradictory purity of a virgin. The Catholic image *par excellence* of the bride, the perfect woman in general, and the church is the Virgin Mary, who possesses the unique combination of attributes of a wife, a mother, and a virgin (Warner 1959:379–388). The concept of the church to which the Catholic bride of Christ metaphor refers has a triple referent (1959:365–376) somewhat different from that to be found in Protestantism. The "church" still refers to the collectivity of all Christian souls, but more properly and more frequently it refers to a single organized institution (Dulles 1974:31–42) and in particular to religious offi-

---

*There are, of course, many different types of nonvirgins, not all of which are positively valued. An additional contrast to both "a virgin" and "a bride of Christ" which is logically possible, although I have never heard it used, is "a bride" of someone other than Christ, such as "a bride of Satan." Instead, the image of negatively valued nonvirginity that is frequently used is that of "a whore," a type of woman whose metaphoric potential is discussed below in relation to the contrast between legitimate and illegitimate sexual relations.

cials. "The priest, the religious, the nun, the deaconess, or the primitive Church, are constituents of the Church in a stricter sense than the other members of Christ's mystical body" (von Hildebrand 1962:100). As such, consecrated virgins, or nuns, who are conceptualized as "brides of Christ" in their own right, serve as both metaphors and metonyms of the church as a whole. Their virginity is an expression of ascetic purity (von Hildebrand 1962:108–112), their marital ties to Christ an expression of spiritual intimacy (Williams 1975:109, 123; Warner 1959:371–373; von Hildebrand 1962:128). Thus for nuns as for the Church in general, it is possible to speak of the "bride of Christ" as being a virgin (Warner 1959:367–379; von Hildebrand 1962:99–142).

Among colonial New England Puritans, sexuality became the "most persistent metaphor" (Barker-Bensfield 1972:72) for the relation of the saved Christian to Christ. "In sermon after sermon the ministers of New England explained to their congregations that the true believer was wedded to his God in a holy marriage" (Morgan 1949:107). Images of courtship and espousal were used to explicate the conversion process, and images of consummation and intimacy to express the nature of salvation and regeneration (Masson 1976:309). "Conjugal communion" between husband and wife was used to express both public worship and the complementary bestowal of Christ's benefits upon His believers. Thus each converted Christian was a bride brought to Christ by ministers whose metaphoric role was that of the "friends" of the bridegroom whose customary function was to arrange the match (Morgan 1949:109–110). From among the many metaphors available to the Puritan minister to denote the role of the regenerate Christian before God, the marriage metaphor was chosen, Masson (1976:311) argues, precisely because only it "could convey the passion with which the Christian convert embraced God and anticipated the joy of ultimate union."

Within pentecostalism, as opposed to more traditional forms of Protestant Christianity, the desired relationship of every Christian to Christ is even more personal, more intimate, and more emotional. Conversion is not the ultimate religious experience, and the pentecostal seeks a closer relationship with Christ, as in the chorus "Draw me nearer, nearer, nearer precious Lord" and the following spontaneous prayer:

> . . . O God we worship Thee, this way tonight. May our hearts, be filled with Thy love, this evening hour, as we draw unto Thee. We pray Lord, that You will draw nearer unto us. Help us Lord, to love Thee, Lord as we have never loved Thee before. Help us Lord to, exalt Thy name. . . (prayer by a man, April 29, 1973).

The ultimate experience of intimacy is that of receiving the Holy Spirit:

. . . O Lord, how close You've drawn us to Yourself. O Lord Jesus, to be able
to commune with Thee Lord, in an unknown tongue. O we praise Thee Lord,
for this wonderful experience. O Jesus we pray tonight, that fire from heaven
Lord, shall fall upon us. O Jesus, we thank You Lord, for the way in which
You met with us Lord, on Tuesday night. We thank You Lord, for coming
upon us Lord, in such a wonderful way. . . (prayer by a woman, November
9, 1972).

Thus, to seek to be a part of the bride of Christ is to seek to have an
intimate personal relationship with Christ.

The third characteristic of a bride is that her relationship is faithful,
pure, and legitimate. A bride, by definition, has not been married long
enough to become an unfaithful wife. She is a woman whose marriage is
still perfect, for whom the honeymoon is not yet over. As such, the
marriage of a bride provides a more appropriate metaphor for an ideal
spiritual relationship than the marriage of a "wife." The faithfulness of
brides contrasts even more directly with the unfaithfulness of whores
and adulteresses, who by definition possess illegitimate relationships
and involvements with incorrect partners. A "whore" is thus the dominant metaphor for an unfaithful church or an unfaithful Christian. To
call another denomination the "whore of Babylon," as some church
members do, is to imply that they are not really "of God," that they are
"serving the wrong master," or that they are "following the Devil rather
than Christ." Bryan Wilson (1961:94), for example, cites a 1938 issue of
the *Elim Evangel* as referring to the Roman Catholic church as "the
mother of Harlots, drunk with the blood of the Saints," a metaphoric
statement that parallels those of the colonial New England Puritans (cf.
Morgan 1949:109). It is interesting to note that in this usage a whore
contrasts not with a virgin but rather with a wife or bride. The metaphor
is being utilized not for its implications of fleshliness but for its implications of unfaithfulness and illegitimacy. The whore image thus functions
not as a metonym for sexuality but as a metaphor for an individual
involved in an improper relationship.

The purity and faithfulness of a bride also contrast with the purity
of a virgin. Whereas a virgin is a woman who is pure of any relationship,
a bride is a woman who possesses a pure relationship. For pentecostals,
sinfulness, not purity, is inherent in the nature of humanity, and living a
sinless life is a human impossibility. Purity may be achieved only
through the establishment of a sin-cleansing relationship with Jesus
Christ. Such an image of purity is more accurately compared to that of a
bride than that of a virgin. Virginity, like the initial state of grace in the
garden of Eden, is a status with which one is born but which is easy to
lose. It is an unusual status in that it is gained by ascription but lost by

achievement. To become a bride, in contrast, is to be able to begin again with a fresh start and a clean slate. Even a whore can regain the purity of a bride although she cannot become a virgin. As such, the bride metaphor is useful for expressing the availability of Christ to even the worst of sinners. In addition, the purity of a bride, like the spiritual purity of receiving the Holy Spirit, is a status achieved by one's willingness to receive. Thus, to call the church "the bride of Christ" is to imply a pure, faithful, and legitimate relationship with Christ.

The fourth characteristic of a bride is that she is a woman. As such, the metaphor is drawing our attention to the fact that the relationship of church to Christ is like that of bride to bridegroom rather than that of bridegroom to bride. This characteristic, of course, follows in part from the fact that Christ is male, but there are other implications as well. The point being exploited here is the nonequivalence of male and female sexual roles and their usefulness for expressing the nonequivalent roles of Christ and the church. The significance of this point was made clear to me by a woman I had confronted with the very difficult task of describing the religious experiences of conversion (becoming a born-again Christian) and spirit baptism (being filled with the Holy Spirit).

Unlike most informants, who begged off requests to describe their experiences with the claim that "the natural man cannot understand the things of the Spirit" (a paraphrase of I Corinthians 2:14), she explained that the difference between the two "felt like the difference [between] being engaged and being married." Baptism in the spirit she described as being "like a loving embrace, like being flowed over from head to toe in love, [like] being filled up" as opposed to conversion, which was "slightly more detached. . . . I had an inner picture of Him over me putting His hand in mine saying come along and follow me. There was some distance between us." In drawing this analogy (conversion: spirit baptism::engagement:marriage), this woman was drawing upon the domain of sexuality to express the relationship of Spirit to church. Just as in the sexual act it is the male who fills, the female who receives, in pentecostal Christian religious experience it is the Holy Spirit who fills the church and not the other way around.

Although the concept of females and males as containers and contained is perhaps a bit too crude to have much overt expression in the churches, the relationship is certainly recognized as shown by the statements of the informant cited above. The relationship between God and church is also commonly conceptualized as one of "being filled" as when an individual asks God in prayer to "fill me to overflowing, 'til my cup runneth over" or sings the chorus:

Burn, burn Holy Spirit
Burn in me
Set my heart on fire
Fill me with the Holy Ghost
With God's full desire. . . .

This same metaphoric analogy (male:female::giver:receiver) appears to have had significant implications in Catholic and Puritan thought as well. Within a Catholic idiom, von Hildebrand (1962:88)* develops a rather elaborate metaphoric justification of a religious double standard in which the priesthood must remain a male monopoly because it involves the metaphorically male function of giving to the church, whereas the metaphorically female receiving function of the human soul can be assumed by males as well as females. Puritan thought also seems to have acknowledged the fact that, as bride rather than bridegroom, the church's role was one of submission (Masson 1976:310). There is some disagreement (Masson 1976:314; Barker-Bensfield 1972:73), however, as to whether this led to an increased cultural concern with female subordination or an increased equality of the sexes through recognition that males as well as females assume a submissive role in relation to Christ. The pentecostal interpretation of metaphoric sex role difference seems to me to involve less subordination than either the Catholic or the Puritan view. It is more that the individual Christian is elevated through Christ than that he or she must accept a subordinate role in relation to Christ.

But the question still remains as to the significance of expressing the

---

*This argument invites quotation at some length: "In the natural order woman represents, in contrast to man, the receptive principle. This finds its clearest expression in the biological sphere, where man may be considered as the giving, fertilising factor, woman as the recipient. . . . In relation to God, however, this characteristic of predominant receptivity is not confined to the female sex. . . . Here God alone is the giver, the creative and fertilising principle, and the human being, as a creature, the recipient, therefore, if you like, 'feminine.' . . . Since woman in her receptive relation to man is the obvious natural image of the soul as receptive or conceiving from and by Christ, and since we speak of the soul as the bride and Christ as the bridegroom, not vice versa, it is woman, not man, that is the natural type of that consecrated virginity, which represents precisely the nuptial status of the soul as Christ's bride. . . . Since within the natural order the male is in the spiritual sphere . . . he is better fitted to fulfil in the supernatural order also the giving function of the priest as the representative of Christ. Nevertheless, . . . as an individual soul he must be just as receptive in relation to God as the woman, for in this order in which the Divine and human meet, the male, inasmuch as he is a human individual, is purely receptive, that is to say, metaphysically feminine" (von Hildebrand 1962:88, cited in part in Warner 1959:365–366. This quotation is copyright by Helicon Press, Inc., 1120 North Calvert Street, Baltimore, Maryland, and is reprinted with permission.).

desired purity of the church as that of a faithful wife as opposed to that of a faithful husband. The answer, I feel, can only be understood by examining the proper relationship of the church to outside forces. Evangelical Christians are not expected to keep to themselves. They are expected instead to "go out into the world to preach the gospel." Thus, externally, they expose themselves to outside forces. Internally, or spiritually, however, they are expected to be faithful to Jesus Christ, to allow themselves to be filled with the Holy Spirit, but not with other spiritual forces such as evil spirits. These two aspects can be metaphorically expressed in terms of differences in male and female sexuality. Thus when expressing the relationship of the church to the outside social world of the "unsaved," it is appropriate to use male metaphors of penetration such as that of an army. When expressing the spiritual nature of the church, however, she is like a bride, faithful to Jesus Christ, not allowing herself to be invaded by other spiritual forces. Thus, to say that the church is the bride of Christ is to say that the church is filled with the spirit of Christ and does not allow itself to be penetrated by forces other than Christ.

The fifth characteristic of a bride is that she is not merely married but in the process of becoming married. Bridal imagery implies an entire dramatic scene: The wedding is about to begin and the bridegroom is about to arrive. This scene, as developed in the closing chapters of Revelations (21:2–9), is the "most highly developed vision of the church as the Messiah's bride" (Minear 1960:55), and the dominant Biblical image of the imminent second coming of Christ. As a "key scenario" (Ortner 1973:1341) of the adventist message, this scene implies a necessary course of action: The bride must prepare herself for her coming wedding.

This theme of preparation for a wedding was the subject of a sermon in the Apostolic Church on December 26, 1972. To paraphrase the preacher:

> It is often said that there is a red line of redemption from Genesis through to Revelations. There is also a line of preparation. We are not here for very long, and preparation is important.
>
> The Bible begins and ends with marriage. Why? Because in all marriage there is preparation. Some people think that they will get to heaven and there will be a big reward. But Jesus demands of all a preparation. The unsaved must prepare to meet their God, and we must prepare ourselves. When Paul preached this message perhaps he was thinking about the second chapter of the book of Esther in which the king goes out into 120 provinces looking for a bride and finally finds her. The theme is the same, a bride sought for the King. We must prepare for Jesus Christ.
>
> There was perhaps a more elaborate preparation for an upper-class wedding

in the East. First, there was the dowry, [what anthropologists would call bride wealth], a measure of the man's love. What about the dowry of a great bridegroom? Christ gave Himself, what a dowry! Christ loved the church and gave himself through the glory of His resurrection. Second was the bath of purification. No expense was too great. One year was spent out of sight in the back rooms, six months of bathing in oil of myrrh. She was willing to take this suffering to take the throne. Then six months of baths in sweet oil. When we are presented there should be no wrinkle and no blemish. Third was the day of presentation. Preparation is unpleasant, but necessary to achieve the standard so we may look forward to a day of presentation. On that day they didn't look at the king but at the bride. Others were chosen but he loved her above all. It was a wonderful day for all, but an attainment for her. She was presented, which means placed alongside Himself. It shows what a high regard Christ has for the church to place her alongside Himself. For the crowds around, it was a day of admiration, for the king one of possession. Christ so loved the church that He gave Himself for it, so we may be presented to Him.

In Revelations three congregations are mentioned, those who shall "sit with me on my throne," those who "are around the throne," and those "before the throne." All were prepared.

But what is the purpose of marriage? Not reproduction but union. The most important goal of the church is unity: unity of nature, life from a common source, unity of faith, unity of truth, unity of worship, unity of life, unity of dominion, unity of vision, unity of divine government.

To summarize the night's message, the congregation was asked to close the service with the singing of three verses of the hymn "The Church's One Foundation": "The Church's one foundation is Jesus Christ her Lord. She is His new creation, by water and the word. From heav'n He came and sought her, to be His holy bride. With His own blood He bought her, and for her life He died. . . ." The Biblical text for this sermon was Esther 2:12–18; the subject, the analogy between a royal wedding and the second coming of Christ; the main message, the need to prepare for this event. What is striking about this portrayal of bridal preparation is that active purification rather than passive virginity is stressed and that intimacy rather than motherhood is presented as the goal for which the bride is told to prepare herself.

A strikingly similar message was preached in the United Pentecostal Church on August 9, 1973, based on a different text, the parable of the wise and the foolish virgins (Matthew 25:1–13). The parable itself tells of ten virgins who are awaiting the coming of the (heavenly) bridegroom. When he finally appears, none expect him, but the five wise virgins are ready with oil in their lamps while the five foolish ones are unready. The main point of this parable, according to the preacher that night, is not simply to state that Christ is coming again but rather to provide a "warning that we who look for His coming should be prepared." The message is that "we should not be like the foolish maidens." When the bride-groom came, "five had vessels filled with oil, I don't know if they were Girl Guides or not, but they *were prepared*. . . . All who are born again have lamps and all have vessels or human frames." The usefulness of these frames, however, depends on "what they contain. . . . The oil represents the Holy Spirit." Many Christians don't have the Holy Spirit, they are "living a barren life," they are "not prepared. . . . While they were away in a backslidden state, not right with God, not prepared for the bridegroom's coming, He appeared."

Again, in this sermon, the central analogy is between the arrival of a bridegroom and the second coming of Christ, and the message is the need for preparation. Again, too, the proper role of a bride is not that of a passive virgin. A virgin is inadequate and unprepared if her lamp is also virginal, if she is not filled with the Holy Spirit. The proper role of a bride is to be like a Girl Guide, to "be prepared." Thus, to say that the church is the bride of Christ is to say that the church prepares itself for the Second Coming and actively accepts Christ.

In quick summary, the New Testament provides a series of female figures as potential metaphoric vehicles for analyzing the nature of the church: whores, brides, and virgins. As interpreted in the pentecostal churches of Edinburgh, these three images are in fact often used as a means of talking about spiritual relationships in the idiom of sexual and marital ones.

5. Conclusion

It is now useful to return to general questions of female imagery. When are metaphoric analogies to the domain of women made? What do they imply about "women" as a medium in terms of which to think about reality? What do they imply about cultural and pan-cultural ways of thinking about women? One theme that has been frequently stressed is that the female life-giving function is a useful way of representing growth, nurturance, motherhood, and reproduction. A second is that female sexuality and sexual vulnerability are useful ways of thinking about questions of purity and defilement. A third, less developed theme is that the female sexual role is a useful way of thinking about the acts of receiving and enticing as opposed to giving or penetrating. What then are the domains for which female imagery has commonly been used? In particular, what are some of the domains that utilize aspects of feminin-ity other than that of life-giving force?

One of the most commonly discussed domains of female imagery is that of nature and the land. Ortner (1974) has argued that the biological characteristics of women make the contrast between femaleness and maleness an appropriate way of thinking about the contrast between nature and humanity or nature and culture. A more culturally specific analysis is Peacock's (1970) comparison of the meanings of *motherland* and *fatherland* in the speeches of former Indonesian president Sukarno. Whereas *fatherland* is used as an image of the Indonesian people in their public, political, and outward-looking sense, *motherland* is used to evoke images of a private intimate world to be protected from outside penetration. The most detailed analysis of the land-as-woman or nature-as-woman motif, however, comes from the literary analysis of Kolodny (1972, 1973, 1975, 1976), who has traced the history of pastoral imagery in American literature. The result of envisioning the land as female, she argues, has been to treat the land as an external "other" and oppose it to a masculine self. Pastoral imagery in American writing has been concerned with the exploration of conceptual tensions between land-as-enticing-seductress, land-as-nurturant-mother, and land-as-ravaged-rape-victim. Thus, this imagery of the land as female "other" has exploited the standard themes of motherhood and purity as well as that of mistress and seductress.

The church-as-woman metaphor discussed in this chapter is a second major example of female imagery to be found in Western intellectual history. It is a particularly interesting one because it has persisted throughout Christian history but its interpretation has shifted dramatically to accompany changes in religious conceptions of virginity, motherhood, and the nature of the church. A central element of Catholic ideology has historically been an acceptance of the Virgin Mary as a dominant image of the ideal woman, stressing the dual themes of virginity and motherhood. The "bride of Christ" thus became an image of virginity and maternity. The *church*, a term that referred more to religious officials and church institutions than to the totality of lay membership, came to be represented as mother church and as virginal, particularly as epitomized by the chastity of priests, monks, and nuns. The transition from Catholicism to reformed Protestantism was accompanied by a less institutional vision of the church and a strong de-emphasis of the role of the Virgin Mary. Thus the intimate wife rather than the virginal mother became the dominant image of the "bride of Christ." In the preaching of colonial New England Puritans, the representation of the church's relation to Christ was one of sensual union, with the minister taking on the role of matchmaker.

In pentecostalism the situation is even more extreme. Not only is there a strong de-emphasis of the Virgin Mary, even in predominantly

Catholic countries (Flora 1975:414, 1976:190), but there is also an accompanying de-emphasis of the role of the minister, a stressing of the "priesthood of all believers," and an increased sense of intimacy between the individual and Christ. The marriage imagery of Puritan conversion becomes the even more intimate pentecostal imagery of being filled by the Holy Spirit. The adventist stress on the imminent second coming of Christ leads to a second use of the same metaphor to represent the spirit-filled bride of Christ awaiting the return of her heavenly bridegroom.

A crucial aspect of this usage is that it is based on an understanding that marital and sexual relations look different from male and female points of view. It is not just that the church is married to Christ but that the church is the bride and Christ the bridegroom. Thus the metaphor indicates that church members are to view their spiritual marriage bond to Christ from a female point of view. We have here a suggestion of an interesting contrast. When groups metaphorically identify themselves as men, *women* may become a metaphor for that which is seductive and enticing, for forces which draw and attract. When groups metaphorically identify themselves as women, *men* becomes a potential metaphor for that which can overpower and fill, for forces which can penetrate and enter the (social) body. In both cases, the nature of biological sexuality provides a structural metaphor for the relationship between seducer and seduced, container and contained, receiver and giver, or that which attracts and that which penetrates.

Thus the pentecostal usage of the bride-of-Christ metaphor uses female imagery, not to label a female "other" in relation to a male self as in mother nature and motherland imagery, but rather to express a female image of one's own identity. To be a member of the church is to be like a woman in relation to Christ. The female image being exploited here is neither that of a virgin nor that of a mother. It is rather an image of potential receptivity. To be female in relation to a male divinity is to be a potential receptacle for receiving a spiritual "infilling."

ACKNOWLEDGMENTS

The research on which this article was based was conducted in Edinburgh, Scotland, between September 1972 and November 1973. Earlier versions of the article have profited from comments by Kathryn March, Ruth Borker, Inge Harman, Roger Rasnake, Juliet Rake, Michelle Rosaldo, and members of an undergraduate seminar at Cornell University taught by Dr. Rhoda Possen.

References

Allen, Gillian and Roy Wallis. 1976. Pentecostalists as a medical minority. In Roy Wallis and Peter Morley (eds.), *Marginal Medicine*. New York: Free Press. 110–137.

Barker-Bensfield, Ben. 1972. Anne Hutchinson and the Puritan attitude toward women. *Feminist Studies* 1(2):65–96.

Black, Max. 1962. *Models and Metaphors: Studies in Language and Philosophy.* Ithaca: Cornell University Press.

Dulles, Avery, S.J. 1974. *Models of the Church: A Critical Assessment of the Church in All its Aspects.* Garden City: Doubleday.

Fernandez, James W. 1972. Persuasions and performances: Of the beast in every body and the metaphors of Everyman. *Daedalus* 101(1):39–60.

Fernandez, James W. 1973. Analysis of ritual: Metaphoric correspondences as the elementary forms. *Science* 182 (4119):1366–1367.

Fernandez, James W. 1974. The mission of metaphor in expressive culture. *Current Anthropology* 15(2):119–145.

Flora, Cornelia Butler. 1975. Pentecostal women in Colombia: Religious change and the status of working-class women. *Journal of Interamerican Studies and World Affairs* 17(4):411–425.

Flora, Cornelia Butler. 1976. *Pentecostalism in Colombia.* Rutherford: Fairleigh Dickinson University Press.

Hollenweger, Walter J. 1969. *The Pentecostals.* London: SCM Press.

Kolodny, Annette. 1972. The unchanging landscape: The pastoral impulse in Simm's Revolutionary War romances. *Southern Literary Journal* 5(1):46–67.

Kolodny, Annette. 1973. The land-as-woman: Literary convention and latent psychological content. *Women's Studies* 1(2):167–182.

Kolodny, Annette. 1975. *The Lay of the Land: Metaphor as Experience and History in American Life and Letters.* Chapel Hill: University of North Carolina Press.

Kolodny, Annette. 1976. Stript, shorne and made deformed: Images of the Southern landscape. *South Atlantic Quarterly* 75(1):55-73.

Linford, Aaron. *Fabulously Rich.* Nottingham: Privately published.

Maltz, Daniel N. 1974. Comment [on Fernandez 1974]. *Current Anthropology* 15 (2):138–139.

Masson, Margaret. 1976. The typology of the female as a model for the regenerate: Puritan preaching, 1690–1730. *Signs* 2(2):304–315.

Minear, Paul S. 1960. *Images of the Church in the New Testament.* Philadelphia: Westminster Press.

Morgan, Edmund S. 1949. The Puritan's marriage with God. *South Atlantic Quarterly* 48(1):107–112.

Ortner, Sherry B. 1973. On key symbols. *American Anthropologist* 75(5):1338–1346.

Ortner, Sherry B. 1974. Is female to male as nature is to culture? In Michelle Zimbalist Rosaldo and Louise Lamphere (eds.), *Woman, Culture, and Society*. Stanford: Stanford University Press. 67–87.

Peacock, James L. 1970. President Sukarno as myth maker. In Jean Pouillon and Pierre Maranda (eds.) *Éxchanges et Communications Mélanges Offerts à Claude Lévi-Strauss à l'Occasion de Son 60ème Anniversaire* (Vol. 2). The Hague: Mouton. 1409–1416.

Rosaldo, Michelle Zimbalist. 1975. It's all uphill: The creative metaphors of Ilongot magical spells. In Mary Sanches and Ben G. Blount (eds.), *Sociocultural Dimensions of Language Use.* New York: Academic Press. 177–203.

Rosaldo, Michelle Zimbalist and Jane Monnig Atkinson. 1975. Man the hunter and woman: Metaphors in Ilongot magical spells. In Roy Willis (ed.), *The Interpretation of Symbolism*. New York: Halsted Press. 43–75.

von Hildebrand, Dietrich. 1962. *In Defence of Purity: An Analysis of the Catholic Ideals of Purity and Virginity*. Baltimore: Helicon Press.

Walker, Andrew G. and James S. Atherton. 1971. An Easter pentecostal convention: The successful management of a "time of blessing." *Sociological Review* 19(3):367–387.

Warner, William Lloyd. 1959. *The Living and the Dead: A Study of the Symbolic Life of Americans*. New Haven: Yale University Press.

Williams, Drid. 1975. The brides of Christ. In Shirley Ardener (ed.), *Perceiving Women*. New York: Halsted Press. 105–125.

Wilson, Bryan R. 1959. The pentecostal minister: Role conflicts and status contradictions. *American Journal of Sociology* 64(5):444–504.

Wilson, Bryan R. 1961. The Elim Foursquare Gospel Church. In *Sects and Society: A Sociological Study of Three Religious Groups in Britain*. London: William Heineman. 15–118.

3

MARIGENE ARNOLD

Célibes, Mothers, and Church Cockroaches

Religious Participation of Women in a Mexican Village

Most analyses of religious ritual in Mexico focus on the mayordomía-cargo system (the sponsorship of fiestas) and, more specifically, on the overt public roles played by men in this male-dominated endeavor (see, for example, Cancian 1965). The religious roles taken by women have not been explored to the same degree. Yet, when one considers that Eric Wolf (1958) has analyzed the Virgin of Guadalupe as the "master symbol" of Mexico, one would expect that women's contributions in the ritual sphere would be great. This chapter explores the symbol of the Virgin and her Mexican cultural meanings, in relationship to roles played by women in Catholic ritual.

The Virgin's nature as a ritual symbol contains contradictory meanings: she is both maiden and mother, both sexually pure and a childbearer. Turner (1967) has noted that ritual symbols often combine and condense contradictory meanings, which then serve to synthesize "real" human experience (29–30). The Virgin serves as such a symbol for the integration of female life cycles and ritual participation in the highland, mestizo village of Cajititlán, Jalisco, a peasant community of 1800 inhabitants located south of Guadalajara. In Cajititlán, unmarried women are ritually linked with the Virgin and after marriage they become associated with the Virgin as Mother. A special category of ritual participation is reserved for spinsters who take on attributes of the Virgin and of androgyny, which accords to them special ritual powers not associated with the Virgin.

MARIGENE ARNOLD · Assistant Professor of Anthropology, Kalamazoo College, Kalamazoo, Michigan. This chapter is based on 16 months' field research sponsored by the Foreign Area Fellowship Program.

1. Célibes (Virginal Women)

A young girl serves a religious apprenticeship from the time of her first communion. On January 4, during the fiesta in celebration of the Three Kings,* all girls who have just made their first communion march in the processional, two abreast, in their white dresses. For several years afterward, girls continue to wear this ceremonial attire on specified occasions. For instance, each night during the month of May, women of the town sponsor masses for La Purisíma (the Immaculate Conception); in this ceremony girls are obliged to wear first communion dresses and offer flowers to the Virgin.

The sponsorship of these public masses is a responsibility of married women. During these masses girls become more active participants in village life, assume responsibilities to the community, and gain knowledge of ritual expertise. Such religious participation constitutes the first experience of a girl outside her family and in ritual she begins to develop a sense of responsibility to, and participation in, the community at large; the community-level ethos is stringently tied to Catholicism as it is practiced in Cajititlán.

Adolescent girls, after serving apprenticeships aiding their mothers in the sponsorship of masses, are given the responsibility of caring for Saint Theresa. Each year the girls of the town take up a collection to sponsor masses for this saint; they are responsible not only for sponsoring the mass but for singing, organizing the processional, hiring musicians, and buying cohetes (fireworks). Thus their role expands from that of participant to that of sponsor. In addition to the sponsorship of masses, adolescent girls also share ritual responsibility with spinsters which is denied to other women. To adolescents and spinsters is given the important charge of assisting nuns in the teaching of catechism classes. Girls are also charged with the sweeping of the church. The priest and nuns draw up a list of 30 groups with three girls in each group and then assign the groups a particular day on which they must sweep the church. This job is considered a solemn responsibility for unmarried girls between the ages of 15 and 20.

One reason for the relatively high participation of unmarried women in religious ritual is the fact that they have extra time to invest in public ritual, while married women have the responsibility of a household and the maintenance of the household's relationship to the supernatural. But their sexual status is ritually paramount: both unmarried girls and spinsters are virgins and as such may ritually be related to the

---

*The Three Kings are the patron saints of Cajititlán.

pure or virginal aspect of Mary. Each year one girl is selected to play the role of the Virgin of Guadalupe as her apparition appeared to the Indian, Juan Diego. Others serve as the "Three Marys," who parade through the town on horseback, carrying the standard of the Virgin of Guadalupe. During the nine-day fiesta season honoring the Three Kings, a different girl serves each day as the Virgin Mary in the processional. It would be unthinkable to the people of Cajititlán that a married or nonvirginal woman should take such parts; the occasion is viewed with solemnity, and being chosen to serve is considered a great honor. No hint of scandal should ever have surrounded the honored one and selection to play a Virgin represents public recognition of the purity of the woman. Her virginity is displayed by wearing a white wedding dress, garb that is reserved for virginal women who have married without elopement.*

The extreme importance placed on purity can best be illustrated by example. During my stay in Cajititlán I was asked by a group of townfolk to portray the Virgin Mary during the annual fiesta. I declined this honor, not wishing to risk jealousy on the part of the young women in town who desired selection. However, although word of the invitation spread through Cajititlán, word of my refusal did not. The morning of the day I had been selected to serve, January 1, I joined several friends at a local store and drank two beers. After I did not participate in the processional, many persons asked me if I had failed to serve because I had drunk beer before the processional. A "virgin-player," it was later explained, could not hope to attain both the sexual purity and motherhood of the Virgin; however, she should emulate the Virgin as much as possible. It is assumed that the Virgin did not stop at a local bar on her way to Bethlehem!

To emulate the Virgin's purity, the girl should fast and take communion after the processional. Although the core cast of the ceremony—Joseph, Mary, the Babe, the Three Kings, and the Angel—all enter the church after the processional, only the Virgin Mary and the Angel, a young virgin girl dressed in communion attire, partake of the eucharist. In these public religious rituals, Mary's symbolic role as virgin rather than as mother is elaborated. While adolescent girls have many roles in, and responsibilities to, the religious community, the most important of these, according to the people of Cajititlán, revolve around their status as virgins.

*A woman's married life often begins with the *robo*, in which she is "stolen" by her future husband and spends at least one night away from home. Although a church wedding usually ensues, she wears a pink or blue dress, rather than a white one, because she is not considered to be a virgin.

2. Mothers

Just as virginity is ceremonially elaborated in female adolescence, motherhood is ceremonially elaborated in adult life. The importance of the mother role is well documented in the ethnographic literature, particularly in the case of the mother–son tie (see, for example, Schwartz 1962; Nelson 1971; Diaz-Guerrero 1955). The reverence that a child develops for his or her mother is very pervasive, the most stinging insult being the *mentada de la madre* (naming of the mother). No one should allow anyone to speak evil of his or her mother. While children are taught that *respeto*, or respect, for one's parents is paramount, they soon learn that more affection can be directed to and received from the mother. As an example of this, it was explained that the mother should go to collect her son if he were drunk in a local saloon, for while drunken sons might be disrespectful to their fathers, it was assumed that they would never lack respect for their mothers.

Most ritual obligations for adult women are related to their roles as mothers and take place in the private family setting. Although women do sponsor masses felt to benefit the entire community and participate in the mayordomía-cargo system in their roles as wives of mayordomos (fiesta sponsors) (Moore 1973; Arnold 1973), their greatest roles are related to the household.* Males carry on ritual felt to benefit the entire community, while a household's female head is entrusted with maintaining the critical relationship of the household to the supernatural. In this capacity, the woman is ritually associated with the Virgin Mother. To women falls the task of beginning the religious socialization of children; mothers tell their children about God and the Virgin even before the children can talk. Children are taken to church at a very early age and mothers cross their children before the children learn to cross themselves. One mother explained the manner in which she taught her children about religion:

> Pointing to the crucifix in the church, I would say, "Allá está tu papá, diocito" (There is your Papa, little God). Pointing to the Virgin I said, "There is the little Virgin, she is your other mother." Then I taught my children to ask God for bread, saying, "Ask your Papa for bread!" Then my children learned to hold out their right hands, just as they did when asking me for bread.

---

*Women of the village tend to formalize the role played by females in this case. That is, when one speaks to men of the town it is stated that there are two *mayordomos* for each fiesta; women claim there are four—two *mayordomos* and their wives, the *mayordomas*.

This nurturant role is also seen in the efforts of women to protect the household against disaster. Women are responsible for taking water to be blessed by the priest on Holy Saturday; this water is kept in the house and used for emergencies: before and after household deaths, and to "remove the devil" if a man becomes crazed by drink or if a person is delirious from fever. Women are also most likely to take palms to be blessed on Palm Sunday; these palms are hung on the wall and are said to protect the household from dangers.

The woman in charge of a household also has a specific task to perform in relation to the Christ Child. Each December 23 and 24, three village women carry an image of the Christ Child from the church to every house in Cajititlán. The women do not enter the house but meet the female head of the household outside the door and hand the Child to her. The mother takes the image to each family member, who kisses it. Then she places the image on every bed in the house to remove the evil in each person's heart. Finally, she returns the image to the three women along with an offering. This ritual is symbolic of the role of the Virgin Mother in bringing the Christ Child into the world, and thus into the hearts and bedrooms (the most intimately personal space) of all people. Women also have specific responsibilities in burning candles on All Saint's Day and in establishing household altars. Most women in town belong to "conferences" whose major work consists of arranging for "visits" by the images of the saints to households. These images are taken from house to house, where they abide anywhere from a day to three days; the female household head "receives" these images, which are said to be indebted to her. She in turn may ask favors of the saints if a family member becomes ill.

In sum, the ritual tasks for married women, unlike the public roles assumed by the célibes, center in the private domain of the household. There, the adult woman maintains a ritually nurturant position toward her household. A mother's ritual gives her supernatural familiarity and authority, which she uses to urge compliance to Catholic doctrine among family members. A woman will refrain from taking communion if she feels her household is not "right with God," if for instance her son is living with a common-law wife. Thus she takes on the burden of her family members' relationships to the supernatural and is subtly able to pressure the offending member into "correct" behavior. In these instances just like the Virgin Mother she is able to intercede between Christ and His followers; certainly few sons would dare risk their mothers' damnation.

3. Cucarachas del Templo (Church Cockroaches)

Although normally women follow a developmental pattern in which they participate in public ritual for a time and then move from this into the private ritual of the household, such a cycle does not describe all female ritual participation. Approximately one in every eleven women in Cajititlán never marries, never lives with a man, and never bears children.* These *muchachas ya grandes* ("old girls") are not accorded full social adulthood within the community although they may be highly respected and even sought out for advice. They remain virgins—both symbolically and literally (as far as anyone knows)—and are continuously linked with adolescent girls. Regardless of their age, they are never called by the respect form *doña*. They aid adolescents in the preparation of altars for the Corpus Christi celebration and give catechism classes. Even during the Lenten season when the priest gives classes to all members of the community, spinsters attend classes given for young girls; during this time, they learn how they should conduct themselves with members of the opposite sex, even if they are 60 or 70 years old. Thus their status as virgins removes them from their age-mates and socially equates spinsters with adolescents. At death, spinster women are dressed as saints and buried as *angelitas* (little angels) without a funeral mass. Loss of virginity is tantamount to ritual loss of innocence, and thus a 60- or 70-year-old woman is buried as if she were a young girl.

While spinsters are often linked with adolescents, they do not often play public roles as virgins. The Virgin Mary connotes not only virginity but also beauty and youth. However, virginity is paramount because some aging spinsters do occasionally portray the Virgin of Guadalupe. In these cases, the spinsters select themselves, promising to *salir de virgen* (play a virgin) in order to fulfill a promise to Her. There is no evidence the community members find this laughable or even incongruous, yet the fact remains that no one asks an elderly spinster to take the role; she must solicit the role herself,† which indicates that spinsters enjoy some degree of ritual autonomy. A spinster with much free time

---

*Based on a census carried out by the author.

†Although I was beyond the age of most "virgin-players" I submit that, as a stranger, a different standard was applied to me. It was said that I looked like the image of the Immaculate Conception in the church (although I saw no resemblance). Furthermore, I was also asked to serve as the town queen for the Independence Day Celebrations—another role usually reserved for girls between the ages of 15 and 17.

becomes a *cucaracha del templo* (church cockroach), practically living in the church, spending hours on end praying for deceased family members and lost friends, a ritual role that is essential to the progression to salvation of a deceased person's spirit in Catholicism. Spinsters also have other responsibilities not shared by adolescents. They are actively sought out to serve as godmothers.* It is believed that spinsters, having no children of their own, will take the duties of godmother seriously, as well as the duties of *comadre* (comother). Thus the spinster also shares some ritual obligations of motherhood.

While they continue to participate in the conference for Saint Theresa, spinsters usually and gradually join more conferences within the town; this process begins most normally when a young woman reaches her mid-20s or early 30s and her chances of being married are lessened. There are currently six such conferences in Cajititlán, only one of which is reserved for married or widowed women (Our Lady of Refuge). The charge for moving the saints' images devolves upon the president of the conference and the *encargada* (the woman in charge of moving the image from house to house). Two categories of women serve as presidents and encargadas—spinsters and widows. The fact that widows fulfill this obligation indicates that such women need not be virgins. Explanations by the villagers as to why widows take these roles centered on the fact that they have more time than other women. In a community in which the extended family is the ideal, such reasoning appeared contradictory since a widow should be participating in the ongoing life of her extended family and caring for her grandchildren. Closer scrutiny of the widows involved in such responsibilities indicated that for the past 15 years widows participating as presidents and encargadas were childless, had children who had moved away or had spinster sons and daughters, and did not have the responsibilities of an extended family. Married women who have the above characteristics do not take such roles, for they still have to care for their husbands. Special ritual participation for women becomes possible when they are freed from familial responsibilities. Further, these widows are also called church cockroaches, signifying that they are symbolically linked with spinsters on account of their own lack of success in producing procreative offspring. Thus, again we find that women are integrated into ritual on the

---

*They are denied the right to be *baptismal* godmothers unless they have a brother, single or widowed, to serve with them. There are many other occasions (first communion, confirmation, marriage, etc.) in which they do serve.

basis of their reproductive status. Substitution of church life for family life occurs to the extent that the church becomes the center of almost all social life for both categories of church cockroaches and they "nourish" the community with ritual as a mother nourishes her children with food.

Spinsters exist between the two ideals of the Virgin. They are still sexually pure but lack youth and beauty and generally do not participate in the public display of virginity characteristic of adolescent girls. However, they can select themselves for this public role and can, in fact, also select themselves for the role of *mayordoma* and sponsor a fiesta, a role usually reserved for married men, which implies that in addition to possessing the ritual power of virginity, they also possess authority associated with spinster androgyny: in old age women past menopause often are able to enjoy privileges ordinarily reserved only for men. Elderly females in many cultures act both male and female roles and often bear special ritual obligations. Spinsters also take on many of the aspects of the Virgin Mother role. They serve as godmothers and intercede through prayer for deceased relatives in the church, and they join a specific category of widows in performing the public aspects of the household rites involving the conferences' images within the household.

4. Conclusion

The contradictory meanings of the Virgin symbol are ritually integrated into the life cycle of Cajititlán women. The Virgin *qua* virgin is enacted by the young and beautiful adolescents of the village, who join men in publicly safeguarding the community's relationship with the supernatural. The Virgin *qua* mother is enacted by the married women of the village, who take on a ritually nurturant role and privately keep the household's relationship to the supernatural on an even keel. The responsibility of a married woman as a religious conference member involves the care of the images while they remain with her in her own home. She receives the image and bids it good-bye but does not participate in the actual moving of the image.

The role of spinster ties the two aspects of the Virgin's character together; the unmarried adult acts out roles that are both public and private, both sexually pure and motherlike. But, in addition, the spinster possesses ritual autonomy (she may "select" herself for the virgin role) and ritual rights ordinarily reserved for males. Her elderly, childless status makes her sexual identity ambiguous and thus she is enabled to participate in ritual at times in the women's domain and at times in the men's.

In a social structure where most public ritual is the duty of men and is associated with communal rather than familial good, only special categories of women take public roles, which are accorded on the basis of reproductive status. Adolescent virgin girls assume roles that function for the community's benefit when they participate in processionals, while widows and spinsters assume public aspects of household rites in organizing the movements of the saints' images from house to house. Such women provide a link between the communal ritual of adult males and the familial ritual of adult females, and symbolically function as androgynous angels. For all female ritual participants, status and authority flow from sexual attributes, but in Cajititlán only childless women possess ritual power that is efficacious in the public domain.

References

Arnold, Marigene. 1973. Mexican women: The anatomy of a stereotype in a Mexican village. Ph.D. dissertation, University of Florida.

Cancian, Frank. 1965. *Economics and Prestige in a Maya Community.* Stanford: Stanford University Press.

Diaz-Guerrero, Rogelio. 1955. Neurosis and the Mexican family structure. *Journal of American Psychiatry* 112:411–417.

Moore, G. Alexander, Jr. 1973. *Life Cycles in Atchalan: The Diverse Careers of Certain Guatemalans.* New York: Teachers College Press.

Nelson, Cynthia. 1971. *The Waiting Village: Social Change in Rural Mexico.* Boston: Little, Brown.

Schwartz, Lola Romanucci Manzolillo. 1962. Morality, conflict, and violence in a Mexican mestizo village. Ph.D. dissertation, Indiana University.

Turner, Victor W. 1967. *The Forest of Symbols: Aspects of Ndembu Ritual.* Ithaca and London: Cornell University Press.

Wolf, Eric. 1958. The Virgin of Guadalupe: A Mexican national symbol. *Journal of American Folklore* 71:34–39.

4

RUTH BORKER

To Honor Her Head

Hats as a Symbol of Women's Position in Three Evangelical Churches in Edinburgh, Scotland

1. Introduction

The position of women in evangelical churches is determined by a number of interweaving factors, the most important of which is the Bible. Although these churches are often regarded as highly male-dominated because of the supposed unambiguous nature of the Biblical texts, I hope to show here that in fact the very absoluteness of the Biblical standard and the ambiguity of meaning built into it generate a marked flexibility in meaning that permits a variety of symbolic strategies by both men and women with important implications for women's position. In this chapter I will demonstrate this semantic flexibility through an in-depth analysis of the meaning of a key symbol of women's position in three Edinburgh churches: the wearing of hats.

The theoretical framework I am using here draws upon work in two major approaches in anthropology: symbolic analysis and the ethnography of communication. Two currents within symbolic analysis are particularly relevant: (1) the focus on the nature of symbols (e.g., Turner 1967) and types of symbols (e.g., Ortner 1973; Harris 1977), and (2) the focus on the use of symbols by individuals in particular social situations (e.g., Turner 1964; Deshen 1970). These are paralleled by two relevant concerns in the ethnography of communication with its concentration on speech: (1) the focus on the structure of the communicative system and the impact of this structure on what is communicated (e.g., Marks

RUTH BORKER · Assistant Professor of Anthropology and Women's Studies, Cornell University, Ithaca, New York.

1974; Levy 1973) and (2) the ways individuals employ their communicative repertoires and actually operate within the structure of the system (e.g., Gumperz 1971). Using this framework I will be examining the constraints influencing an individual's interpretation of symbols and the symbolic strategies an individual employs in communicating his or her religious belief and experience as framed in those symbols.

In order to do this I have made a distinction between two general types of meaning: core and situational. By core I mean that constant set of meanings that exists in the "abstract"; it is the background meaning people keep in their heads and bring to bear in interpreting any specific usage. I am here using the word *core* much as a linguist would use the word *referential* or *dictionary* in speaking of word meaning. By situational meaning, on the other hand, I mean those aspects of meaning involved in a specific use of a symbol in a specific time and place. A major element in this meaning is often the particularization of the core meaning. What is of interest is how this particularization is shaped by the social, experiential, and personal constraints operating in the situation itself.

Before examining these two sets of meanings for hats, it is necessary to briefly look at the social position of women in the churches, which is an important element in the symbol's meaning. The Biblical basis for core meanings and these meanings themselves will then be examined, followed by a consideration of a number of specific situations and the meanings involved in them with a focus on individual strategies of interpretation and usage.

The three churches studied were an extremely large Baptist church (in fact the largest in Britain, membership about 900), a small and elderly Open Brethren assembly (membership about 45), and a small Seventh Day Adventist church (membership about 50). Each of these churches is evangelical, by which I mean that their members believe in the truth of the Bible as God's word to man and they believe the purpose of the church on earth is to spread the gospel message—that man is basically a creature of sin, incapable of "saving" himself, and bound for hell and that salvation is only possible by spiritual rebirth through the personal acceptance of the atoning sacrifice of Jesus Christ on the cross, recognizing that "Christ died for *my* sins." It should be noted that the salvation message is the same for men and women. All three share this common evangelical understanding of the New Testament, such that differences between them can most fruitfully be seen as variations on a single theme. These differences are not on a single dimension, such as strictness to laxity, but rather result from differences in emphasis on multiple dimensions within an overarching framework (cf. Borker 1974 for a fuller discussion of the similarities and differences in their interpretation of the gospel).

The social position of women in the churches is an extremely complex one, both in response to and conducive of the semantic complexity discussed below. Although on the surface women seem to be placed in a subordinate position, in most churches women's position is not as simple as it appears.

Looking at the official level of church organization, women are seemingly excluded from positions of authority. In the Brethren, which in many ways is the most extreme in differentiating a member's role by sex, women are not allowed to be elders (there are no ministers) and in fact women are not allowed to speak when men are present. Despite the fact that they maintain they practice the "priesthood of all believers," in practice only male members participate in the meetings as they feel led by the Holy Spirit to do so, while the women worship in silence. However, women are completely in charge of the Women's Meeting, which is one of the primary evangelistic activities of the church, and the speakers are frequently women. In addition, women are Sunday school teachers (although not Bible class teachers dealing with the older children) and girls receive the same rigorous Bible training as boys. In the Baptist church women are not allowed to preach or teach from the pulpit, but they can otherwise participate in meetings. As in the Brethren, women are not allowed to be elders (or ministers). The Women's Meeting, which is primarily directed to church members, is headed by the pastor's wife and again the speakers may be women. The Adventists, in contrast to both, permit women considerable participation in the church organization. Although they as yet have no women pastors, women can speak in church and hold a variety of positions of authority, e.g., head of the Sabbath school and church treasurer. In all the denominations women can be missionaries, where they are frequently in the position of teaching and even preaching to men and are always serving as official representatives of their churches.

Women's influence is not completely exhausted by these official positions. Frequently women exercise considerable informal authority through their husbands or fathers, and some older women by virtue of their long Christian service and experience wield considerable influence on their own. Even in situations in which women are restricted in actual participation, hymns written by women are read and sung and generally used for spiritual edification.* Finally, there is considerable variation in belief among the members of the various churches as to the

---

*Even in the most conservative Brethren assemblies where women cannot sing solos during gospel services, hymns written by women will be read and sung. The "contradiction" involved in keeping a woman from speaking while others speak her words was first pointed out to me by a member of the Brethren.

proper role of women and this leads to a certain amount of situational variation in their actual participation depending upon the persons present.

2. The Biblical Basis of Meaning

As is always the case with evangelical Christians, the meaning of hats is first looked for in the Bible. However, as the Bible is a complex system of interlocking multivocal symbols, words with a multiplicity of meanings, the meaning of hats is by no means unambiguous. For evangelicals the Bible is not just a book of words but rather The Book consisting of the Living Word, and as such one of its primary characteristics is that through the Holy Spirit it speaks to different individuals as is appropriate for them in their particular situations.* The Bible thus provides both a general and universal truth and a full guide for action and belief for each individual.

In discussing the Bible the Baptist minister wrote, "The Bible alone must be our authority in all matters of faith and conduct; . . . what the Bible says must be the deciding factor in any decision that has to be made; . . . every opinion must be examined in the light of what the Bible says" (Prime 1967). Elsewhere the same minister presented these general principles for Bible study: "Know the background of the passages which you study. Watch the context (verses before and after the passage considered). Use Scripture to explain Scripture. Remember the Bible is God's Word. Ask for the help of the Holy Spirit" (Prime 1972). On this last point he went on to elaborate: "The Holy Spirit, who caused the Scriptures to be written, is given to every Christian to teach and to instruct him in the things of God. . . . Spiritual understanding, thank God, is not a matter of intellectual ability but rather a matter of submissive wills and minds bowing before God as the Scriptures are studied, and being taught by the Holy Spirit" (Prime 1972).

There are four passages in the Pauline epistles that are central for evangelical Christians in determining the meaning of hats and the position of women. The first of these passages deals explicitly with the question of head coverings, while the others, which deal more generally with the role of women, are often cited in attempting to explain the

---

*Ann Kibbey Levy (1973) has presented a detailed study of the Puritan understanding of how the Holy Spirit speaks through the Bible to individuals that shows many similarities to the understanding of this by evangelicals that I found (Borker 1974).

first.* Because of their importance I shall quote each in full. All quotes are from the Authorized, or King James, Version of the Bible. The first and most important is I Corinthians 11:1–16, in which Paul writes:

> [1]Be ye followers of me, even as I also am of Christ. [2]Now I praise you, brethren, that ye remember me in all things, and keep the ordinances, as I delivered them to you. [3]But I would have you know, that the head of every man is Christ; and the head of the woman is the man; and the head of Christ is God. [4]Every man praying or prophesying, having his head covered, dishonoureth his head. [5]But every woman that prayeth or prophesieth with her head uncovered dishonoureth her head: for that is even all one as if she were shaven. [6]For if the woman be not covered let her also be shorn: but if it be a shame for a woman to be shorn or shaven, let her be covered. [7]For a man indeed ought not to cover his head, forasmuch as he is the image and glory of God: but the woman is the glory of the man. [8]For the man is not of the woman but the woman for the man. [9]Neither was the man created for the woman; but the woman for the man. [10]For this cause ought the woman to have power on her head because of the angels. [11]Nevertheless neither is the man without the woman, neither the woman without the man, in the Lord. [12]For as the woman is of the man, even so is the man also by the woman; but all things of God. [13]Judge ye in yourselves: is it comely that a woman pray unto God uncovered? [14]Doth not even nature itself teach you, that, if a man have long hair, it is a shame unto him? [15]But if a woman have long hair, it is a glory to her: for her hair is given to her for a covering. [16]But if any seem to be contentious, we have no such custom, neither the churches of God.

Later in the same letter, Paul states in I Corinthians 14:34–35:

> [34]Let your women keep silence in the churches: for it is not permitted unto them to speak; but they are commanded to be under obedience, as also saith the law. [35]And if they will learn any thing, let them ask their husbands at home: for it is a shame for women to speak in the church.

Then in I Timothy 2:8–15 Paul writes:

> [8]I will therefore that men pray every where, lifting up holy hands, without wrath and doubting. [9]In like manner also, that women adorn themselves in modest apparel, with shamefacedness and sobriety; not with braided hair, or gold, or pearls, or costly array: [10]But (which becometh women professing godliness) with good works. [11]Let the woman learn in silence with all subjection. [12]But I suffer not a woman to teach, nor to usurp authority over the man, but to be in silence. [13]For Adam was first formed, then Eve. [14]And Adam was not deceived, but the woman being deceived was in the transgression. [15]Notwithstanding she shall be saved in childbearing, if they continue in faith and charity and holiness with sobriety.

---

*Christians will use a wide variety of verses to illuminate other verses and this provides for an almost endless source of variation in the meaning that may be given to a particular verse.

The last text is of a somewhat different nature. It is very short and, contrary to the others, denies rather than asserts the distinction between men and women. This is Galatians 3:28, which reads:

> There is neither Jew nor Greek, there is neither bond nor free, there is neither male nor female: for ye are all one in Christ Jesus.

While these are not the only verses relevant to the question of hats and the position of women, they are primary in the minds of church members and are sufficient to spell out the core meanings of the wearing of hats.*

3. Core Meanings

In my discussion with them, church members drew out three principal meanings of the wearing of hats from these passages: (1) subordination, (2) dignity or modesty, and (3) formality. I have called these Biblical meanings core in the sense that unless a Christian can base his argument on Biblical citations, he has no argument. Thus when in interviews I asked the direct question "What does the wearing of hats mean?" I was answered either with an explicit or implicit reference to these or other Biblical passages. The point is that for these evangelicals a question about the meaning of hats called for a response explicitly in terms of the Bible. Biblical citations form a necessary framework in which particular meaning will be framed, much as the "dictionary" meaning of a word gives focus to its usage in a particular situation. Like dictionary meanings, these Biblical core meanings are generally agreed upon—in fact, all individuals I interviewed gave one or more of these meanings and no others.

3.1. Subordination

The dominant meaning of hats for most church members is the subordination of the woman to the man, both within the church and in the home. This relationship between the sexes is summarized for most in Paul's statement: "The head of every man is Christ; and the head of the woman is the man"; i.e., as man is to God, woman is to man. There

---

*The meanings of hats and hair are closely connected for many evangelicals. In recent years a number of general studies on the symbolic importance of hair have appeared, e.g., Leach's study of magical hair, Hallpike's on social hair, and Firth's on the relation of public and private meanings of hair. In this discussion I am concerned not with the search for universal meanings in symbols such as hair or coverings but rather with the meanings a symbol has for a particular group of people in particular situations.

are two different models used by church members in conceptualizing this relationship of subordination, each based on linking I Cor. 11 with other verses in the Bible.

For some, subordination is a result of the need for order and does not imply inferiority. It refers to a "surface" difference in function (i.e., a difference in what they do but not in what they are). The usual analogy made is with the Trinity: while the Spirit is subordinate to the Son and the Son to the Father, all are equal. This model for subordination is the result of an explicit linking of I Cor. 11 with Gal. 3:28. If there is "no male nor female in Christ," Paul could only be referring to a surface distinction resulting from the need for order in Corinthians. Essentially this is the model of social difference and interdependence implied in the Durkheimian notion of organic solidarity.

For others, however, the important illuminating passage is I Tim. and the subordination of women is interpreted as a function of their spiritual weakness as shown in the fall of Eve. This is essentially a model of spiritual inequality. In it the role of the woman is restricted and separated from that of the man as a consequence of her lower and to some extent polluting nature. This theme is commonly discussed in the anthropology of the symbolism of women (e.g., Ortner 1974).

3.2. Dignity

The second core meaning of hats is that of dignity or modesty and to some extent it mediates between the other two, subordination and formality. It is primarily concerned with woman's position in society, a position to some extent derived from her subordinate relationship to man. A basic element is that a woman's quiet acceptance of her "proper" position creates for her a power or authority. To some extent church members make an equation between wearing a hat as "honoring her head" (i.e., the man) and as "having power on her head." In fact only through her fulfillment of her proper role can a woman exercise authority from God and so influence others toward God, as seen in Peter's advice to wives of non-Christians (I Peter 3:1–2). Conversely, not to accept this position implies immodesty and shame. An important element in dignity–modesty is the nonassertion of self that is demonstrated in covering one's head as opposed to the brazenness and immodesty in adorning oneself and one's head with gold, pearls, and braided hair that women are warned against. Part of wearing a hat is that "women are instructed not to call attention to themselves or to dress so as to cause someone to stumble." There is a connection made between a woman's modesty and her godly influence, especially on men. The principle involved is essentially that of "honor and shame" as has been discussed for the Mediterranean (e.g., duBoulay 1974).

3.3. Formality

The final meaning of hats is primarily concerned not with the relationship between men and women but with that between humans and God. While the need to exhibit formality is supported Biblically by quoting the equation of God and king, the fact that *hats* on women express this formality is traditional. Until recently in Scotland, hats were a normal part of women's apparel, especially when "dressing up." Thus it indicated the formality of an occasion, while not wearing one indicated informality, and for some Christians not to wear a hat to church was irreverent in that it failed to define the situation with sufficient respect. As one informant summarized it, "Head coverings are associated with reverence, even if the principle is not there in black and white."

That the equation of formality and hats is cultural is clearly seen in the insistence by many evangelicals on hats as opposed to other coverings, e.g., scarves. A woman in the Brethren, struck by what she felt was the absurdity of this confusing of Biblical and cultural elements, used to tell me jokingly that one day she was going to wear a wig and not a hat just to get people's reactions.

These three core meanings of wearing a hat provide a basis for agreement among church members, but because of their ambiguity they also provide a basis for disagreement. Agreement results from the shared view that the Bible is the primary referent of meaning, the fact that this Biblical meaning can be expressed in a number of key words and phrases (e.g., *subordination, dignity, modesty, formality*), and the assumption that agreement over phrases is the same as agreement over meaning. Disagreement results from the fact that the meanings of these words and phrases are in fact ambiguous. This real ambiguity in meaning that may exist behind the apparent agreement can be of crucial importance in the attributing of meaning in particular situations, as will be discussed below.

4. Situational Meanings

In this section I will be looking at a number of specific situations that demonstrate how particular meanings emerge from this framework of core meanings, by examining how individuals "select" meanings to fit the situation and even change them by "playing" with the system. Three types of variations in situational meaning of hats will be considered: (1) variations between churches, (2) variations in strategies and meanings in a particular church setting, and (3) variations in the strategies and meanings for a single individual from one setting to another. In the first category I will compare churches as well as examine how the meaning attributed to hats marks off one church from another. In the second, I will be contrasting two Bible studies, one in the Baptist and one in the Adventist church. In the third I will be examining the strategies of women in the Baptist and Brethren groups in actually wearing or not wearing hats to different meetings at their churches.

In looking at the variation between the churches, the subordination of women is clearly the dominant meaning. Among the Adventists, where women come closest to sharing an equal official position with men and many question the modern relevance of women's subordination, only a few older women wear hats and it is never brought up as an issue.* Among the Baptists, with their intermediate position on the role of women in the church, there is a corresponding intermediate position with regard to the wearing of hats and people both for and against wearing hats express concern over the problem. Among the Brethren, with their position of very restricted participation for women in the assembly, the wearing of hats is mandatory for women members.

Although subordination is the most relevant meaning in the context of interchurch variation, there is significant variation between men and women within each church regarding the appropriate model for understanding this. In the Brethren, men tend to hold the "spiritual inequality" interpretation of subordination while women tend toward that of "social difference." In the Baptist church, on the other hand, the reverse is true. Men tend to hold the "difference" interpretation, while women tend toward that of "inequality." This is related to the different experience of the sexes within and between the churches resulting from differences in the social organization of sex roles (Borker 1976) and it produces a striking difference between the churches in the self-conceptions of women. Brethren women, who have a strong sense of the different spheres and functions for men and women, with no sense that these imply inferiority, exhibit considerably more self-confidence than do women in the Baptist church, who often view their position as a

---

*An important factor in the Adventist attitude toward hats is the strong influence of the American church, where hats became of little significance years ago. American influence is quite marked both in terms of members of the Edinburgh church going to American Adventist meetings and institutions and in terms of the number of American church members visiting the Edinburgh church. For example, the minister in charge of the young people's meeting when I did my research was an American who was in Edinburgh to get a Ph.D. in theology.

result of their spiritual weakness. Here we can see a dramatic indication of the impact of social experience in framing the meaning of Biblical symbols and the importance of sexual separation in women's religious self-concepts (cf. Fallers and Fallers 1976).

The interchurch variation has resulted in hats having a boundary-marking function in distinguishing members of different churches. Grace Harris (1977) has made a distinction between inward- and outward-looking symbols that is useful for discussing this boundary-marking process. An inward symbol is one that serves as a rallying or unifying symbol for the people within a particular group, while an outward symbol is one that marks one group off from others; it "stands" for the group. Hats for the Brethren have taken on both these functions as the wearing of hats has declined in other churches. As an inward symbol it signifies to the Brethren, both men and women, their adherence to the Bible, to God's way. Hats have come to represent for them their doctrinal purity, as opposed to other churches that are willing to give in to the standards of the secular world. Hats thus mark the boundary between the assemblies and the other evangelical churches.

At the same time hats serve as an outward symbol of the Brethren to many Baptists. For the Baptists, hats signify the Brethren tendency to be like the Pharisees, overemphasizing outward form at the cost of the inward *meaning* of the individual's relationship to God. To use de Saussure's terms, they feel the Brethren are giving more importance to the signifier than to the signified. They feel the Brethren position has resulted in driving women from the church,* that they "strained for the gnat and swallowed the camel," as one informant put it. Given the situation within the Baptist church, with its division over this issue and the resulting need to de-emphasize it (see below), it is not surprising Baptists should see the Brethren in this light.

Moving from general differences between the churches to specific church settings, it is illuminating to contrast the interpretation of hats in similar settings in two different churches. The setting, that of a Bible study, presents certain situational constraints that are the same for both cases. Yet the meanings selected are very different due to other situational factors, in this case the differences between the churches in the consensus of interpretation and in the social position of women in each of the churches. The first of these studies I will discuss in some detail as an illustration of the processes involved in determining core meanings and applying them to a situation.

*Baptists often gave the example of Brethren assemblies that posted signs saying women without hats would not be admitted and explained that this violated two fundamental principles of the evangelical message, in that it meant judging women on the basis of behavior and keeping women who needed to hear the gospel from in fact hearing it.

The pastor of the Baptist church devoted one of the regular Thursday evening Bible study classes to an examination of I Cor. 11:1–16. He had chosen the topic of women and hats in response to a missionary's query on the subject and the attendance was extremely high (200+, as opposed to a usual 125), reflecting the degree of interest in the topic.

In order to understand the strategy he employed in this study it is necessary to keep in mind a number of factors about the Baptist church. One such factor was size. With a membership of 900, many members did not know one another personally and so were forced to rely largely on outward signs in making judgments about each other. The large size also increased the importance of the pastor, whom all knew and who, despite his comparatively short tenure at the church, knew almost everyone in the congregation at least by name. Thus he served to link together the entire membership.

A second important factor was the minimum of doctrinal consensus required of members of Baptist churches in Scotland. In order to become a member one only needed to have undergone conversion and believer's baptism: to have experienced a personal acceptance of Jesus as savior and to have been baptized by immersion after a profession of faith. It was therefore important for the operation of the church that other doctrinal issues did not emerge as sources of conflict and factionalism within the church, something about which the pastor would be particularly concerned. This danger of factionalism was particularly marked due to the church's size, which in itself led to the formation of subgroups within the church.

The wearing of hats and the position of women was one such source of potential conflict, being an issue over which there was wide variation in interpretation and in the translation of belief into action. The most striking aspect of this variation was the almost universal wearing of hats by older women, the equally universal absence of hats on young women, and the split among the women in their 30s and 40s. It should be mentioned here that comparatively few of the young people (between the ages of 16 and 27) went to the evening Bible study as they had their own Young People's Meeting, including Bible study, on Wednesday. Thus the audience at the meeting was somewhat biased in favor of hat-wearers. The pastor in this meeting employed a symbolic strategy explicitly concerned with influencing others toward a particular set of meanings and actions that he felt was the correct interpretation for the *church*.

The pastor laid out four steps in approaching the passage: (1) "understanding the passage," i.e. a verse-by-verse examination aimed at determining core meanings, (2) examining the context and background of the passage, (3) working out the principles involved, and (4) applying the principles. Although separating these steps in theory, in actually going over the passage the pastor tended to stress the principles being expressed as well as putting the chapter in context. This was partly a result of the difficulty in trying to isolate core from situational meaning and partly a result of his overall strategy.

The format of this first and major step in the study was to read each verse and then discuss its meaning. Essential to this step was the assumption that word meanings are basically unambiguous and so one could determine *the* meaning of a sentence or verse. He began with v.1–2, which he interpreted as Paul's setting the issue in its proper perspective as a nonfundamental of the Christian faith.* This in fact constituted a major part of his strategy of interpretation and presentation. This strategy was twofold in purpose: (1) to downplay the importance of the issue, thereby eliminating it as a legitimate basis for doctrinal division in the church, and (2) to influence others toward a particular and rather conservative interpretation he regarded as correct. He did this by stressing "general principles," upon which all should supposedly agree, while not setting categorical translations of these into action.

The first and for him most important of these principles was that of subordination stated in v.3. Using the analogy of the Trinity, he distinguished subordination from inferiority,† a confusion he felt was often made in modern society. The next four verses were then seen as a further statement of this subordination principle, which generated an opposition between men and women, but one of a restricted nature. He felt men were only more like God in that they could exercise authority, whereas women could not, and that in fact being the "glory of the man" provided the woman with dignity through being served and protected from danger by her husband, to whom such behavior was "instinctive." Thus he introduced early the focus of his interpretation of v.10 and by doing so further emphasized it.

His analysis was as follows: Women should acknowledge their proper relationship to men, though he felt Paul did not want to "encourage extremes"; head coverings are a clear symbol of this subordination

*These two verses need not have been included as part of the complex of verses. The chapter divisions in the Bible are arbitrary, i.e., the Bible was written in verses and books but these were not originally divided into chapters. Thus it was an individual decision on the pastor's part that these verses "went with" the others. This again provides for another possible range of variations in the meaning of the Bible passages themselves, the definition of immediate context.

†He is thus here favoring the social difference as opposed to the spiritual inequality model of subordination.

but, conversely, as such they are also a symbol of women's authority, i.e., a woman with a proper sense of her dignity exercises "authority under her husband." He felt the angels referred to (v.10) were guardian angels who are concerned that "we do right" and who set an example for women by veiling their faces before God. In his framework, v.11–12 became an extension of another principle, that of complementarity, and another warning against an extreme position. In his words, "One's relation to Christ affects all others, Paul is not saying anything to detract from the basic equality of the sexes; God is not creating rivalry but complementarity." In concluding the pastor went on to discuss the three verses on hair and to stress that v.16 again warned against making this a major issue in the church.

The context in which he placed the passage again fit with his playing down of the problem for the modern church.* He pointed out the special problem of the Corinthian church, located in a city renowned for its immorality and one where women uncovered in public were regarded as morally loose. He elaborated on this by explaining the meaning of veils in Middle Eastern society, stressing that veils symbolically made a woman invisible. He made it quite clear that the word for covering used in Greek clearly referred to veils, that Corinth's cultural background was very different from that of modern Edinburgh, and that hats in Edinburgh were not equivalent to veils in Corinth. Although he here presented the foundations for the interpretation that these passages apply only to Corinth, he never suggested this as a possible interpretation. His acknowledgment of this context did, however, temper any criticism that might be leveled against such an interpretation.

Given the structure of his interpretation thus far, the principles and applications flowed quite naturally. The primary principle was that of subordination of woman to man and "this should find expression in Christian worship," although this was difficult "in our culture, which has almost no way of expressing subordination." Second, he felt women should be marked by modesty and the Christian should be "sensitive" to what is regarded as "right" in his society, reiterating that hats were not veils. From the point of view of someone interested in the position of women, it is worth noting that here he did not expand on the principle of complementarity.

In discussing the application of these principles he began with a statement of another issue entirely—that of the position of women in the

---

*He had in fact started the process of contextualization at the very beginning of the meeting as a whole, by using as his introductory Bible reading (such a reading is given at the beginning of all meetings in the Baptist church) the passage from Acts dealing with Paul's visit to Corinth (Acts 18:1–17).

church—by pointing out he had refused to allow the wife of a missionary (who had led one Sunday morning service) to give the children's
address because "women should not teach when men are present." He
in fact strengthened this point by acknowledging that others might dis-
agree with him and warning that if they did it must be "on the basis of
Scripture and not prejudice." The reason for this seeming digression is
clear in terms of his overall strategy. To avoid potential conflict he had
presented himself as taking the most reasonable position with regard to
the passage's meaning. Throughout the study he had presented his as
the most reasonable interpretation, avoiding extremes in either direction,
and to do this he had throughout presented aspects of both positions,
usually favoring the conservative more strongly. Here he was stating his
agreement with one major aspect of the conservative application of the
complex of verses on women before rejecting another—that women
must wear hats. Rather he suggested each woman should consult her
husband and then follow his wishes, thus expressing the principle of
subordination. It was a perfect solution, as it meant that a woman could
express subordination both by wearing and not wearing a hat and it
posited no "blame" on a husband for either favoring or not favoring a
wife's hat wearing. Essentially, it said any agreement reached between a
husband and wife was okay.

The pastor accomplished a number of objectives through this
strategy. Given his position of influence, he successfully managed to
head off any attempts to press this as an issue and provided a
framework in which it became impossible to know a woman's interpretation of the passage from whether or not she wore a hat. In addition, he
presented his interpretation in such a way—by avoiding literalism and
stressing underlying principles—that it appeared the most reasonable
view and as such was impossible to invalidate or even to seriously question. Finally, he provided a framework in which both the conservative
and other views could be incorporated as Biblical and thereby avoided
alienating either camp. Perhaps one sign of his success is that informants I spoke with always thought the pastor agreed with them no
matter how different their views were from each other.

I would like to contrast briefly this Bible study with a much shorter
one dealing with I Corinthians 14 that occurred in the young people's
meeting of the Adventist church. Here the church context was completely different. The Adventists did not make a major distinction between the roles of men and women in the church. To begin with, the
minister in charge of the meeting asked one of the young women to read
v.33–36 and to comment on them. This in itself set forth part of his own
interpretation and strategy as it involved having a woman speak. After

the woman's suggestion that Paul seemed to oppose women preaching, he, as well as another minister attending, went on to suggest a number of contextual interpretations for the verses, all of which restricted their application to the present, e.g., that this was a cultural carry-over from before becoming Christians, that it referred to the particular moral situation in Corinth, that as the chapter dealt with the health of the church the verses might be a warning addressed to some specific women in Corinth who were causing disruptions by asserting themselves and asking foolish questions in church. The entire thrust of interpretation was toward particularizing the meaning to Corinth. The minister even went so far as to jokingly mention that some scholars had cast doubt on the authenticity of these verses, feeling they might have been added by a medieval scribe. This was not presented as a serious interpretation (in fact it would be horrifying as such to an evangelical) but rather served to emphasize the general strategy of particularization and to imply a danger in attempting to apply them rigidly today. This strategy resulted from the general lack of relevance seen for the church of any of the core meanings associated with this entire complex of passages. In particular, women were not perceived as subordinate within the church and to some extent could not be, as the church itself was founded by a woman, Mrs. Ellen G. White.

The differences in these two strategies of attributing meaning are not a matter of crass calculation, of only seeing what one wants to, but largely stem from very real differences in situations that in fact generate different meanings. I have here been able to suggest only some of these situational factors, such as degree of consensus among church members, the official position of women within the church organization, and differences in church history.

Individuals employ symbolic strategies across church settings as well as within a single setting. I would like now to examine the types of strategies women in the Baptist and Brethren churches use in different settings and the ways in which different core meanings are made relevant for the individual in this context.

The women in the Baptist church for whom hats are most problematical are the middle-aged. For the older women there is a correspondence between their interpretation of Biblical meaning and their behavior, both religious and secular. For them hats represent subordination and formality, which are required in both the secular and religious domains. Not only do they always wear hats to church, many of the older women wear hats whenever they leave their homes. For the young women, on the other hand, a correspondence also exists, but their interpretation and behavior are different. Within their cultural framework hats express formality, and within their general religious framework formality in worship is de-emphasized and hats are not worn. Rather than stressing that church is a place to meet with God the king, as do the older women, they stress meeting with God as friend, a situation demanding informality or at least a feeling of being "comfortable," which would not exist if hats were worn.

Neither situation holds for the middle-aged. They were raised believing that women wear hats to church and that not wearing a hat is a sin. They related to me that with the change in Scottish culture they no longer have a "conviction" that wearing hats is necessarily a God-ordained universal as opposed to a man-made tradition. At the same time they are ambivalent as to whether one's relationship to God as king or friend should dominate. For these women, hats have often been a significant factor in their reevaluation of their concept of sin and of their relationship to God. The extent and depth of the meaning of hats for them were quite clear to me in their discussions. They would often speak at length about the process by which they gave up wearing hats or the "compromises" they had reached. In many cases women had in effect rank-ordered services according to their degree of "sacredness" or solemnity (which in turn warranted a corresponding degree of formality) by setting up a continuum of meetings in which they would or would not wear hats. In essence, they had made formality the dominant meaning involved in actually wearing hats in particular situations.

For some of these women the additional factor of not "offending one's brother" entered into their decisions, especially for those who were wives of deacons and elders. Sometimes this factor provided a solution to their dilemma. Although they no longer felt not wearing a hat was sinful in itself, they still found it hard to overcome the feeling it was wrong. This provided them with a good Biblical reason for continuing to wear hats but avoided a firm commitment to particular meanings for the symbol itself.

Whereas, among the Baptists, the ability of women to "manipulate" the system or to express themselves within the system emerges from lack of consensus in the church and from the nature of hats as multivocal symbols with many different alternative meanings, among the Brethren, the ability of women to use hats "strategically" comes from the very rigidity of the equation of form and meaning in which hats are multivocal symbols that mean many things at once. This potential for the strategic use of hats in the Brethren context is best illustrated by an examination of a case of a young woman who attended services at the assembly but did not wear a hat.

This woman was raised in a Brethren assembly and regularly came to most church services with her mother, who was a member. She had undergone a conversion experience in her teens and was accepted as a Christian by most church members, but she was not asked to join the church because she would not wear a hat. The point is that despite the clear equation between hat wearing and being a female member of the assembly—in fact, because of this fixed equation—the position of this one woman was totally ambiguous. There was no way of determining from her actions her attitudes toward the church and church doctrine. There was no way of determining whether she wasn't a church member simply because she did not want to wear a hat or because she did not want to be a church member as well. The rigidity of the rule protected her from ever being asked about her religious beliefs.

5. Conclusion

In this discussion I have been considering the conception of women's position in one important variant of Western Christian culture —evangelical Protestantism. I have done this by examining in depth the meaning of one central symbol of the position of women—the wearing of hats to church. To discern and understand these meanings I have made a distinction between core meanings, with their Biblical basis, and situational meanings, in which the Biblical core is understood in terms of one's experience and the social situation in which one is placed.

Core meanings are those agreed-upon meanings that are drawn from the Bible and that provide a basic frame for situational meanings. Three such core meanings of hats are dominant: subordination, dignity or modesty, and formality. Two of these, subordination and dignity, relate to general themes in studies done on cultural conceptions of women, in particular the examination of notions of power, pollution, modesty, honor, and shame. The third meaning, on the other hand, relates to the general issue of the relationship between humans and their divinities. I have tried to show that it is distorting and misleading to stop the analysis at the level of core meanings. These meanings are in many ways ambiguous and are only given substance through the use of the symbol in particular situations, which themselves generate fields of potential meaning.

After looking at general differences between the churches in the meanings they attribute to hats, I focused on the strategies different individuals used in particular situations to communicate particular interpretations of the meaning of hats. Specifically, I discussed how two pastors, concerned primarily with the need of harmony in their churches, employed symbolic strategies aimed not so much at expressing a particular conception of women's position as at creating consensus among church members, both male and female. Also I discussed how women among the Baptists and the Brethren used symbolic strategies for a variety of purposes: to express their relationship to God, to indicate membership or nonmembership in a church, to communicate a particular conception of their position in the church, and to express the nature of the relationship between wives and husbands. I have tried to demonstrate throughout this analysis that understanding the meaning of hats as a symbol of women's position involves the examination not only of women as objects whose nature and position are defined by fixed cultural conventions, but also of women as part of the social arena of pastors and other individuals interpreting these symbols, and finally of women as social actors in their own right defining cultural realities through their strategic use of hats as symbols.

ACKNOWLEDGMENTS

I would like to thank John Gumperz, Jane Monnig Atkinson, and my husband, Daniel Maltz, for their comments on an earlier version of this article. It is based on research conducted in Edinburgh from September 1972 to October 1973.

References

Borker, Ruth A. 1974. Presenting the Gospel: Religious communication and expressive strategies in three evangelical churches in Edinburgh, Scotland. Ph.D. dissertation, University of California, Berkeley.

Borker, Ruth A. 1976. Strategies of activity and passivity: Women in evangelical churches. Paper presented at the annual meeting of the American Anthropological Association, Washington, D.C.

Deshen, Shlomo. 1970. On religious change: The situational analysis of symbolic action. *Comparative Studies in Society and History* 12:260–274.

duBoulay, Juliet. 1974. *Portrait of a Greek Mountain Village*. New York: Oxford University Press.

Fallers, Lloyd and Margaret Fallers. 1976. Sex and role in Edremit. In J. G. Peristiany (ed.), *Mediterranean Family Structures*. Cambridge: Cambridge University Press.

Gumperz, John. 1971. *Language in Social Groups*. Stanford: Stanford University Press.

Harris, Grace. 1977. Inward-looking and outward-looking symbols. In A. Bharati (ed.), *The Realm of the Extra-Human: Ideas and Actions*. Chicago: Aldine.

Levy, Ann Kibbey. 1973. Puritan beliefs about language and speech. Paper presented at the annual meeting of the American Anthropological Association, New Orleans.

Marks, Morton A. 1974. Uncovering ritual structures in Afro-American music. In I. Zaretsky and M. Leone (eds.), *Religious Movements in Contemporary America*. Princeton: Princeton University Press.

Ortner, Sherry B. 1973. On key symbols. *American Anthropologist* 75:1338–1346.

Ortner, Sherry B. 1974. Is female to male as nature is to culture? In M. Z. Rosaldo and L. Lamphere (eds.), *Woman, Culture and Society*. Stanford: Stanford University Press.

Prime, Derek. 1967. *Questions on the Christian Faith Answered from the Bible*. London: Hodder and Stoughton.

Prime, Derek. 1972. *Methods and Means of Bible Study*. Mimeo.

Turner, Victor W. 1964. An Ndembu doctor in practice. In A. Kiev (ed.), *Magic, Faith, and Healing*. New York: Free Press.

Turner, Victor W. 1967. *The Forest of Symbols: Aspects of Ndembu Ritual*. Ithaca and London: Cornell University Press.

5

Riv-Ellen Prell-Foldes

Coming of Age in Kelton

The Constraints on Gender Symbolism in Jewish Ritual

Societies and communities most often turn to ritual mechanisms and performances when enmeshed in conflicts that defy resolution. Both Victor Turner (1968) and Max Gluckman (1965) have argued, for example, that in stateless societies rituals remove conflict to a mystical plane, embracing the widest norms of unity and loyalty, in order to overcome crises that may not allow for resolution. Rituals might be understood as forms or mechanisms of redress particularly appropriate to either the types of conflict within groups that may grow out of contradictions in social organization, or types of groups that deny conflict in their ideologies (Moore and Myerhoff 1975).

This chapter will address the choice of a modified, and in part innovative, Jewish Sabbath service whose intent was to redress the exclusion of women from ritual practice within a contemporary urban West Coast prayer community. Their exclusion grew from what women and most male members agreed was an inherent failure of traditional Jewish symbols and prayers to include women in a capacity equal and equivalent to men. The ritual to be explored was not ostensibly "radical," breaking entirely with traditional forms. Rather it was created for a single performance by participants who consider themselves traditional or *halakhic* (law-oriented) Jews, and was designed to integrate their contemporary concerns with a traditional, conservative, and religious setting.

The difficulty of structuring change into traditional religion, and in particular prayer and ritual, inevitably raises the question of the elastic-

Riv-Ellen Prell-Foldes · Instructor of Anthropology, University of Minnesota, Minneapolis, Minnesota.

ity, flexibility, and accommodating nature of symbols. Are rituals and their constituent symbols successful and appropriate mechanisms for redress because they "cloak" conflict and exclude questions about the moral order, or is it their unique capacity to dramatize statements of concern? Is there a limit to the multireferential quality of symbols; in certain contexts and social settings might symbols fail to embrace all conflicting parties or interpretations of events? In that case, has the ritual failed as a redressive mechanism? These questions will be raised in light of the case study of what the Minyan, the urban Jewish prayer community, came to call "The Women's Service."

1. The Minyan

The Minyan is the name of the urban prayer group located in Kelton, a major university neighborhood. It is a voluntary community that meets weekly for Sabbath morning services and for all the worship portions of the holidays of the Jewish liturgical year. The Hebrew word for the quorum of ten necessary for prayer is *minyan*; it traditionally denotes ten men. The Minyan takes as its name the elemental social body for Jewish prayer, suggesting the centrality of community prayer to its ideology and functioning. The Minyan is an open group that allows anyone to pray with the community. It has a core group of 25. During the research period from 1973 to 1975, participation varied each Sabbath but usually averaged 40 people. Virtually everyone in the group was involved in nearby universities in the capacity of students, faculty or alumni, or in the local Hillel Foundation, a national Jewish campus organization.

In the context of American Judaism, the Minyan is a somewhat unusual institution because, unlike large synagogues, it does not depend on a rabbi for leadership and because it allows women equal participation. Communal prayer groups have become more frequent in the last eight years, forming a branch of a modern Jewish movement called "New Jews" (Sleeper and Mintz 1971). From its founding in 1971 to the research period, the Minyan counted four rabbis and ten rabbinical students among its members. However, it has not depended upon any one of them for leadership in the conventional sense, and the group's most capable worship leaders often have been religiously well-educated Jews who are not rabbis. In fact, the Minyan conducts its Sabbath and holiday services on a rotating leadership basis primarily in the homes of members. All roles for the service, including the *hazan* (cantor), rotate weekly.

While the group idealizes the possibility that all members should be able to fulfill all roles equally, members nevertheless admit that this ideal has not been realized. Those roles that require considerable religious knowledge and skill, such as leading the service effectively or reading the Torah (Pentateuch) scroll in the more difficult unvocalized Hebrew, are filled by a small and readily identifiable minority. This skilled group, until recently all males, largely overlaps the founding members of the Minyan, who were ironically termed the "Founding Fathers" (and later, "Founding Fathers and Mothers" to reflect the reality of both male and female founders) by the larger group. Therefore, the Minyan, whose structure is formally leaderless and whose manifest ideology is egalitarian, recognizes an expert elite whose services in part allow the group to function.

In addition to worship, the Minyan regularly includes a discussion on a topic generally appropriate to prayer, but ranging from politics to one's work. During the service there is a discussion of the weekly Torah portion,* which usually includes secular contemporary issues rather than more traditionally Jewish scholarly issues. As innovative as these discussions are in the context of Jewish worship, the Minyan considers itself a traditional (rather than Conservative or Orthodox) prayer group. In their manifest ideology, members selectively choose among traditions, symbols, theology, and laws in the religion for their practice during Jewish festivals and Sabbaths. That is, they acknowledge and actively believe that Judaism is changing and changeable by their own choices. Their choice of observance, in fact, agrees in part with their own politics and values in their secular lives. They are thus committed to the political and social relevance of their context to religion, but within a traditional Judaism.

The Women's Service was a ritual held by the Minyan in the spring of 1974. Its purposes were many, but in general it was a concrete form through which a network of women in the Minyan articulated a concern with what was called nationally "the woman's role in Judaism" (Adler 1973). Certainly affected by modern American feminism and a general concern expressed in the New Jews movement with authority relations in the American Jewish religious structure, women were reassessing their essentially domestic role in Jewish ritual through conferences, newsletters, and journals. Women's services, many considerably more radical in altering the traditional liturgy than that conducted in the Minyan, had been held for two years in similar groups nationally. But the task of this discussion is not only to analyze a "Jewish woman's com-

---

*The Torah is divided into portions that are read weekly, except for festivals and particular Sabbaths, when sections relevant to the event are used.

plaint" but to demonstrate its effects in the microstructural context of a community. Consequently, the history of the events that members felt precipitated the ritual is included as well as a discussion of the role of women in Jewish tradition and the rise of Jewish feminism. This use of the "extended case method," tracing events backward in history to uncover their emergence, then moving forward in time to understand their development, provides the structure for this exposition and analysis of the ritual (Gluckman 1973:612).

2. The Impact of the Social Field

Victor Turner has argued that "social dramas"—or extended cases, as they are called here—are played out in "social fields," contexts consisting of various components, including events in the group history, subgroups, personalities, and other categories. Their barriers and interconnections are likely to predate the ethnographer and form the widest social units in which a drama is placed (1968:90). Within the widest social field is the arena, which is the setting for the drama, the setting that allows the crisis to develop into publicly accepted redress. Here action is definitive; the implicit problems and probable crises lurking in the social field are crystallized (1974:134–135).

One of the most significant contexts in the Minyan's social field is Jewish law and ritual. These are constantly taken account of, even when certain traditions are rejected. In this extended case, ultimately it was these traditional laws and rituals, apart from their manifestation in the Minyan, that were the subject and focus of the ritual. Jewish law and commentaries upon it provide the context to which feminists have looked to ascertain the legal and traditional view of the woman. That body of laws enjoins upon people observance of norms restricting "commonly" agreed-upon evils like "theft, fraud, and shedding of blood." These "universal" precepts are only part of the entire corpus of Jewish law, though, because there is a subset of laws appropriate and unique to Jews concerning ritual practice (Maimonides 1912:75–78). Jewish feminists have turned their attention to their exclusion from that subset to emphasize their plight. The law seems to view women as sexual temptresses from whom men must be protected, or contrarily, whom men must protect from themselves. This attitude is the foundation for the segregation of the sexes during worship, when women are not only isolated but often physically hidden from men. In addition, the Jewish woman is seen as procreator, child-rearer, and homemaker.

These two views of the woman are tied directly to her biological functions. As a current Jewish feminist writes:

> The woman's meager [observances] . . . are, for the most part, closely connected to some physical goal or object. A woman's whole life revolved around physical objects and physical experiences—cooking, cleaning, childbearing, meeting the physical needs of children. Without any independent spiritual life to counterbalance the materialism of her existence, the mind of the average woman was devoted to physical considerations. It was, thus, natural that Jewish men should come to identify women with *gashmiut* (physicality) and men with *ruchniut* (spirituality) (Adler 1973:81).

Women were conceived in the law as biologically suitable for the biologically based role of mother and wife. Thus many religious commandments, or *mitzvot* (*mitzvah*, singular), central to Jewish life and observance were accordingly not assigned to them.

Every Jewish male is required to observe 613 *mitzvot* as outlined and embellished upon in Jewish law. These are divided between negative *mitzvot*, those things one must not do such as murder, steal, and commit adultery, and positive *mitzvot* like study of Torah, daily prayer, and special behavior during rituals throughout the year. A Jewish female is enjoined to observe all negative *mitzvot* but is required to observe almost no positive *mitzvot* directly tied to time, such as wearing a prayer shawl. It is reasoned that she cannot be obligated to observe time-bound *mitzvot* like prayer at three separate times daily, because time-bound observances might conflict with a woman's primary responsibility to care for her children.

Only three *mitzvot* exist that are normally associated with women. The first female *mitzvah* is lighting Sabbath candles; the second is *niddah*, the ritual purification a woman performs at the completion of her menstrual period before she may resume sexual intercourse. Through *niddah*, a ritual enjoined upon women to cleanse them from what was conceived as a polluting state, women guard the purity of their husbands and families. The third *mitzvah* is *hallah* and is also related to the Sabbath. It requires that a person, when baking the Sabbath twisted loaf (or other foods categorized as bread) tear off a small piece and burn it in the oven while saying a blessing. While this act is reminiscent of the ancient priest's act at the sacrifice at the Temple, it is appropriate to women because they are associated with the domestic realm and food preparation. The first and third *mitzvot* may also be performed by a man in the absence of females, but the middle one may not. (For further discussion of the place of women in *halakhah* [law] see Adler 1973; Hyman 1973.)

Clearly, the Minyan members, and many women members in particular, were displeased with both the larger problem of equality for Jewish women and its manifestation in the Minyan. Yet their decision to hold a service was not precipitated by an overt crisis or conflict. The service appeared as a redress of a potential, rather than realized, conflict. The advent of an opportunity for a form of redress without an overt breach of norms in the group presented itself, along with some visible relief that the seemingly inevitable conflict over this issue between women and others in the group had not materialized. What form the feared conflict might have taken was never apparent. Perhaps it was only fantasy that any member believed women members would actually withdraw from the group or demand liturgical changes so radical that even sympathetic members would be unable to agree. Rather, a series of events preceded the planning of the ritual which were occasions to make known the concern of women without any particular incident developing into a demand that might then have produced a conflict.

The concrete manifestation of this issue in the Minyan may be traced to its first anniversary, when a vague dissatisfaction among women in the group developed over their participation in the group and their relationship to it as women. They coped with this dissatisfaction by organizing as a group to discuss problems within the Minyan specifically, avoiding the wider issues of concerns that arose directly out of halakhic Judaism. Their focus was on a general feeling of exclusion from discussions, and their inability to compete or contribute because of a lack of religious education. In particular, they were angry at "dominating" and "authoritative" men in the group, feeling that the assumption of these men was that they had less to say because they were women. The meeting was a cathartic one, in which these few women expressed anger rather than organizing in any way for future action, and indeed, they never met again. But they did decide at this meeting that they had to educate themselves as Jews in order to be taken seriously. Until this time a sexual grouping had never been acknowledged as significant in the Minyan, particularly because its manifest ideology directly countered the traditional Jewish view that women did not have the same religious needs or duties as men. The form of their meeting was akin to a "women's group" or a "consciousness-raising" session. It was cathartic; it located the problems that each experienced outside of the individual women, in part with certain men, and also with the dearth of women's religious education resulting from generally held cultural values. They expressed frustration and anger at their treatment as women, portending a conscious recognition of sex. Crucially, these problems were no longer perceived as individual problems; they were now the problems of their sex and their culture.

In the spring of 1973, eight months following this meeting, a group of West Coast Jewish women, a few Minyan women among them, organized a Jewish feminist conference. There, as in many of their publications, Jewish feminists raised the legal and ritual view of women and how to change it. The conference, organized in the Western United States as one the year previously had been in the East, was a culmination of efforts to create concern for Jewish feminism as an issue, and a beginning for organizing ongoing study and consciousness-raising groups. As a result, women in the Minyan organized and participated in such groups in addition to their prayer community in order to explore their own role in Judaism. As a result, the locus of this quest was directed toward the Minyan from 1973 to 1974. With the arrival and more assertive participation of several women—some overtly committed feminists and others who were so traditionally skilled as to be able to assume more demanding roles in the worship service—"the woman's role in Judaism" became a significant public topic. Minyan discussions increasingly focused on the limited Biblical vision of women. Jacob, a rabbi and Founding Father, summarized this change in the group before the Women's Service was held. He said:

> There was even a time, by the way, when I had the feeling that the women were going to take over the Minyan. They had become so together and so confident and so many of them could do so many different things, that I thought it was going to become a women's Minyan. . . . It might well be that if one took a count of who in the Minyan can fulfill all the offices [leadership of the service], there might be more women than men.

Women had indeed become more visible in the Minyan. During the same period, though to a far less intense degree, men in the Minyan, particularly Founding Fathers and husbands and boy friends of feminists in the group, self-consciously attempted to integrate women by being sensitive to including them more in discussions and encouraging their religious participation. Some liturgical changes were made; certain blessings recited around the Torah (Mi Sheberakh) were rewritten to include the blessing not only of the Biblical "patriarchs," which is traditional, but of the "matriarchs" as well. But all this activity and orientation to women's issues did not satisfy a concern that was experienced about the "women's role" in the tradition. One informant described the situation prior to the planning of the Women's Service.

> Though women enjoy equal rights in the Minyan's ritual observance in terms of counting in a Minyan, serving as hazzanim [prayer leaders] and dis-

cussants, being called for *aliyot* [blessings of the Torah], and reading from the
Torah, nevertheless, a pronounced feeling of male dominance remains.
Many attributed this in the past to women's lack of education or familiarity
with the tradition, but as women in the group became more knowledgeable,
the problem did not cease. Rather it emerged more definitively as a feeling of
exclusion from a traditional liturgy filled with masculine imagery, that is, in
the metaphors and attributes associated with God and therefore more acceptable to men.

At last, by 1973, the problem reached the most cosmic level. No longer
were women complaining of their place in an organization, or even of
laws that the Minyan together had chosen to change, but they felt it
was the *experience* of worship, the language of prayer, and the culture
out of which the *siddur* (prayer book) was produced that made women
feel alien.

The many elements of the social field impinging on the events of the
arena are apparent in the group history. Secular feminism, a movement
that every person in the Minyan was familiar with and that women and
men identified with, had tremendous effect on the inception of the
women's service, its form, the women involved, and the men who supported it. Likewise Jewish feminism, which became nationally promi-
nent in 1972 with a New York conference, produced publications and
ideas and led to the local conference that also affected behavior in the
Minyan. Thus movements of national scope touched the community
and shaped events in the arena.

3. The Planning of a Redressive Ritual

The generalized dissatisfaction with women's place in the group
and in Judaism met with a fortuitous possibility as a result of a Fall 1973
Sabbath retreat. In a general Saturday afternoon meeting in which the
liturgy for the Minyan Sabbath service was set, a member named
Martha asked others to join her in planning a slightly modified service,
an occasional option of the group. Only four women volunteered. The
potential of this accident escaped no one. There was spontaneous and
instantaneous recognition that this service would be oriented to women,
and that it would imply an indictment of Judaism and/or the group. A
raucous burst of laughter and nervous joking followed an uncomfortable
silence, which betrayed the trepidation of members regarding a "wom-
en's service." The tensions, the issues, and the people involved in
feminist issues had become fused in the Minyan. The electric reaction in

the room caused by five women volunteering to lead the service illustrates how profound the issue of women really was. Unrealistic fears were expressed, then and throughout the planning, that the service might be extremely radical, too political, and might in some way ruin a Sabbath. The women who volunteered later expressed an instantaneous fear and excitement that they must do something important, something more than "bitching," to legitimate the claims against the tradition they had been discussing for more than a year. The intense response seemed to grow out of a sense that a crisis, whose potential existed in the social field of which the Minyan was a part, had been imminent. The period of planning the redressive ritual was, for all those involved, overshadowed by the possibility of conflict.

The months that followed the retreat in which the Women's Service was ostensibly being planned were filled with the breakup and formation of network after network of planners. Only one woman of the original planners stayed involved in the service through all of the groups. From September to March the service belonged to any woman who was interested, and loose coalitions of women came together and separated. The reasons given by every woman for the constantly changing and overlapping groups of planners were conflict with scheduled meetings and personal laziness in the face of the enormity of the task of creating a service that would address Jewish women's problems in the tradition.

The initial group of planners had attempted in their three meetings to rewrite some prayers, thought about planning a discussion rather than holding a special Sabbath service, attempted to locate "role models" for alternative views of Jewish women (another common secular feminist approach to the sexism problem), and found each task enormous and hopeless. Their most touching revelation occurred around rewriting prayers. As God is addressed in the masculine "you" in Jewish prayer, they faced first how to address God in an alternative service. They had no desire to be "radical," so they did not take the simple solution to reverse language and use a female pronoun. Instead, they decided to rewrite prayers and refer to God as "one," leaving it neuter. As Martha, who had a fluent knowledge of Hebrew, sat down to translate the prayers she recalled that there was no neuter in Hebrew and therefore no alternative. It was just such an incident that led the first group to disillusionment and dissolution.

One woman from that first group served as a bridge between these planners and the other loosely connected groups. Jean was not a particularly verbal member of the Minyan but was nevertheless outspoken

about her feminism. In the *Purim* pageant* she was cast as Queen
Vashti, a role she assumed in a costume of a women's liberation poster
attached to her shirt. In a later group Deborah was a key planner. She
was a Reform rabbinical student,† but neither was she religious in a
conventionally observant way (observing dietary laws or Sabbath restrictions), nor was she religiously educated before she entered rabbinical
training. She was a relatively active, admired, recent Minyan member
and her interest in such a service developed from the previous *Simḥat
Torah*,‡ where she "viscerally responded" to a radical sense of exclusion
as a woman in Judaism.

Miriam, the third member of the trilogy of planners, was also a
Reform rabbinical student. She was a Founding Mother and had gone to
school at the local university and into the rabbinate on Jacob's suggestion. She had moved from a reticent, religiously uneducated female
member to a rabbinical student "expert" in the course of her years of
Minyan membership. She was not, in her own words or in the views
of other planners, a feminist, but she was concerned with the issue of
women in Judaism. Miriam did not play a key role in the service itself,
but she worked with Jean and Deborah, all three of them employed by
Hillel at the time in the planning of the service.

These three women were joined intermittently by Gail and Barbara,
the group's most outspoken and vocal feminists. They both participated
actively in Jewish feminist study and consciousness-raising groups.
They were self-conscious feminists, almost strident about their beliefs,
and they were also educated and committed Jews interested in the integrity of the service and a place for women in it.

---

*Purim (the feast of lots), a Jewish festival, is celebrated in memory of the fictionalized
triumph of Jews over a Persian statesman who had sought their destruction. It is an early
spring carnival-like festival, which is celebrated through masquerades, pageants, and the
reading of the *megillah*, a burlesque elaboration of the Biblical story of Esther (Schauss
1970). The Minyan celebrates *Purim* in conjunction with the local Hillel by not only
reading the megillah, but presenting a humorous dramatization along with it. In the
megillah Vashti, Queen of Persia is mentioned. She met her downfall by a refusal to be
submissive to her husband Xerex's wishes. His subsequent marriage to Esther was responsible for saving the Jews. Traditionally, her haughtiness is condemned, but in the
1974 pageant Jean played her as a feminist heroine.

†At the present time, commencing a decade ago, women are admitted only to the Reform
and Reconstructionist rabbinical seminaries.

‡*Simḥat Torah* (rejoicing in the law) is the holiday that concludes the long cycle of festivals
that begins with the Jewish New Year. It is the eighth day of the *Sukkot* festival, which
follows the Day of Atonement. The festival marks the end of the reading of the Torah
scroll and the immediate beginning of it with Genesis. It is a joyous festival marked by
unusual intimacy with the Torah. A discussion of the 1973 celebration of the festival in the
Minyan occurs later in the chapter.

Finally, a group of women who had participated or been made aware of the service were called together for a final plenary session on the week of the service. They were women Deborah characterized as "deserving to be involved; *kovod* (respect) required it." They were women with whom any such service must reckon. They included Founding Mothers, a Yiddish professor, and Linda, the woman whose home it was to be held at and who was an active and interested participant. At this final meeting they discussed details, made suggestions, and were extremely enthusiastic. While the first three planners were weary and wary of all the plans by the time the service occurred, these women expressed a sense of power and excitement.

What precisely constituted the goals or purposes of their planned ritual is a complicated matter. Generally they all agreed that they had come together to modify a ritual in order to address a problem rather than to permanently change a state of affairs. They alternately called their rationale for the service throughout the months "coming to terms with sexism in Judaism," "to focus on the role of women," and "to raise consciousness in the group." Clearly they had hoped for recognition of their concerns; but such an acknowledgment meant an unconditional indictment of Judaism. However, changes in the Minyan were not implied by such an indictment. In seeking redress for the general and imprecise grievance of the woman's position in Judaism, they sought many shades and types of it. Their many purposes, in fact, underlie the implicit and occasionally contradictory meaning in the notion of redress. At least three general types—transformative, reiterative, and compensatory—may be identified within the Women's Service, and they serve as the framework for its description and analysis. On this occasion these general types of redress simultaneously articulated contradictory goals, emphasized different aspects of social life, and ignored others. Most perplexing perhaps is that while some types of redress sought to change behavior and transform symbols, other types sought no such changes.

Redressive mechanisms may attempt to *transform* situations by altering affairs that brought about a conflict. One might characterize this as a conventional understanding of redress. But redressive mechanisms may offer more subtle alternatives. They may simply *compensate*, that is, allow parties to acknowledge a problem without undertaking to alter the causes of a conflict. Finally, redress may *reiterate* the social order, denying or minimizing a conflict, suggesting without any public change or acknowledgment that the status quo has returned. Even if a solution is achieved it would not be publicly recognized as redressive. In the Women's Service all of these types of redress were sought and all succeeded in different degrees. But all were sought in the framework of a traditional Minyan Sabbath service with important modifications.

Why did the women select religious ritual in which to redress their grievances? There were many other means available to them such as conducting classes and lectures, or meeting apart from the Sabbath, and ritual seemed a very defeating, if familiar, medium for them all. They grew tired of the task, and often felt the problem was overwhelming. Their discouragement was hardly surprising as their concerns were unredressable in the transformative sense. The members of the Minyan, women included, had no interest in discarding traditional Jewish liturgy. Ritual succeeded here in offering a form that did not require conclusions, actions, or concrete proposals. Ritual was an appropriate vehicle because a complex, multileveled statement was required. Sally Moore and Barbara Myerhoff (1977), in a discussion of secular ritual, have attempted to isolate the crucial characteristics of the ritual form. In short, they view ritual as a social activity rather than belief or intention. Emphasizing its behavioral qualities, it is stylized and precise, giving it a sense of the nonordinary which frames, selects, and focuses attention on elements that are frozen and condensed from mundane social process while simultaneously binding participants to one another. Under normal circumstances rituals are closed to negotiations of their boundaries; they are beyond question, and what they draw attention to is beyond question. They argue, therefore, that ritual provides the ideal form for dealing with the terrifying and risky because it may be contained in a shape and form that is on the participants' own terms. The terrifying and risky for participants is, they suggest, the recognition inherent in every ritual that "lurking beneath the smallest and the largest of them, the more banal and the most ambitious [is] the possibility that we will encounter ourselves making up our conceptions of the world, society, and our very selves. We may slip into that fatal perspective of recognizing culture as our construct. . . ." (1977:22). Ritual's precision and predictability combat that fear even in improvised or made-up rituals that Myerhoff has called "nonce" rituals, which inevitably borrow from and endow themselves with the authority of traditional rituals (1977). Thus steeped in the familiar, the new may appear unchanged and changed at once.

Following this view, the ritual vehicle was ideal then for a service that sought to both change and maintain tradition simultaneously, to underscore certain problems in Jewish life without invalidating all of it. The framing aspect of ritual and its special ability to tolerate paradox offered a form appropriate to the message. Myerhoff has written on this special quality of ritual to cope with paradox: "Ritual must take this [highly precise] form because of its function—which obviously differs from its professed aims—that function is to present symbols in a context such that the opposed meaning and contradictions they embrace do not and cannot become evident" (1974:239).

Myerhoff had in mind that contradictory meanings embraced by the orectic and ideological poles of a symbol outlined by Victor Turner (1970:28); here I am describing not only the various meanings accrued by a symbol but also the often contradictory messages and purposes behind a ritual which make it the vehicle of paradox *par excellence*. In turning to the actual ritual event, I discuss it in terms of the three purposes or types of redress sought. This organization, rather than a chronological one, will, I hope, clarify both the esoteric quality and the quantity of the data.

4. The Ritual Event

The modifications of the Minyan Sabbath service introduced by the women on this occasion had wide and radical implications, but their commitment to and respect for tradition was evident in their maintenance of the majority of the liturgy and structure of a regular service. In the place of the 30-minute pre-praying *(davening)* discussion that normally began the Sabbath service, the women planners introduced an event that discussed in turn the individual role each one had taken. The regular *shachrit* (morning service) was modified and divided into three sections: (1) reciting psalms, (2) an alternative *amidah* (the central "standing" prayer), and (3) reading the Torah; a discussion of the service was substituted for a Torah discussion, and a second postmortem discussion of the service, led by various women, followed.

The transformational aspects of redress which the ritual structured and succeeded in accomplishing might be characterized as providing a kind of *rite de passage*. The women used the ritual to demonstrate, underscore, and frame their status in the group and in Judaism, and through a particular statement made some small impact on the place of women in the Jewish tradition within the Minyan. In fact, it is ritual in its active, behavioral dimension, which allowed the women to take every role in the service, demonstrating public competence in their religious education and skills. On this occasion roles were not filled simply by members who happened to be women, but by Jewish women, and their Jewishness and femaleness were equally significant. The women not only took the conventional Minyan roles for a Sabbath, they talked about the process of creating a Women's Service in the Minyan during the service. They explained what roles they would take, and the learning they experienced in the planning process. The women claimed that their modifications were not designed or performed to prove something, and that the "rehearsals" were far more significant than the "performance." Their introductory statements carried a covert meaning: "If this fails or you don't like it, we've already succeeded." This whole introduction to the service, in addition to the women assuming all regular Sabbath roles, was a statement through ritual form that the highly prized goal of competence had been acquired by women.

As is so often the case in ritual, even the setting of the service reinforced the meta-message that the role of women in the group as participants had been transformed. As Linda said in retrospect:

> I loved the fact that people took it [the service] so seriously. I loved the fact that people got dressed up for that service, which was really exciting for me. A lot of people said that it was like a *Bat Mitzvah*. People were so nervous. It was a little late and people were concerned about when it was going to start and said, "They're getting dressed" [like at a *Bat Mitzvah*]. Deborah was madly reading the Torah scroll [for practice]. Everyone was very concerned and discussing strategy.

Linda referred to a *rite de passage* in Jewish life, a marking of manhood or womanhood in a religious sense. The *Bar Mitzvah* (*Bat*, feminine) entails preparation and education and culminates in the acknowledgment of the right of the adolescent to participate fully in Jewish ritual life by being called to the Torah. In the Minyan, it constituted a formal acknowledgment of a new status for women, and their anxiety indicated the extent and significance of this performance as a successful demonstration of their preparation and a formalization of what had developed over two years in the group. An informant underlined the changes that she felt resulted in the group after the service:

> It succeeded in the point that it was the culmination of finally bringing women to the forefront in the Minyan. It was a coming out. Everyone knew that a lot of work had gone into it—and reading, and thinking, and meetings. And somehow all of that serious work was coming out of "we're no longer sitting on the couch squeaking." We can speak out equally because we've come to grips with the very essence of the Minyan (the *siddur*) and that is what is in the pages we read and reread. We took the text and we came up with a point of view. We're on valid footing.

While this informant's view of the outcome of the service was considerably more optimistic than that of others, even Deborah, the most sparing in her optimism about the results, felt that women would no longer solely be expected to cook, nor would anyone call them "girls" again.

These examples called up by Deborah are both concerns of secular feminism. From one of the most optimistic conclusions to one of the most pessimistic ones regarding the Women's Service, there was a general sense that the attitude toward women in the Minyan had been altered by the service, despite the fact that all participants since the Minyan's inception had idealized the official equality of women in the group. Public manifestation of the change also occurred within the ritual context. In the months following this service there was a serious effort in the Minyan to change grammatical forms so that both male and female Biblical figures were invoked where traditionally only males had been, and on one particular holiday *(Simḥat Torah)* several men met with Deborah in order to plan an alternative to imagery in prayers previously perceived as sexist.

Transformative redress is concerned with altering a state of conflict, moving it to a new level in which parties are, if not satisfied, willing to accept decisions or other events planned to directly resolve the crisis. In the women planners' presentation of themselves as fully competent participants in Jewish worship and Minyan discussions, they made a statement through ritual that they had changed their status. This change was reflected in an alteration of Jewish liturgy, to some extent, to more seriously include Biblical matriarchs and to reduce some "sexism" on a particular religious holiday. It was action, a property of ritual that allowed the women to *behave* competently rather than merely ask for belief in their competence, that made this formalization of role transformation possible and effective. But transformative redress constituted only a portion of the intent and outcome of the Women's Service. Reiterative redress—that is, redress that ironically is oriented toward denying a need for change, denying that a group requires either new mechanisms or that situations require any change in social relations—characterized a large portion of the ritual. When the planners had organized to plan a service, they initially sought to rewrite every prayer in the *siddur,* and they contemplated changing every Hebrew masculine reference to God to the Hebrew feminine. They quickly gave up this task, they said, because of the sheer enormity of it. But unstated publicly, though evident to all participants, was their interest in remaining Jews within a traditional Minyan despite the tremendous problems this posed for feminists.

The work of ritual for this service was to reveal change while masking it: to give the familiar a new form, to make the new comprehensible and acceptable and show the old capable of growth. They sought to introduce the new, not so much in newly written prayers, though there was one major attempt at that, but by introducing nonprayer forms into the service in which women related to God in a "womanly voice." That is, the planners sought some examples of a "woman's language" rather than the "male language" of the *siddur*. These new forms provided alternatives to the *siddur*. What was reiterated in these new forms was that the Minyan was capable of incorporating any change, that the old ways were more than sufficient.

The women's alternative prayer forms were introduced into the service where the psalms *(Pesukey Dezimra)* are normally *davened* as preparation for prayer. The psalms are the section for limited innovation in Minyan services; on occasion poetry or prose are substituted. In the Women's Service the prayer preparation section was replaced by seemingly contradictory forms, the poetry of a modern Hebrew poet and a Yiddish *tkhine*, a private petitional prayer written for and frequently by women, and the traditional "Song of the Red Sea." The poetry of Yocheved, Bat Miriam was included because it was directed toward an unknown "you" in both the masculine and feminine pronouns, and had been interpreted as a unique effort of a Jew to speak to God in modern language. The gender switch in the poet's address to "you" suggests an interest in a variety of God's images besides the customary masculine one. The poetry sharply contrasted with the second new prayer form introduced, the *tkhine*, a supplementary conversational prayer in Yiddish, which was written for immigrant women at the turn of the century, emphasizing seemingly stereotyped roles of wife and mother. The setting of the *tkhine* they chose was the Sabbath candlelighting. What united these apparently contrasting forms and languages was their use apart from their content, as a "woman's language" or a vocabulary about God outside of the *siddur*. The only section from the *siddur* used during psalms was the *shirah* (the song), whose authorship is attributed to Miriam, the sister of Moses. The song was believed to have been sung in celebration at the Red Sea following the drowning of Pharaoh's soldiers at the exodus. The Minyan members rarely include this psalm because of its celebration of violence and an ethnocentrism that leaves them uncomfortable. Despite its content, it was not perceived as contradictory within a feminist service. In the Women's Service the *shirah* represented another example of "women's language," that is, a woman's unique attempt to communicate joy, even, the women said, if it was for "an unfortunate reason."

When the poetry, prayer, and *tkhine* were *davened* in the ritual at the planners' request—that is, when they were actually chanted like prayers—they were elevated to the sacred. "Women's language" and prayer became a single language. New content became prayer when placed in traditional structures. The new "psalms" both emphasized and self-consciously masked change in their ritual form. The old was made new; the new became traditional. Hebrew, Yiddish, and English translations were made, in one sense, a single language through *davening*. One planner characterized this process as "fitting new things into old frameworks." In summary, the effort to create a "women's language" represented the reiterative aspect of the Women's Service as a redressive mechanism. In this sense, the service sought to stay within the tradition, to show that the ritual, if not its "script," the *siddur*, was modifiable, expandable, and open to change, without requiring serious transformation. Members could comment on "how lovely" the poem was, and could feel, as an informant paraphrased, an "isn't that nice, a creative service" feeling. None of this implied change; none of this really implied an indictment of the Minyan or the Jewish tradition, though of course it all appeared in a service that was on the whole such an indictment.

One task of ritual is to present events as timeless, to mask and limit change, to reiterate the past within the present. This aspect of the Women's Service demonstrates, however, that ritual may also serve to present change, newness, and difference in a form that suppresses its very possibility. Some of the goals of the Women's Service went beyond the scope of reiterative mechanisms. What the reiterative mechanisms could not contain was the introduction of a feminist ideological element that often assumed a liberalism and humanism antithetical to Judaism or any traditional religion. This element may best be understood in the desire for compensation, in that while an acknowledgment of a problem was called for, action for change was not demanded. What the women planners wanted in part was a reexamination of Judaism at the level of belief, which Moore and Myerhoff point out (1977) is precisely what is avoided in ritual forms. Organizers confessed that their goal could vaguely be stated as a changed "consciousness" in the Minyan.

"Consciousness raising" is a secular strategy and tactic of the American women's movement. In addition to political action and equality, the goals of this movement included a "new consciousness" from which political action would spring. Consciousness meant a new way of seeing and experiencing the relationships between men and women, women and women, and women and themselves. As one informant put it: "It is the process of acquiring an attitude, life-style, and commitment to action to deal with institutionalized interpersonal sexism in an understanding of roles." When one's consciousness is "raised," one is jarred into understanding the old ways as "sexist," "unliberated," and above all inappropriate. Implicitly, a new consciousness demands an admission or recognition of guilt or fault in one's prior behavior.

Although it implies change in the future, it does not itself constitute that change. Clearly a redressive mechanism seeking compensation is completely compatible with a goal for a change in consciousness, which was the women planners' rationale for their service. With a new consciousness among Minyan members, the problems of exclusion women experienced would be acknowledged and accepted as legitimate, but without a guarantee, indeed even a suggestion, that once they were acknowledged change would follow. Neither a permanent transformation of symbols nor a specific course of action would be demanded.

Ritual is rarely a forum for stating problems. The "nonce elements" of this service, those Myerhoff characterized as improvised, were drawn out of secular feminism and uncomfortably juxtaposed with the sacred, timeless qualities of the Sabbath morning ritual. In contrast to the suggestion that ritual "promotes shared public time, setting aside individual experience" (1977), this attempt to "raise consciousness" was above all designed to emphasize how limited a share Jewish and Minyan women had in the public sacred experience. The "consciousness-raising" elements in the ceremony inverted the function of ritual and prayer. They were highly self-conscious. They were ideological and tied to belief rather than concretely performatory. They suggested that the entire ritual was open to question, contained conceptions that were time-bound, made-up, and necessitated change. While they maintained the stylized, even dramatic elements of ritual, they violated, with great effect, the crucial elements of ritual that bind participants to a potential unity. By denying unity, they "raised consciousness" and demanded compensation.

The central sections of the Morning Service were the focus for "consciousness raising." The intent of the changes in the service was to communicate that Judaism has made women "other." It was an effort that one planner called "irresponsible" because it alienated everyone from the liturgy, at least at the moment of the service. Alienation, however, was the very process by which consciousness was "raised." The following analysis takes up three particular sections of the service; the *amidah* prayer, the Torah service, and the discussion that followed the Torah service.

The *amidah* is the central prayer of Jewish liturgy, modified slightly on the Sabbath. It is called *amidah* (standing) because it is recited while standing and is at the center of the service in both its location and its significance. No one in the Minyan has rewritten or modified it for any service. The Women's Service, and Jean in particular, chose to take up this prayer for modification in English translation. Jean said that what she found missing from the *amidah* was "the recognition of matriarchal figures and attributes, the inclusion of 'feminine' characteristics which are usually underplayed as to their importance, the humanization of language and symbol, and the observance of customs and law in ways which are mindful of individual needs."

The *amidah* was not only an effort to find a language in which women might pray; it created a feminist theology. In her version Jean introduced the Biblical matriarchs along with or instead of patriarchs, and replaced the "warlike, powerful" images of God with concepts Jean associated with the feminine: "tranquility, nurturance, maternality, and peacefulness." Here new images and language replaced the old, unlike in the psalms, where they were subsumed within the old.

Examples from the new *amidah*, contrasted with its traditional form, illustrate this effort. These feminist images and qualities seemed to emerge completely from a stereotypic view of woman as mother. Jean's images were certainly not those of Miriam, who sang when the Egyptians drowned. For example, she changed the phrase "God who is great, mighty and awesome" (De Sola Pool 1960:196) to "God who is great in infinite smallness and mighty gentleness." A similar change consisted of "Thou art the rock of our life and shield of our deliverance" (De Sola Pool 1960:204) to "Yours are the cradling arms of life and the womb of our safe deliverance." The feminist *amidah* populated the cosmos with matriarchs and sought new imagery for a God symbolized as "king," "father," "master." The simple exchange of one quality for another, a matriarch for a patriarch, expressed a need to compare and contrast, to above all notice and experience what women felt. It was a prayer that did not present a new kind of meditation, as in the psalms; it was *the* prayer, and it suggested in unmistakable terms that in its traditional form it excluded women.

Inevitably, these simple exchanges, which highlighted the exclusion of women from traditional ritual, entailed a "feminist theology." If what was indictable about Judaism were its "masculine" and "exclusionary" images, then Jean's *amidah* had no choice but to advance an alternative liberal and humanistic vision of the religion as feminist. Along with her substitution of one gender-related quality for another, Jean incorporated other messages implied in her liberal humanist stance which radically contradicted important theological precepts in the *amidah*. Her perspective is the most evident, for example, where she reconceptualized the Biblical charge to observe the Sabbath according to God's precise commandments, which are repeated in the *amidah*, to read, "The people of Israel shall keep the Sabbath, observing it in a way which befits each person's needs. . . ." Also, that section of the *amidah* which voices the messianic hope that the Temple will be rebuilt and reoccupied in

Jerusalem was replaced with the supplication "Help us to build the temple of justness soon and in our day, where we may always worship." With this change, Jean is no longer describing the historical Temple of Israel, which was the focus of the sacrificial cult, but a metaphorical concept of universal justice independent of the messiah.

The implications of Jean's *amidah* raise the issue of the precision of symbols and their ability to accommodate contradictory referents in social contexts. Rituals, Moore and Myerhoff argued, are precise in order to avoid the realization that they are in fact made-up artifices. That Jean could rewrite prayers implied that she then could make not only the simple substitutions but the more radical theological changes as well. To approach issues of belief through ritual is an endeavor that undermines the traditional and unchanging quality of ritual. For one's social group to accept those beliefs in the vehicles of symbols demands that they, for many reasons, accept the referents as well. Whether or not the Minyan found the referents Jean introduced in her new theology consistent with their own experience of the prayer was taken up in the discussion of the service. Jean's *amidah* was presented to the Minyan as an alternative to be voluntarily *davened* in English along with the traditional version, and its active *davening* by the majority of men and women was an acknowledgment of her view, even an effort to try the new cosmology.

The Torah service follows the *amidah* and was the second area of compensatory redress. In the Minyan's service the *ḥazan* brings in the Torah and marches it around the room to be kissed by participants as a sign of respect. Thereafter the scroll is "undressed" from its protective and ornate "garments" and is read intermittently as congregants are called up for blessings over it. Following the weekly portion, at the close of the reading, two members of the congregation are called to lift the scroll and then retie and "clothe" it before it is put away. Then follows the reading of the *Haftarah*, a section from the books of the Biblical Prophets. The ritual is punctuated with sung prayers about God, Moses, the place of the ark in Biblical wars, and the oneness of God.

Not only did the Torah as an object and symbol and the service around it have the larger Jewish significance but, for planners, they had import within the Minyan itself. At *Simḥat Torah* in 1973 the Torah was conventionally symbolized throughout the ritual as female. The central metaphor of the holiday is marriage, and certain men who are honored are called groom *(ḥatan)* of either the Torah or Genesis *(Bereshit)*. The festivities include seven *hakafot*, or circumambulations of the synagogue, during which the Torah is passed from one man to the next in the act of ritually dancing with "her." *Torah* is a feminine Hebrew noun and is symbolized as the bride to Israel, who is "her" bridegroom. In fact, this "sexual" relationship is one of the metaphors by which the human–God relationship is explained. That relationship is described as one of dominance–submission, and metaphors include king–people, and often lover–beloved or husband–wife. It was the latter that was emphasized on *Simḥat Torah* and the most problematic one for Deborah. She, like many other women planners, wondered, if Jewish males identified themselves as both groom/lover and beloved/bride, what possibilities remained for women to symbolize their relationship to God?

The Torah service gathered a number of activities together in the Women's Service, all oriented to "consciousness raising," and was the one most appropriate to that activity. The handling of the Torah, forbidden to women by custom, was already changed in the Minyan. However, the treatment of the Torah as a female during *Simḥat Torah*, even metaphorically, was achingly alienating for Deborah as a woman. The Torah service became her focus. Though Deborah read the scroll for this Sabbath, it was the very presence of women in a portion of the service normally dominated by skilled men that was the most jarring reminder of their frequent exclusion.

The tone of the service was set when Deborah brought the scroll into the room and read a personal statement:

> A pause in our service
> Time to take the Torah out of the ark.
> It's an unfamiliar pause for me
> Usually I sit and watch my men friends approach the ark
> Touch the Torah
> hold the Torah.
> Can I lift her?
> Will I know how to hold her?
> Why do I call the Torah "her"?
> Is it because the word itself is feminine?
> Or because we think of God as male
> and his gift to his people as somehow female?
> Why?
> How do I relate to Torah
> I who have never been close to her?
> The Torah is the central symbol of Judaism
>   but I've hardly read from her.
> The Torah is the central symbol of Judaism
>   but I've hardly held her.

Deborah's statement, not unlike Jean's *amidah* translation, attempted to directly make members aware, even uncomfortable, that the Torah is a symbol and an object that is perceived as female, and that many are unfamiliar with it. In timeless rituals there is no place for such fears and doubts. She successfully made them public and overt so that members would be forced to confront the discomfort.

The most obvious reversal of women's peripheral status occurred in the various roles associated with the Torah. These activities had been open to all members in the Minyan, but certain regularities had developed. For example, men almost always lifted the Torah because of its weight and size, and women then took the allied role of redressing the Torah in its garments. For this service an especially small Torah was borrowed from a local synagogue, and a woman was called to lift, and a man to redress and wrap it. Each aspect of the Torah service became significant because every decision to carry it out was made by gender rather than by individual. This systematic choice, the planners knew, would be apparent to all members, who were forced to see that women had noted their lack of participation—forced or not—and now they, in a limited sense, returned the gesture.

The Torah service consistently pointed, in the most overt manner, to the exclusion of women from the Jewish cosmos, from prayer, and from full religious membership. The women's purpose in their service was to use ritual as a forum to demonstrate and experience the possibility of a new female role in Judaism and in their own community. They pointed to the arbitrariness of ritual boundaries and asserted that everything was open to question. They consciously chose to say that traditional symbols could not accommodate their demands. As such, they were making a statement, one that might be considered contradictory to their own and anthropologists' increasingly sophisticated analyses of symbolic systems.

Anthropologists, particularly since Levi-Strauss, seem inclined to view symbolic forms as ways of organizing the world. Whatever efficacy a rain dance may have, it is as much if not more an object of study because of what it tells us about the participants' views of the world, their organization of the cosmos and of their society. As Levi-Strauss said about totems, "They are good to think with." He explained that they were "condensed expressions of necessary relations which impose constraints . . . [that] are not unlimited" (1970:36). Therefore totemism is a metaphoric system through which the universe is perceived and conceived for both participant and analyst.

In the "consciousness raising" task of the Women's Service, sophisticated participants who were frequently proud that they understood the myths, the wars and violence, and the ethnocentrism of text as metaphoric, as "condensed expressions" of the universe, chose in this instance to concentrate on the most literal sexual meaning of ritual symbols and activities. They designed their service to express that what was metaphoric in nature was exclusionary in social practice. It became clear that metaphoric meanings were only possible if all involved embraced the same social reality—both its spoils and its disadvantages. Literalism seemed an appropriate tool for those members of the community who chose to opt for a new role, who felt they could not afford to be "even metaphorically" excluded. These women were not engaged in a struggle to redefine the symbols, metaphors, and divine attributes invoked in this service; rather their goal was to change "consciousness." Their emphasis upon the literalness of symbols made them more techniques of "consciousness raising" than weapons in a battle to seriously redefine them.

The nonritual element of the Women's Service was also given over to "consciousness raising." The complete incursion of the secular occurred following the Torah service, when the regular weekly text discussion was replaced by a discussion of the service itself. They wanted to know if they succeeded, a question traditional services and ritual never raise! They sincerely enjoyed the performance, members said, but all the liturgical changes left them feeling uncomfortable and awkward. All uniformly agreed that no changes could be incorporated into the Minyan's traditional service as a result of this event. The discussion of the service formed the final experience of "consciousness raising": confession. Members admitted a "changed consciousness," and agreed as they always had to the truth of the women's grievances, yet said that, consciousness aside, they could not change their service.

Even though the Minyan was committed to an egalitarian ideology, it placed the commitment within traditional Judaism. A feminist theology and a restructuring of the language of prayer were rejected while the commitment to include women was redoubled. At least one explanation for the Minyan's inability to incorporate even minor changes offered by the women grows from the understanding that the addition of gender-related referents to Jewish prayer strained the capacity of symbols to incorporate the contradictory *significata* of a liberal humanism within their underlying commitment to traditionalism.

Yet, the planners did not fail; their success took the form of compensation. The ritual was held, was performed decorously and taken seriously, and people felt different. They had never asked the group to give up the liturgy of the *siddur*. Such redress, which compensates without transforming, was described by Linda when she said: "Consciousness; I'm so confused now about what the word means. Maybe it just means simply a person's existence is taken into account finally. And people just finally say: 'Hey, you're here, and I know you're here, and we're glad to have you!' " Some of the planners, Linda and Deborah in particular, felt their goal had been wrong because they had not de-manded action. But that was a retrospective view. At the time there was a sense of satisfaction by planners and members alike.

A postmortem discussion following the service reintegrated the planners into the Minyan outside of the ritual sphere. Until the women gave up their goal to state their case as a group united through gender, reintegration was impossible, for to dramatize exclusion was to keep the Minyan engaged in uncertainty. Within the ritual, women had pre-sented themselves as Jews and women, and neither part of that identity was subordinate. They were marginals at the hand of Judaism, Jewish liturgy, and their own community. However, no marginal voice was heard in the discussion conducted after lunch, when the women re-turned to their undifferentiated status as visualized in Minyan ideology, as all equal despite varying education or Jewish theology to the contrary. Then the Minyan as a group turned from the substantive, divisive evaluation of the service to such unifying tasks as assigning responsibil-ity for making sufficient copies of some of the alternative prayers, and choosing an appropriate occasion for a more general discussion of symbols.

5. Conclusion

The women began their ritual by distancing themselves from other members and concluded the day with a gesture of reintegration. Their choice of a ritual to make their statement about the woman's role in Judaism was one that allowed both stances. Rituals provide, within social settings, precise boundaries of tradition, which allow one to dare great feats with safety because the form itself suppresses any denial of tradition. But this ritual also underscored the inability of traditional symbols to accommodate all referents, to expand their meanings in order to embrace contradictory *significata* that undermined their collec-tive nature. Though symbols give concrete expression to the collective, there are a limited number of interpretations of that collective in a given social group, and the women's challenge to the role gender occupies in Judaism necessarily stopped short of a demand for its embodiment in liturgy.

A ritual that both respected and violated the customary boundaries of a Minyan Sabbath, then, was the most appropriate mechanism to present women as fully competent Jews, to present the Minyan and their religion as capable of change and growth, and to simultaneously present themselves as alienated and abused. The planners' demand for a changed consciousness was met, and the group's expected and mutual choice to return to their traditional ritual did not overtly challenge the success or significance of the Women's Service. Ritual orchestrates action, and because it does not ask for abstract statements of belief it allowed women members a dramatic moment to present themselves as "come of age" in their social context, if not to alter their tradition.

ACKNOWLEDGMENT

The author acknowledges the critical assistance of Steven S. Foldes, Mischa Penn, and Barbara G. Myerhoff, and dedicates this essay to the memory of Edith Lieberman.

References

Adler, Rachel, 1973. The Jew who wasn't there: *Halacha* and the Jewish woman. *Response: A Contemporary Jewish Review* 3(18):77–83.

De Sola Pool, David (ed. and trans.). 1960. *The Traditional Prayer Book for Sabbaths and Festivals.* New York: Beehrman House.

Gluckman, Max. 1965. *Politics, Law, and Ritual in Tribal Society.* Chicago: Aldine Publishing Co.

Gluckman, Max. 1973. Limitations of the case method in the study of tribal law. *Law and Society Review* 7(4):611–643.

Hyman, Paula E. 1973. The other half: Women in the Jewish tradition. *Response, A Contemporary Jewish Review* 7(18):67–76.

Levi-Strauss, Claude. 1970. *The Savage Mind.* Chicago: University of Chicago Press.

Maimonides (Moses Ben Maimon). 1912. Concerning the difference between the saintly man and him who has self-restraint. In Joseph Gorfinkle (ed. and trans.), *The Eight Chapters of Maimonides on Ethics.* New York: Columbia University Press.

Moore, Sally F. and Barbara Myerhoff (eds.). 1975. *Symbol and Politics in Communal Ideology, Cases and Questions.* Ithaca and London: Cornell University Press.

Moore, Sally F. and Barbara Myerhoff (eds.). 1977. *Secular Ritual: Forms and Meanings.* Assen: Von Gorcum Press.

Myerhoff, Barbara. 1974. *The Peyote Hunt: The Sacred Journey of the Huichol Indians.* Ithaca and London: Cornell University Press.

Myerhoff, Barbara G. 1977. We don't wrap herring in a printed page: Fusion, fictions, and continuity in secular ritual. In S. F. Moore and B. Myerhoff (eds.), *Secular Ritual: Forms and Meanings.* Assen: Von Gorcum Press.

Schauss, Hayyim. 1970. *Guide to Jewish Holy Days: History and Observance.* Samuel Jaffee (trans.). New York: Schocken Books.

Sleeper, James A. and Alan L. Mintz. 1971. *The New Jews.* New York: Vintage Books.

Turner, Victor W. 1968. *Schism and Continuity in an African Society.* Manchester: Manchester University Press.

Turner, Victor W. 1970. *The Forest of Symbols. Aspects of Ndembu Ritual.* Ithaca and London: Cornell University Press.

Turner, Victor W. 1974. *Dramas, Fields and Metaphors: Symbolic Action in Human Society.* Ithaca and London: Cornell University Press.

6

LORNA RHODES AMARASINGHAM

The Misery of the Embodied

Representations of Women in Sinhalese Myth

Within Sinhalese religion, in both Buddhist doctrinal tradition and mythical traditions associated with village exorcism, women are treated metaphorically as vehicles for impermanence and sorrow. This consistent depiction of women may provide a link between the "great" and "little" traditions through a common metaphor that is expressed more or less concretely in different contexts.* Both practical and doctrinal Sinhalese Buddhism reveal the way in which certain philosophical assumptions about reproductive processes contribute to a negative image of women, and the elaboration of this image in mythology suggests some general questions about the relationship between mythical representations and women's lives.

After discussing some of the basic premises of Buddhist belief and the way in which they inform the Buddhist view of women, I will examine the role of women in myths that relate the origin of demons who are exorcised in village ritual. I have taken most of these myths from Wirz's (1954) *Exorcism and the Art of Healing in Ceylon,* a study of low-country curing practices, and from Barnett's (1916) *Alphabetical Guide to Sinhalese Folklore.* I am not attempting here to present a picture of the beliefs of any one village or area, but rather to compare textual material from two traditions that prevail throughout the Sinhalese area of Sri Lanka.

---

*In this I follow Obeyesekere, who has suggested that there are "common sets of assumptions," which link great traditional Buddhism and the practical religion of Sinhalese villagers (1963a:153).

LORNA RHODES AMARASINGHAM · Department of Social Psychiatry, Harvard Medical School, Boston, Massachusetts.

The Sinhalese, who make up 70% of the population of Sri Lanka, are Theravada Buddhists. The majority of Sinhalese live in agricultural villages centered on wet rice cultivation. The Sinhalese caste system, while similar in principle to that of India, is far less rigid, with the majority of the population belonging to the highest caste, the cultivators. The mountainous central area of Sri Lanka, which was the last to come under colonial domination and still remains the more traditional part of the country, is called the "up country," while the coastal areas are the "low country." The Sinhalese practice a "surprisingly orthodox" Buddhism (Gombrich 1971:40), and villagers are generally aware of the major elements of doctrine. Buddhist monks, usually as residents of a local temple, embody and perpetuate the tradition, as do such teaching devices as temple-paintings, Sunday school books, and stories of the Buddha's previous lives.

The orientation of doctrinal Buddhism is toward eventual salvation and release from the world. Villagers, however, also practice rituals that are designed to ease and prolong life in the world. The exorcist rituals that are the context for the myths I will deal with here are aimed at alleviating suffering, and particularly illness, in this world by taking steps to ensure the cooperation of various supernatural beings. While at one level the relation between these rituals and Buddhist doctrine is one of contradiction (see Obeyesekere 1968 for an elaboration of this point), I will concentrate here on the consistent ways women appear in both of them.

The first of the Four Noble Truths of Buddhism is that "Everything Is Suffering." The word for suffering, dukkha (Pali; Sinh: duka), has a wider range of meaning than our word, implying not only the suffering produced by old age and death but a condition that is inherent in the very nature of the world. According to Buddhist theory, everything we know, both in the external world and in our own minds, is conditioned, or the result of past intentions. The law of karma (Sinh: karuma, karmaya) is simply a statement that actions and thoughts have a result or "come to rest" in the future. The processes of birth and death themselves are included in this conception; rebirth, in the Buddhist view, is the result of the desire for life, which creates the conditions for continued existence. Suffering, then, means more than just pain; it applies to the impermanence, emptiness, and insubstantiality that are associated with the continuation of karmic existence itself (Rahula 1959:19).

The Buddha pointed out a way of salvation from the round of birth and rebirth and the frustration associated with it. He taught that ignorance of the true nature of things produces craving (tanha) or desire for the unreal appearances of the world, which makes people cling to existence and thereby perpetuate it. The escape from repeated rebirth and continued suffering lies in a transcendence of good and evil through detachment from desire.

The achievement of this transcendence rests entirely on the individual and consists of a series of renunciations that are designed to wean him from the world.* One of the earliest steps on this path must be the giving up of the sensual pleasure embodied in women. Women are thus represented as one of the great barriers to salvation. "As long as even the slightest thought of lust of a man towards women remains undestroyed, so long is his [the disciple's] mind tied, even as the sucking calf is bound to its mother" (Conze 1959:58). Sex is not sinful in the Christian sense; it is rejected because it represents a strong tie to the world of impermanence. The disciple Ananda asks the Buddha: "How shall we behave to women?" and the Buddha answers: "Not see them!" Ananda: "And if we have to see them?"—the Buddha: "Not speak to them!" Ananda: "And if we have to speak to them?"—the Buddha: "Keep your thoughts tightly controlled!" (Conze 1959:58).

It is not enough for the disciple to avoid contact with women; he must discipline his mind so that he no longer desires them. One way to do this is to picture to himself the true nature of women, that is, the impermanence of their attraction. The disciple is exhorted by his master:

> What now, ye monks, is the delight of the embodied? This: a king's daughter, a Brahman maiden . . . fresh with the freshness of her sixteen or seventeen years; not too big, not too small; not too slim, not too stout; not too dark, not too fair; does not such shining beauty, ye monks, at that age seem simply entrancing?
> Indeed yes, O Master!
> What now, ye monks, is the misery of the embodied? Only let us look upon this sister at a later time, in her eightieth, ninetieth or hundredth year; broken, crooked, shrunken, trembling, shuffling along, supported upon crutches, infirm, withered, toothless, with bleached wisps of hair, bare tottering head, wrinkled, the skin full of spots; what do you think monks; is not what was once shining beauty wholly departed, and misery now come in its place? (Dahlke 1908:244).

Thus women can be particularly apt object lessons on the impermanence of all things, simply because they are among the most desired. Women also are intimately connected with the life of the householder; a life of attachment, which must eventually be transcended. "With fetters bound

---

*Buddhism is unusual in explicitly placing the ultimate goal of human life beyond or outside of culture. Perhaps Sherry Ortner's formula "female is to male as nature is to culture" would have to be reworked to fit the Buddhist context; or perhaps here, as in other systems, women are assigned "polarized" meanings, which allow them to represent both embeddedness and transcendence (Ortner 1973:84).

is household life; full of impurity; like the open air of heaven is the life of
the ascetic" (Dahlke 1908:244). The ability to give up, both physically
and emotionally, the land, wife, and children who tie him to impermanence is the mark of the saint; in the *Vessantara Jataka* the Buddha in a
previous birth demonstrates his detachment by giving away his wife and
children. Women represent involvement in life because they are the
ones who give birth and thus perpetuate the karmic round. Birth is used
as a metaphor for all becoming; thus women are more grossly implicated
in the ensnarements of the world than men, and have a harder time
untangling themselves from it. It is an inconsolable woman who comes
to the Buddha with her dead son in her arms and begs for help; he tells
her, "Bring me a mustard seed from a house where there has been no
death," thus causing her to realize the inevitability and omnipresence of
suffering.* Thus in the great tradition certain meanings are given to
women: sensuality, desire, and attachment. And since in Buddhism
these imply suffering, death, and rebirth, women become images also of
the impermanence and inevitable corruption of life. And most importantly, because women embody birth, they become a metaphor for the
karmic energy that maintains suffering in the world.

The orientation of Buddhism toward eventual salvation, and its
rather abstract imagery, can be contrasted with the more direct approach
to suffering of the village rituals. However, in its very concrete depiction
of the causes of suffering, the exorcist tradition also makes use of
women to carry most vividly the connection between birth and impermanence. The supernatural beings who inhabit the universe of the
Sinhalese villager are as subject to the law of karma as he is. The gods
are relatively pure beings who, through accumulation of merit (good
karma), have risen to a position of power in one of several different
heavens. The gods can cause trouble for men who do not propitiate
them (for example, by sending epidemics), but they can also be called
upon for help. The gods, like men, aspire to eventual release from the
round of birth and death; thus they appreciate offerings of good deeds
which can help them to increase their merit. Although the gods will
eventually use up the merit that has landed them in heaven and be
reborn as men, this has the advantage that only as a man can one
achieve *nirvana* (transcendence).

Of the beings capable of causing suffering to men, the most feared

---

*While Buddhism uses women as an image of worldly concern, it should also be noted
that the Buddha did make possible the participation of women in the religious life of
Buddhism. Nevertheless, the idea that it is harder for women, involved as they are in
birth and death, to achieve salvation seems to have had more force at the village level than
some of the more positive aspects of doctrine.

and the most vividly represented are the demons *(yakas)*. Demons, in the Sinhalese context, are beings who have accumulated bad karma in their previous or present lives and have thus fallen to a lowly and miserable state. They are malevolent, powerful, and impure. They molest humans in their search for food, and they haunt undesirable and lonely spots like graveyards.* The demons have "wild, savage, gross and beastly natures [and] pass their time near the surface of the earth, revelling in scenes of blood and misery, bringing disease and death to men. . . ." (Goonewardena 1866:14).

Rituals to propitiate the gods and placate demons are based on the common relationship that all beings have with the Buddha; this relationship gives men a certain bargaining power with which to deal with supernatural beings. Although the Buddha himself is no longer active he has delegated power to the gods and extracted from the demons a promise to submit to requests made in his name. The demons, like the gods, recognize their karmic nature and realize that they gain merit by accepting offerings of food in place of the human flesh they really crave; they also recognize the moral superiority and thus the power that the gods and the Buddha have over them.

The performance of a ritual exorcism of demons takes place after a patient has been diagnosed as suffering from the attack of a particular demon or group of demons.† The performers are low-caste men; they usually form a small troupe and are related to one another by kinship ties. A ritual lasts all night and includes drumming, singing, and dancing. The following events are usually included:

1. A description of the Buddha's original act of control over demons and invocations to the gods to be present and to aid men in their struggle to free themselves from demonic attack.
2. Invocations to the demons to be present and to partake of offerings.

---

*In theory, demons are not actually present on the earth; they are banished by the Buddha and are now forced to limit their harm to attacks from their exile in the demon-world. They achieve their effect on men by the use of their "look" (gaze) or by the creation of apparitions. However, in practice people speak as though demons were present in the world and as though they could possess a person by entering his/her body.

†The patients of exorcist rituals are often women, though no study has been done on the proportion of men to women patients. It should be noted here that there are no notions of witchcraft practiced exclusively by women, and that most ritual practitioners (with the exception of some fortune-tellers) are men. The demon-exorcising rituals are not too rigidly tied up with particular illnesses, though some demons are specifically implicated in certain disorders of women. Since Western medical care and native homeopathic remedies are readily available, rituals (which are expensive) tend to be performed for chronic and psychogenic disorders.

3. Recitations of myths that describe the nature and origin of the particular demon or demons involved in the illness.
4. Enactments in which the performers act the part of demons; these are often comic.
5. The offering of food to the demons, with explicit reminders of their obligation to accept it.
6. The extraction of a promise from the demon to leave the patient.

It is apparent in the exorcist rituals that the demons' cannibalistic tendencies are an extreme and excessive form of hunger and desire; the purpose of the ritual, then, is to bring these voracious creatures under control by convincing them that an offering of food is an acceptable substitute for a human being.

It is the third aspect of the rituals, the recitation of origin myths, that I want to concentrate on here. Obviously the rituals say a great deal more about demons than is included in these myths, but the myths reveal some of the important ways in which human beings, and especially women, are related to demons. Before looking at the myths themselves, I want to point out something of the logic behind them. Clearly the notion of karma implies that the idea of the supernatural for the Sinhalese is not as removed from this world or as extraordinary an eruption into it as our own idea of the supernatural. The supernatural beings are subject to the same laws as men and do not arise spontaneously or miraculously, but are of similar origins to men. Supernatural beings do not represent the highest goal to which humans can aspire, and since they share the ambitions of men they can be dealt with through reciprocity and bargaining.

Further, in the Indian tradition the world may dissolve and be recreated many times. The Sinhalese have stories similar to the story of the Biblical flood, in which two brahmans appear as the first couple (Barnett 1916:54). But there is no central story in which the origin of evil itself is given; good and evil, men and women, humans and demons are assumed to be always present or potentially present in the world. Thus in stories that recount the origin of particular demons, the existence of suffering and evil are already taken for granted. James Boyd has pointed out that while in Christianity illness is a disruption of the essential goodness of creation, in Buddhism illness represents something inherent in the very nature of the world. "Illness and disease are manifestations of a basic condition which one must radically break through. To realize the truth of suffering is a step on the path to Enlightenment rather than an obstruction of it" (Boyd n.d.:8). This view of illness and suffering makes their presence in the world inevitable. Therefore, only the particular causative agent (the specific demon responsible for a specific incident of suffering) needs to have an origin.

Since the demons are produced by the same forces that generate men, the problem that the origin myths deal with is how demons, starting from human origins, became demonic. To have an origin on earth, demons must be born of women; the myths, then, center on the nature of this birth and the subsequent events that make a human child into a demon. Finally, the myths are recited at rituals whose aim is to control demons; thus they must contend with the problem of the control of demons and demonstrate that men, with the help of the gods and the Buddha, can force demons to behave in acceptably harmless ways. However, there is no suggestion of permanently eliminating them from the world.

The eleven myths given in the Appendix are all accounts of the origin of male demons and of their eventual subjugation and control.* What follows is not an attempt to delineate the structure of these myths, but rather to look for the thematic patterns in them which point to a relationship between women and demons. The fact that demons have an earthly origin raises the question: What is the role of women in this origin? How are women connected to the kind of behavior that makes demons dangerous? I will illustrate what I think are recurring emphases with specific examples from the myths that are given in full at the end of the chapter.

1. Generation

The focus of the stories is the generation of demons, that is, how they came into existence.† It is this emphasis that answers the question of how demons can arise from earthly circumstances in accord with the law of karma. Invariably, the circumstances that surround the cre-

---

*There are female demons (yakkiniyo), who are mentioned in some of these stories and who also appear in a few myths of their own. However, they are rarely implicated in affliction except in diseases of children. As the question of female demons deserves more space than I can give it here, I have limited this account to the origin of male demons.

†In all but three of the myths the parents or ancestors of the demons are royalty. One reason for this theme of royal origin may be that it is pure blood that confers power. The demons are powerful; thus, although they have fallen into a demeaned state, they must have an origin that takes into account their ability to exercise power over others.

In rituals, the royal parentage of some demons enables performers to address them with the kind of language suitable for kings and thus flatter them into acquiescence to the aim of the ritual. The dual nature of the demons, symbolized in their royal birth, enables the performers to take an ambivalent but effective role toward them.

ation of demons are strange, though usually not beyond the range of ordinary human possibility. In myths 6, 7, 9, and 10, the birth of the demon is brought about by a union between two people who are not of the same status:

> [The king] went into the bush where the soothsayers were living and upon seeing the fair young woman, he was seized by a strong passion. On the following day the king sent a messenger to have Andima brought to the palace. . . . (6)
>
> [The queen] was childless, but the king adopted the son of a laundress who used to wash at the court and who was the king's mistress. . . . (7)
>
> The washer . . . ran away where he pretended to be an exiled prince and married the king's daughter. (10)

In two of these cases, a king has relations with a woman lower than he is; in the case of the washerman, he succeeds in marrying above his station. In the story of Maha Sohona (9) the king Parakrama Bahu is referred to as a *yaka* (demon) from the beginning; when he lusts after Gotembara's wife (again, a case of someone below him) he immediately has an unfavorable influence on her, although he has not yet acquired his final form.

In all of these stories in which an unusual marriage or affair takes place, women are desired by men. The women seem to be completely passive, doing nothing to influence the fate that men's desire places on them. While four of the myths begin with marriages that are inappropriate because of distance, another three (3, 4, 11) involve incestuous unions:

> The two children could not marry outside because they were *yakas*. (3)
>
> "How can we wed our sons and daughters to these children who have no parents and whose origin we don't know!" So there was nothing left but to have the two children marry one another. (4)
>
> When Dala was born astrologers foretold that he would marry his own sister . . . he feigned sickness, saying that he could live only if his sister cooked for him. . . . Thus he gratified his desire. (11)

In the first two of these stories, it is made explicit that incest occurs when the desire to keep marriage within the family (among those who are alike) is taken to its logical extreme. In the third example, it is clear that the man desires his sister; she is the passive object of a desire that is foretold as inevitable.

In addition to these unions, which involve human beings, there are also several instances of nonhuman agents cohabiting with women, causing the women to become pregnant and give birth to demons:

> She took a huge cobra with her into her bedroom. (1)
>
> A sunbeam fertilized her. . . . (4)
>
> She saw a cobra sleeping in her bed. (5)

In the first of these examples the woman acts in such a way that she influences events; in the second and third, however, the women are the passive recipients of sunbeam and dreams. In a symbolic sense, these seem to be extreme cases of wrongly placed desire expressed through the medium of the bodies of women.

Another recurrent event around the birth of demons is the death of their mothers just as they give birth:

> . . . his mother was already dead and abandoned at his birth. (2)
>
> [The queen] was hanged on the *puberiga* tree but before her death she gave birth to a boy. . . . (5)
>
> The king . . . ordered that she be killed and impaled, as used to be done with criminals. However, she was already pregnant, and during the execution she gave birth to a boy. (6)
>
> The king ordered that the queen be brought to the place of execution and had her hanged and cut to pieces. But the child remained alive. . . . (4)

In the first story no explanation is given for the death, but in the other stories the mother is an innocent victim of a misunderstanding. The juxtaposition of death and birth generates a bloodthirsty or vengeful child, although the mothers were generally passive victims. The effect on the desires of the child is made most explicit in the fourth myth, in which the demon avenges his mother's death by devouring all the people who inhabit his father's (the king's) city.

The death of the mothers of demons is brought about by the deception of jealous or greedy women in three of the four stories in which the mother dies:

> One of the maids, hoping to be rewarded, informed the king that while he had been away, a stranger had slept with the queen. (4)
>
> The maid felt deeply offended and resolved to take her revenge. She went to the king and said ". . . you are not to see your son. The queen will have him brought to your brother's house. . . ." (5)
>
> The other sixteen wives felt slighted. . . . (6)

In all of these cases of deception, women resentful of the one who is pregnant succeed in telling a story that causes the pregnant one to be killed.

In some of the stories, the mother of the demon-to-be experiences unnatural cravings during her pregnancy*:

> Then, all kinds of queer desires began to take hold of her. . . . (1)
>
> While she was pregnant the mother wanted to eat human flesh and drink blood. . . . (3)

---

*For a discussion of Sinhalese pregnancy craving, see Obeyesekere, (1963b).

These cravings presage the arrival of a being who will himself be given to craving unnatural things. Again, the women are perceived to be passive in relation to the longings that overtake them.

Finally, in one story it is the greed of the mother, under the influence of her pregnancy craving, that leads to her death and thus the strange birth of her child:

> The servant . . . asked the queen to let her have one of the fruits. But the queen did not fulfill her wish and ate them all herself. The maid felt deeply offended and resolved to take her revenge. . . . (5)

The offense to the maid leads to the maid's deception of the king and thus to the death of the queen, who nevertheless gives birth before she dies.

The generation of demons, then, seems to occur around four major circumstances: (1) as a result of unnatural sexual relations, either too far outside the appropriate social group (inferiors, superiors, or animals) or too close within the family (incest); (2) as a result of unnatural craving (eating things not appropriate as food); (3) when birth and death coincide; and finally (4) as a result of the greediness of women. These circumstances are saturated with desire or craving. The coincidence of birth and death that produces a demon seems a particularly strong statement of the relationship between birth, brought about by desire, and its karmic counterpart, death. Women, as the vehicles through whom this karmic cycle is realized, here embody the kind of uncontrolled desire that makes such a juxtaposition possible; the demonic product of this juxtaposition in turn embodies, even more intensely, desire in its most excessive form.

2. Development

Although unnatural desire surrounding its mother and its birth sets the stage for the creation of a demon, it is only in the course of subsequent events that its true nature is revealed.* Usually the children are not referred to as *yakas* until some decisive event after their birth con-

---

*Several of the stories have interludes that seem designed to suggest that the outcome is inevitable or predetermined. For instance, an astrologer predicts the cruelty of the child (5) or a brahman makes a prophecy that comes true (1). In only one case does a prediction prove wrong (5). The use of prediction to imply inevitability may be a way of affirming the strength of the karmic law.

firms their status. In some of these stories a person becomes a demon through contact with animals; here, as in the juxtaposition of birth and death, we can see a connection between unlike entities, which symbolizes the potentially nonhuman future of the demon.

> The lad caught [the cobras] and then wound them around his waist, arms and legs. He caught a viper . . . and drank the blood and venom. (1)
>
> Then Senasuru took the head of the dead wolf and set it on the headless body of Jayasena. . . . (9)

The most common confirming quality that turns a child into a demon is the eating of human flesh, and especially the flesh of the dead mother:

> You were born out of a corpse and you feed on flesh. . . . (2)
>
> Kalukumara defeated the prince . . . and drank his blood (3)
>
> The child remained alive; he fed on the flesh of his mother and grew. (4)

Since it is a characteristic of all demons to attack people by feeding on their flesh, this recurrent theme serves as an explanation of their predilection. But it should be noted that demons are usually human children before they become demons. This implies that when they later attack humans they are feeding on their own kind, or at least they are not entirely beyond the pale of human existence; this cannibalism is the essence of the misplaced desire that constitutes their nature.

The fact that a human child is or will be a demon is indicated in the stories by his unusual characteristics—he is either excessively large, small, handsome or strong. This seems to be a further display in terms of physical qualities of the excess that characterizes his nature.

3. Aggression

All the stories contain some kind of aggression. One violent act that has already been mentioned is the killing of the mothers of demons by their husbands or consorts. Another form of aggression is the revenge taken by the sons for the mother's death:

> My mother was tortured and killed . . . I am going to take revenge! (2)
>
> One day, he heard of his mother's tragic fate and how the king had her killed. He resolved to avenge her. (4)
>
> One day, he learned [his mother's fate] from a stranger and from that very moment it continued to trouble his thoughts. (5)

> When he heard about his mother and her fate he took it so much to heart that
> he died . . . the boy . . . asked permission to take revenge for the death of his
> mother of his previous life. (6)

The aggression can be seen as a logical and inevitable result of the death of the mother and the events leading up to it. Often, revenge is taken directly against the father who is responsible for the mother's death, but in many of the stories it also extends to other, more innocent victims. Violence can also occur in the stories without being a reaction to a previous murder:

> Six kingdoms will he conquer, among them that of his father, whom he will
> kill. . . . (1)

There is one striking and unusual act of aggression in the myths which produces a particular kind of demon. After vanquishing his father's enemy a king's adopted son visits a land of Amazonian women. The young prince is torn limb from limb by these women, whose desire for him is manifested violently as soon as he appears:

> Unaware of any danger, he resolved to go to this country of Amazons. . . .
> However, upon reaching their capital he was at once surrounded by all the
> women. . . . They dragged him hither and thither and . . . tore him to
> pieces. . . . (7)

This prince, Kalukumara, is reborn immediately as a demon and pursues women and girls exclusively. When he captures them he afflicts them with diseases and sees to it that they are childless, for he devours their children. Thus the aggressive desire represented by the Amazonian women transforms a man into a demon by entangling him, in a particularly violent way, in the cycle of birth and death, so that he is forever afterward bound to intervene in the process of birth itself.

4. Control

Finally most of the myths end with an account of the control over the demons that is exercised by the gods or by the Buddha. This control is essential to the use of these myths in ritual; the moral of each story must be that the demons will surrender to a superior moral power, a power that can be invoked by ritual practitioners. What is important is control over the demons themselves, not over the situation that produced them. The demons have to be convinced, either by force or by logic, that what they are doing is wrong. This process of reasoning with the demons and/or overcoming them with superior power is the same process that exorcist rituals reenact in dealing directly with the damage produced by demons.

5. Conclusion

The important motifs in these myths then are these: A demon is a human who is created out of a situation of uncontrolled desire, often for food or sex, and who continues to manifest this desire in excessive ways; violence, which emerges from desire, is an element either in his birth or in later development; and importantly, women play a central role not only in actually giving birth to the demon but also in expressing, activating, or encouraging the desires that are the essence of his demonic character. In the Buddhist texts we saw that women represent the desire for continued existence, symbolizing in their ability to attract sexual desire and to give birth the attachment to life itself. In the abstract doctrine, all craving leads to all suffering, and women can be convenient metaphorical vehicles for this message, lending to the processes of relationship, nurturance, and birth a negative meaning consistent with the total doctrine.

In the myths, suffering is represented by a few symbolic agents. The general relationship that desire has to suffering is made concrete in specific images of demonic craving. The demons, according to the logic of karma, have an earthly origin and, like men, they are produced by (or through) women. Yet the women who are implicated in the birth of demons are not evil or dangerous in any obvious way. They do not seek contact with the supernatural nor do they usually attract the desires of some evil being. The early events in the myths take place on what seems to be a rather mundane level: kings commit adultery, serving girls tell lies, queens have pregnancy cravings. In each story there are one or two seeds of potential trouble, but even these ominous occurrences are not much more than the ordinary desires and deceptions of people.

Perhaps this is the point. The demonic, rather than arising suddenly out of some horrible event, as we would expect it to, emerges gradually out of the everyday mishaps and miscalculations of life. The crucial factor in its development seems to lie not in the nature of the events themselves but in the fact that they are, in some way, excessive. The queen desires not ordinary luxuries but human flesh. The king reacts to the possibility of his wife's unfaithfulness not by investigating but by immediately killing her. These acts of excess set up a chain of events of which demons are the inevitable result. Women are symbols of this potential for excess in daily life. On the one hand, they provoke desire.

Kings desire laundresses; washermen desire princesses. Just by existing women call forth a desire that, while fruitful in the appropriate time and place, can just as well be misplaced and disastrous. Women also express desire, desire that is in these stories often perverse—for snakes or human flesh or, in the case of the Amazons, for a defenseless man. Women become double images, reflecting both active desire and also the passive reception of the desire of others.

Thus just as women serve as suitable symbols for generalized desire, so in the myths they make effective symbols of specific excess. Birth, in which they are most directly and exclusively involved, here is subject to accidents, perversions, and deceptions. It produces suffering, not theoretically but directly. If, however, the women in the myths are productive of suffering, they exhibit this potential in a singularly passive way. The demons generated by the strange births described above are beings who intend evil and who consciously crave gross and inappropriate things. Their desires have a logical motivation, either of revenge or of early and intimate contact with evil which creates an inclination to perpetuate it.

The women, on the other hand, while generative of these embodiments of demonic urge, do not display any conscious intent in their desires. Often they are purely passive instruments of men's desires. In only one story is a woman's greed a factor in the plot; in the others, women's cravings seem almost automatic and beyond their volition. The actions of the women are not defined as good or bad, and the character of the mothers of the demons does not define their fate. In fact, it is the "good" women who are often killed and there seems to be no notion of "blame" attached to women who produce demons. Thus the image of women is one of desire that is not under conscious control, not subject to any rational order. There seems to be no relation between the woman's consciousness and the nature and intensity of the desire she arouses or projects.* This is true most obviously in the cases where a woman becomes the passive object of a man's desire, but even in those myths in which women express desire they seem to do so in an unthinking, unconscious way. For example, in the incident of the ferocious Amazons, the women react to the presence of a man with an immediate and almost animal-like attack.

Demons, on the other hand, are morally conscious. Even though they are evil, they can be controlled by an appeal to their reason. They are deliberate in their intention to cause suffering and can explicitly state

---

*I think that this theme also occurs in the Buddhist texts, where the emphasis is on the desires of men rather than the consciousness of women.

the reasons for the particular affliction they cause. Again, this is apparent in the Amazon story, in which Kalukumara afflicts women because of the circumstances of his death. This deliberate and conscious quality in the demons allows people to intervene in the process of destruction by appealing to images of authority; it is this possibility for control that makes curing rituals possible. This suggests that the myths represent desire, which is the root of suffering in them as it is in Buddhism, in two forms. In its "natural" form, as imaged in women, it is unconscious and uncontrollable, arising out of the circumstances of life concretely imaged in female sexuality, in unpredictable and dangerous ways. But in its "man-made" form, that is, as imaged in demons with a history and a rationale for their actions, it can be dealt with through authority figures symbolizing renunciation and control. Demons can be reasoned with and will submit to a higher order; the processes that produce the demon are not subject to the same kind of intervention.

Thus the central problem of Buddhism—desire and its relation to suffering—is imaged in women both in doctrinal material and in exorcist myths. The myths, in addition, use male and female figures to represent the degree of control over suffering which men can hope to acquire. They indicate that while the ordinary person may safely continue with his ordinary cravings (for proper food and the proper wife), these can become destructive if they are not subject to conscious control. The women who produce demons represent desire in its thoughtless and unmanageable form; the demons themselves are concrete embodiments of moral evil; as such, they are conscious beings who can be directly influenced by men.

The concrete worldly result of the excess embodied in demons is the illness they cause. The result of the excess embodied in women seems to be the dissolution of normal human relationships—the instability of so many of the unions described in the myths. A theme of inevitable dissolution, separation, and death runs through the stories, carrying the implication that all relationships based on, or influenced by, inappropriate or excessive desire are doomed. The frequent theme of violence juxtaposed with birth seems to reflect the abortive nature of these unions; birth and death occurring at the same time indicate the two directions —dangerous fertility or dangerous violence—in which excess can go.

Finally, an obvious question presents itself: If women represent uncontrolled desire in both doctrinal Buddhism and in folk mythology, what is the relationship between this negative cultural image and the lives of Sinhalese women? Certainly both Yalman and Obeyesekere have pointed out attitudes in Sinhalese society which correspond with those presented here. As Obeyesekere has said, women are regarded by village men as seductive, untrustworthy, and unclean (1963b:326). But we still do not know enough about the subjective daily experiences of women, or about the very complex ways in which these (and other, more positive) mythical representations may influence them, to offer direct correlations.

6. Appendix

(1) Suniya (From Wirz 1954)

A long time ago there was a town in Northern India, called Devanuvera. Here reigned a king named Panduhas Rajjuruvo with his queen Tuserin Bisavun. One day, in the eighth month of her pregnancy, she went to the lotus pond to bathe. There she saw a large, beautiful lotus flower, floating on the water. She picked it and enjoyed its fragrance. And thus it came to pass that the child she was bearing grew up to be an extremely handsome boy. After her bath, the queen returned home. Then, all kinds of queer desires began to take hold of her. She longed to copulate with cobras and other snakes, and she took a huge cobra with her into her bedroom. The king came to know about this and was very much disturbed. He called a brahman to consult him. The brahman said, "The child will grow up to be a very cruel person. Everyone will go in fear of him and he will be the horror of the whole population."

A second and a third brahman were asked but they both answered the same. Then the king inquired about his own fate and the brahman replied, "When the child is seven years old, he will disappear into the forest and capture all kinds of snakes, drink their blood and absorb their venom. Through this he will acquire supernatural powers. After this your son will set off for another country, wage war and kill people. Six kingdoms will he conquer, among them that of his father, whom he will kill to make himself lord of the country."

Such were the words of the brahman, but the king would not believe his prophecy.

The child was born and grew up. He was extremely handsome and was the pride of his father. However, when he was seven years old, he secretly left his father's house and went into the jungle to a big termites' nest. Here there lived four times four and twenty cobras. The lad caught them and wound them around his waist, arms and legs. Then he caught a viper, raised it to his mouth and drank the blood and venom, thus becoming endowed with supernatural powers. He wound another, very long snake, around his whole body from feet to neck, and another one round his loins. Thus equipped, he mounted a white horse which was eight feet tall and fifteen feet long, took in his right hand a sword fifteen feet long and in his left a fire-pan, and resolved to return home and overthrow his father. In the meantime he had become a powerful *yaka*. The god Sakra saw him coming and asked what his intentions were; he said he was going to Naraloka to kill people. Sakra begged him to desist from his purpose. Finally, Sakra promised to endow him with a power to make people ill, but at the same time he must promise to revere Buddha and obey him. . . .

(2) Atura Sanniya (From Wirz 1954)

He was born in Visala Maha Nuvara and his mother was already dead and abandoned at his birth. At that time it was not yet customary to bury or burn the corpses, as is done nowadays. They were carried into the bush and left. Owing to this strange circumstance, he already possessed supernatural powers when he was born and was thus a *yaka*. When a child, he was already given to devouring corpses and as he grew up he began to lie in wait for living persons in order to devour them. He gathered other *yakku* around himself, eventually a whole army of 7,700 and placed himself at their head. . . . With this army he roamed through the country, killing people and devouring them. At the same time, a famine broke out, and people died in crowds. The *yakku* pounced on corpses and devoured them. On seeing the evil caused by Atura Sanniya and his gang, Gautama Buddha went to see Isvara, and both of them deliberated as to how an end could be made of the *yakku*'s doings. They discussed the matter with Vesamunu Rajjuruvo, and the three of them descended to earth by Atura Sanniya, who had just fallen asleep. He was awakened by the radiance of Buddha's halo, but he felt only the heat which emanated from it, without seeing anybody, for the three of them had remained in front of the house. When one of his servants reported that three men were standing outside, who had presumably come to beg for alms, Atura went to the door himself and saw the three waiting. Buddha approached him slowly and Atura grew afraid. "What do you want?" he asked angrily, blocking the passage. Buddha replied, "I know that you are very powerful as I also know about your birth. You were born out of a corpse and you feed upon human flesh. Stop doing that! That is all I wanted to tell you." "My mother," answered Atura, "was tortured and killed by the king. I am going to take revenge and that is why I have come here!" They argued for a long time. Again and again Buddha entreated Atura to desist from his doings, but Atura did not yield. At length, Buddha directed upon Atura and his companions five

differently coloured rays from his head. The rays burnt into their skins
and they began to lament and to cry for mercy. But Buddha said, "You
must leave this place and stop your doings. However, I will concede you
one favour: you may make people ill, but you must not take their lives.
You must, however, return their health to them when they turn to you
with *mantra* and when they present you with offerings which you will
receive as a reward."

(3) Kalukumara (From Wirz 1954)

A god called Kalukunda had a pond in which there were seven
lotuses, one in the middle and six around it. The flower in the middle
produced Kalukiriamma. She had two children, Kalu Yaka and Yak-
shini. The two children couldn't marry outside because they were *yakas*,
so they married each other. The one born from these two was Kalukumara. While she was pregnant the mother wanted to eat human flesh and
drink blood. Later Kalukumara wanted to come to Ceylon and received
permission from Isvara. After he came to Ceylon a king called Gopala
Rajjuruvo had a son who went to the river for a bath and at that time
Kalukumara was also at the river. They had an argument and fought;
Kalukumara defeated the prince and broke his neck and drank his
blood. The king sent giants to catch him. Kalukumara's mother saw
what was happening and asked the king not to kill her son. She explained that he had permission to cause diseases in small children and
pregnant women. But after she left he killed him anyway for revenge (by
torturing him). Kalukumara died angry and came back as a ghost to
torment the king's wife, causing her to become mad and vomit. Isvara
saw the reason for the illness and told the king Gopala to make an
offering to Kalukumara. After he did so the queen got better and ever
since Kalukumara has attacked pregnant and young women until offerings are made in their behalf.

(4) Kola Sanniya (From Wirz 1954)

Once upon a time there lived a princess named Ariyagat Kumari. A
sunbeam fertilized her and she became pregnant. After some time, she
gave birth to a shapeless piece of flesh. Her relatives did not know what
to do about it and the king ordered the thing to be placed in a pot and
carried to the river. There it was to be placed in the water, so that the pot
might drift away to the sea. At the same time, Gautama Buddha also
went to the river to meditate. He saw the pot floating on the water and
took it out. On opening it he saw the piece of flesh which in the mean-

time had divided itself. He brought the vessel, together with its contents to his temple and hung it up. When he examined it again after some time, there were two children lying in the pot, a boy and a girl, sucking their fingers. Buddha brought them up and they grew. When they were sixteen years old, Buddha wanted them to marry so that he would be rid of them. But the people said with one voice, "How can we wed our sons and daughters to these children who have no parents and whose origin we do not know!" So there was nothing left but for Buddha to have the two children marry one another. He led them into the woods, far from anywhere, built them a cottage, and left them to their fate. Soon after, the woman became with child and gave birth to twins, who, in their turn, married each other and likewise brought forth twins who married one another. And they multiplied until, at last, they filled the whole wood and took possession of the whole country. Some time later, they elected a king, who was named Sangapala.

Soon afterwards, the king had to go to war. His wife was already pregnant, but the king was unaware of it. When he returned, the time of her confinement had already come. The king was enraged, for he assumed his wife had had intercourse with another man. He inquired and asked his servants but nobody could tell him anything. One of the maids, however, hoping to be rewarded, made up a story and informed the king that, while he had been away, a stranger had slept with the queen. The king trusted the maid and gave the order that the queen be brought to the place of execution and had her hanged and cut to pieces. But the child remained alive; he fed on the flesh of his mother and grew. Even when the boy was bigger, he fed exclusively on corpses and on all the criminals who were put to death. All this led to his becoming a *yaka*. One day, he heard of his mother's tragic fate and how the king had her killed. He resolved to avenge her. He went to the king's palace, in front of which grew a *nuga* tree. He dug a hole under the tree, hid in the ground, and lay in wait for the people who wanted to enter the palace. He overpowered them, dragged them to his cave, and devoured them, as many as a hundred men in a day and even more. So it went on, day after day, and gradually the whole town became empty. Nobody was able to offer any resistance. . . .

[Buddha eventually made a bargain with him which led to his control. . . .]

(5) Kola Sanniya (From Wirz 1954)

Once upon a time there lived in Northern India a king named Sangapala Rajjuruvo and a queen Asupali Kumari Kavi. While the queen was expecting a child, she longed for a mango and sent one of her maids for some of the fruit. The servant did as she was told, and asked the queen to let her have one of the fruits. But the queen did not fulfill her wish and ate them all herself. The maid felt deeply offended and resolved to take her revenge. She went to the king who lived in another palace and said, "Your consort has conceived a boy. She will be confined ten months, but you are not to see your son. The queen will have him brought to her brother's house, who will bring him up, and when he is grown he will seek your life." Such were the servant's words, and the king believed her. He sent for one of his executioners and ordered him to hang the queen. Following the custom of that time, she was hanged on the *puberiga* tree, but before her death she gave birth to a boy. The king had the child brought to his palace where he was to be carefully attended by a nurse.

When the prince grew up, the king gave orders that his mother's fate was to be kept concealed from him; but one day, he learned it from a stranger and from that very moment it continued to trouble his thoughts. Soon afterwards he went secretly to see Gautama Buddha and told him what he had learned about the fate of his mother, and at the same time vowed to avenge her death. He died, however, when a youth, but was reborn through a queen in Visala. His mother had likewise been reincarnated in Mandana Nuvara where king Vijitranama Rajjuruvo and his consort Suterita Devinanse were reigning. The queen gave birth to a girl, who was Asupala Kumari Kavi, the mother, reborn. This girl was called Padmi Mantri and was married when she was sixteen to the king Sangsu Rajjuruvo, the lord of Visala. She bore a son, the same as her previous one who was thus born for a second time.

Before her confinement the queen had three strange dreams. She saw a cobra sleeping in her bed, the sun rising in great splendor and the moon with many stars. Astrologers were summoned to the palace and consulted as to the meaning of these dreams. The first one said, "The dream of the cobra means good luck. The queen is going to have a boy." The second said, "The dream of the rising sun means bad luck. The boy will be very cruel. He will associate with *yakku* and *raksho* and will torment and kill people!" The third astrologer declared, "The dream of the rising moon and stars indicates good luck; the queen is going to have a boy who will be a wise and benevolent monarch."

Soon afterwards the prince was born, and the king saw that his son was educated with the utmost care. He was a handsome boy and was called Kola Kumara. Even at an early age, he displayed unusual physical strength, but also displayed unusual occult powers, about which his father did not know. Only when he was older did this begin to be

known, and did it come to the king's ears. He began to seek contact with demons and, leaving the palace soon after, set out for the north country.
[Later, Buddha succeeded in removing them from the country.]

(6) Aimana (From Wirz 1954)

Once upon a time a man called Desaguru and his wife Andima came from Kashirata (Benares) to Lanka. They were soothsayers and wanted to settle down near Anuradhapura. At that time, Parakrama Bahu reigned in Polonnaruva. The king heard about the two people and re-solved to go to see them in order to have his future foretold. He went into the bush where the soothsayers were living and upon seeing the young, fair woman, he was seized by a strong passion. On the following day the king sent a messenger to have Andima brought to the palace where she was to live. She became the king's favorite wife. But the other sixteen wives felt slighted and conceived a scheme to do away with Andima. When, soon afterwards, the king went on a campaign, they gathered all their jewels and hid them in order to tell the king on his return that Andima had robbed them. The king believed this story and ordered that she be killed and impaled, as used to be done with crimi-nals. However, she was already pregnant, and during the execution she gave birth to a boy. The child was taken to the palace and brought up there. When he grew up he heard one day about his mother and her fate and took it so much to heart that he died from grief. In the meantime, Andima had been reborn, and again in Kashirata. She once more gave birth to a boy, who was a reincarnation of her former child. The boy throve rapidly and distinguished himself, already in his youth, by his extraordinary strength. When he was sixteen years old, he came to Tammana Adaviya on the west coast of the island of Lanka. In this place, there lived three *yakkiniyo*. They were called Rati-kandi, Ginikandi and Mini-kandi and were the daughters of Kuveni and of King Vijaya. Accompanied by these three *yakkiniyo*, the boy went to Vesamunu Rajjuruvo in Uttarakursdivaina and asked him to grant him permission to take revenge on Parakama Bahu for the death of his mother of his previous life. The king granted his desire and bestowed on him the power. So he became a *yaka*, and was henceforth called Aimana. Together with the three *yakkiniyo*, he then set out for Polonnarava. When they arrived, the king was informed that four people, one man and three women, had come from abroad to see him. But he refused to let them enter the palace and gave orders that they be sent away. Then Aimana recited a *mantra* so that the queen became ill. She grew increas-ingly thin, lost her beauty, and remained childless. The king consulted the brahmans but they did not know what to advise him. They could only tell him that the queen had fallen victim to a demon. Ultimately there appeared one who recommended that the king prepare offerings and pronounce a *mantra*. The king followed this advice and the queen recovered.

(7) Kalukumara (From Wirz 1954)

A long time ago there lived a king in Anuradhapura who was called Puotala Rajjuruvo, with his wife Mutumala Bisavun. She was childless, but the king adopted the son of a laundress who used to wash at court and who was the king's clandestine mistress. The boy was called Nilaya and distinguished himself by great intelligence; but as he grew up, it appeared he was also possessed of unusual physical strength. The king was a very kind monarch, and very popular on account of the interest which he took in the welfare of his subjects. During his father's reign, the country had been overwhelmed by Panji-Rajjuruvo, sovereign of a powerful state in Northern India, who had carried off twelve thousand people as prisoners. . . .

The king had a big, heavy walking-stick which nobody but himself was able to lift. One day, however, the king discovered the stick upside down on the spot where he used to leave it. Greatly surprised, he made inquiries as to who could have done it and who had entered his room during his absence. None of the servants could tell him anything other than that no one had been in the room except the boy and it must have been he who reversed the heavy stick. The king sent for the boy without delay and asked whether it had been he who had put the stick upside down. Ashamed, he confessed that he had done it and to the king's amazement demonstrated on the spot that he had the strength to lift the stick. Puotala resolved at once to keep the boy in his palace, bestowing high titles upon him, and made him a general in his army. From then on, he was called "the huge giant" and was feared by everybody.

Soon afterward, the king decided to undertake a campaign against Panji-Rajjuruvo, to be carried out by Nilaya and which would have as its main purpose the liberation of the 12,000 Sinhalese taken into captivity by Panji-Rajjuruvo. So, Nilaya, at the head of a strong army, set off at once for India, taking the king's heavy stick with him as his only weapon. When they arrived at the northern point of Ceylon, he struck the water with his stick, so that it fell back, allowing the whole army to enter India dryshod. Unhindered, they entered the country of Panji-Rajjuruvo, vanquished him after a short struggle, and liberated their countrymen.

Along the borders of Panji-Rajjuruvo's realm, however, there extended another strange country, which was inhabited only by women, and which, for this reason, was called "Istripura" (country of women). Unaware of any danger, Nilaya resolved to go to this country of the Amazons, about whose strange inhabitants he had been told. However, upon reaching their capital, he was at once surrounded by all the women. Each of them wanted the strong young man for herself. They dragged him hither and thither, pulled his arms and legs from his body, and finally completely tore him to pieces. Nevertheless, he was reborn as a demon who henceforth pursued women and girls, lying in wait for them, and afflicting them with diseases and ailments of all kinds. Moreover, he saw to it that they remained childless, killing and devouring their unborn children.

(8) Riri Yaka (From Wirz 1954)

Like most demons he comes from Northern India. His father was Valiya Rajjuruvo and his mother Sitapraha Meseri. At the time of her confinement she lost a great deal of blood and the child itself appeared in the clot, but it was so tiny and delicate that it did not measure more than a finger's breadth. It was a boy, who later never attained adult size, but remained a dwarf. Nevertheless he had extraordinary physical strength and none could equal him in this respect. Very soon, however, he developed all kinds of evil habits. He attacked people, bit their carotid arteries and sucked their blood which flowed out. They began to be afraid of him and to avoid him and it was believed that he was a *yaka*. The people then went to Saman Deviyo and entreated him to help them. Saman Deviyo summoned the Riri Yaka and asked why he harmed people. He answered, "I was born out of the blood of Sitapraha Meseri and I was ordered by Vesamani Rajjuruvo to kill people, so I am only doing what I was told." Then Saman Deviyo reasoned with him for a long time, to try to convince him that what he did was bad and that he had to stop it, but it produced just the opposite effect. Riri Yaka became angry, began to shout and stamp the ground and swelled into giant form. So Saman Deviyo ordered him to be put in irons and to be bound to the sun wheel where he eventually surrendered. Saman Deviyo let him free but only on [certain conditions]. . . .

(9) Maha Sohona (From Wirz 1954)

In the year 2038 (Buddhist chronology) there was a king Parakrama Bahu who lived and reigned in Polonnaruva. He was also called

Jayasena Yaka and not only the people feared him but also the gods. In the many battles he fought he was always victorious.

At the time there was a district Runuraha in Lanka which was ruled over by a king Kavan Tissa. Among his commanders he had a man, extremely able but of short stature, who was called Gotembara. After King Kavan Tissa died, he was succeeded by Dutugemunu who waged a war with Elala of Anuradhapura, the Tamil king. Later Dutugemunu was also engaged in a war with Gotembara, the Sinhalese being thus in a general conflict with the Tamils. Gotembara was the victor. He decided to celebrate his victory with a feast to which he invited all his warriors. Upon hearing this, Jayasena set out at once to see what was happening and took three thousand of his soldiers with him. He hoped to be invited to the feast and also to have the chance to declare himself to Gotembara's wife with whom he had fallen in love. He neglected no opportunity of courting her. The consequence was that she fell ill under the influence of the *yaka*. When he heard this and found out that Jayasena had committed adultery with her, Gotembara challenged him to a duel which was to be held near Polonnaruva in the country of Jayasena. However, Gotembara considered the whole thing a trifle and, thinking himself certain of victory, made no preparations, while Jayasena brought with him a crowd of combatants. One morning, as Gotembara, clad only in his loincloth, was going to bathe, he remembered that it was the day of the duel. One of the gods warned him and advised him not to go to the duel as it would mean his certain death. But Gotembara paid no attention to the warnings. When he reached the place, he found an enormous army of men which Jayasena had brought with him. Jayasena presented a formidable aspect, a big, strong man in full armor, while Gotembara, small and insignificant, faced his adversary completely alone and unarmed. Nobody thought other than that the fight must be decided in a few moments in Jayasena's favor. But it was not so! Gotembara cleverly avoided all the blows that Jayasena aimed at him, and going back a step or two, took a run, sprang eighty feet in the air, and gave his opponent such a blow with his foot that the latter's head flew off his shoulders. In this way he vanquished his enemy. Jayasena was lamented and buried by his relatives. A friend of his, Senasuru Hamaduruvo (Saturn), who was playing football when he heard of Jayasena's death, set out immediately to attend the funeral. On the way he met a wolf which he killed. He cut off the head and took it with him. When he came to the spot where the duel had taken place, the people were already preparing to bury Jayasena. Then Senasuru took the head of the dead wolf and sat it on the headless body of Jayasena, while reciting a suitable *mantra*. The body was thus brought back to life as a *yaka*, with a human body and a wolf's head, who from then on haunted cemeteries where he attacked people who came to bury their dead. . . .

(10) Tota Kadavara (From Barnett 1916)

The washerman of the king of Baranas, having lost one of his master's garments, ran away to Kasi where he pretended to be an exiled prince and married the king's daughter, who bore him two sons. When the sons played at washing and serving, the king became suspicious and asked the washerman to draw a map of Baranas. The washerman forgot his role and drew his own house in the washerman's quarter. He was put to death and reborn as a demon. He attacked his former wife with sickness and she was cured only when offerings were made.

(11) Dala Raja (Dala Kadavara) (From Barnett 1916)

To obtain a son a queen Ramsaveti offered Isvara an ivory image from the tusk *(dala)* of a living elephant. When Dala was born astrologers foretold that he would marry his own sister. When therefore a sister was born, she was hidden in a cave. Dala heard of this and feigned sickness saying that he could live only if his sister cooked gruel for him. He thus gratified his desire. The princess, being with child, hanged herself, but was saved by Sakra who made her invisible. The king ordered his son to be ousted by an elephant, which in charging him split its tusks and rendered him senseless. Senesuru (Saturn, who had been beaten in gambling by Dala) threw poison on him, turning him into a demon with three heads.

References

Barnett, L. D. 1916. Alphabetical guide to Sinhalese folklore from ballad sources. *Indian Antiquary* 45:46.

Boyd, James. n.d. Satan and Mara: Christian and Buddhist symbols of evil. Unpublished paper.

Conze, Edward. 1959. *Buddhism, Its Essence and Development*. New York: Harper & Row.

Dahlke, Paul. 1908. *Buddhist Essays*. New York: Macmillan.

Gombrich, Richard. 1971. *Precept and Practice*. New York and London: Oxford University Press.

Goonewardena, Dandris De Silva. 1866. On demonology and witchcraft in Ceylon. *Journal of the Royal Asiatic Society* (Ceylon Branch) 4:13.

Obeyesekere, Gananath. 1963a. The great tradition and the little in the perspective of Sinhalese Buddhism. *Journal of Asian Studies* 22:2.

Obeyesekere, Gananath. 1963b. Pregnancy cravings *(dola-duka)* in relation to social structure and personality in a Sinhalese village. *American Anthropologist* 65:2.

Obeyesekere, Gananath. 1968. Theodicy, sin and salvation in a sociology of Buddhism. In E. R. Leach (ed.), *Cambridge Papers in Social Anthropology.* Cambridge: Cambridge University Press.

Ortner, Sherry B. 1973. Is female to male as nature is to culture? In M. Z. Rosaldo and L. Lamphere (eds.), *Woman, Culture and Society.* Stanford: Stanford University Press.

Rahula, Walpola. 1959. *What the Buddha Taught.* London and New York: Evergreen Books, Grove Press.

Wirz, Paul. 1954. *Exorcism and the Art of Healing in Ceylon.* Leiden: E. J. Brill.

Part II
Dual Aspects of Women

Archetypic Nurturance

7

Lois Paul

Careers of Midwives in a Mayan Community

1. Introduction

Midwives in the Zutuhil community of San Pedro la Laguna in highland Guatemala are both ritual and obstetrical specialists. Like shaman-priests generally, the midwife mediates between her patients and supernaturals, performing rituals to safeguard her patients. She herself is recruited by supernaturals and her calling is validated by a shaman. Exercising the role of midwife in San Pedro, in comparison with other communities, involves large case loads and requires a high level of activity and professional commitment. Incumbents are recruited from the category of women still in their prime—married women who begin their careers between the ages of 35 and 40. These women must overcome their own reluctance, their husband's objections, and society's envious ambivalence toward their social ascendancy (Paul and Paul 1975).

The problematics for the individual woman in San Pedro revolve

---

EDITORS' NOTE: A short and conceptually narrowed version of this article was published in *Ethos* shortly before Lois Paul died. That publication, entitled "Recruitment to a Ritual Role" (L. Paul 1975), deals exclusively with one of the two major themes of the present version, that of the normal process of becoming a midwife in San Pedro la Laguna. Like this chapter, it includes the case of Juana, a typical, indeed prototypical, midwife, and it lays out the economic and other background factors that usually characterize those "normal" women who end up in midcareer as sacred midwives. This chapter includes as well the contrasting and instructive case of Maria, a deviant or "abnormal" woman who half solves her psychological problems, along lines suggested by Silverman (1967) for shamans, by becoming accepted as a midwife in a neighboring Indian town. Lois Paul was a research assistant in the Department of Anthropology at Stanford University, Stanford, California. Ms. Paul died on December 21, 1975.

around the cultural definitions of male and female behavior. The activities of the midwife are incompatible with the behavioral norms that apply to ordinary women. Midwives are born with the sign of their divine destinies but are socialized like ordinary women as daughters, wives, and mothers. San Pedro women enjoy the right of bilateral inheritance but are in fact generally subordinate to men and restricted to the domestic domain where they work long hours grinding corn, weaving, washing, carrying water, bearing children, and tending domestic animals.

Females are socialized to attain high levels of skill and mastery, to be responsible and nurturant, even as children, with those younger in their charge. They grow up feeling competent and efficacious but only within the limited domestic sphere. With their seniors, and particularly with males, they are expected to be obedient, compliant, passive, and unquestioning. Trained in extreme modesty, they typically approach menstruation, marriage, and first childbirth experiences in varying degrees of ignorance, which expectably results in fright, anxiety, and trauma. To contain women's exercise of competence and efficacy within the domestic sphere, San Pedro society traditionally has depended on segregation of males and females, supervision of females, the assignment of legitimate sexual pleasure exclusively to males, the mystification of sex and reproduction for females, and the psychological mechanisms of fear, shame, and guilt as social controls (L. Paul 1974).

The role of midwife, on the other hand, demands that a woman be aggressive and authoritative in unfamiliar situations, that she observe none of the usual space or time boundaries applicable to other women, that she display unusual fortitude. She must withstand the terrors of night and of contact with the supernatural. She must overcome feelings of disgust and fear at the sight and handling of blood, of the newborn fetus, of potentially polluting birth substances. She must overcome intense shame and modesty concerning the sexual organs and act upon the bodily organs and substances of strange women.

She must be able to suppress her own panic and lend strength to her patient as she struggles with a difficult breech delivery or delayed ejection of the placenta, relying on ingenuity, herbal remedies, magic, nerve, and physical strength, rather than the wonder drugs, anesthetics, and forceps of the modern delivery room. She knows she will have to take command at the moment of delivery, overruling advice of anxious parents who may be her seniors in age, and she fears taking responsibility for another's life. Characteristically, Pedranos learn to avoid blame by avoiding involvement in the affairs of others. The midwife's high status and supernatural credentials usually ensure her authority, but high status and material rewards can expose the midwife to the envy of neighbors.

In San Pedro, as in the highland Maya area generally, there is a marked ambivalence toward hierarchy and any demonstration of assertiveness or ascendancy that accrues to the individual office holder rather than to the office (Colby 1967:416–418). By accepting the role of midwife the woman exposes herself to the envy of neighbors and the possibility of sorcery. An older woman informant explained: "It is a sin for one who is born with the *virtud* (power) to refuse to go out and help women, but people also gossip about midwives; they say their husbands don't know how to support them. People are always envious of the things others do." A midwife's husband loses a certain amount of "face" in the eyes of other men as his wife gains more autonomy in her new role and men make gibes about his manliness. To safeguard the lives of her patients a midwife must observe the cultural taboo on sexual intercourse required of ritual specialists generally in the Maya area. Midwives in San Pedro should abstain from sex four days before and after a delivery.

To overcome these obstacles, selection of midwives in San Pedro is based on birth signs and other evidences of supernatural choice. This accounts for the high prestige and respect accorded those women who become midwives in San Pedro (Paul and Paul 1975:716–719). Not all of those born with signs of divine election, however, actualize their calling, despite the risk they run of suffering supernatural punishment if they refuse the call. Who are the women who accept the supernatural mandate? What are their social and psychological characteristics? By what process do they come to accept this extraordinary identity? The literature contains few detailed descriptions of the process of becoming a folk curer (Landy 1974:103). The literature is particularly sparse in regard to the midwife's route to her role. In Mesoamerica periodic religious and legal harassment of native ritual specialists since the conquest has contributed to a general attitude of secrecy and suspicion toward outsiders. Accounts of the recruitment process, therefore, tend to the stereotypic.

Biographical data on two Pedrano sisters are presented to illustrate contrasting routes to the role of midwife. Juana (names are fictitious) is the very model of a midwife in San Pedro. Maria, her sister, defined as a deviant personality by San Pedro culture, seeks to stabilize her own equilibrium by becoming a sacred professional. The writer came to know Juana and Maria while living in San Pedro for a year in 1941, long before either of the women became midwives, and has had contact with them on repeated field trips since 1957. Most of the information was secured at the time the events in their lives occurred; early childhood data were recounted by the principals themselves or by relatives and neighbors.

In 1941 two midwives served a population of 2000; one has since died, and the other is now the oldest practicing midwife. By 1975, the population of San Pedro has more than doubled, and is served by seven midwives, all familiar to the writer.

2. Juana, a Prototypical Midwife

Juana, who was 51 in 1975, has been practicing for 15 years. She is the most popular midwife and has the largest clientele.* By Pedrano standards she is the "ideal" midwife, comely, virtuous, quiet-spoken, self-assured, competent, dignified, and compassionate, with indisputable supernatural credentials, and by now her skill in dealing with difficult deliveries that other midwives have given up as hopeless has become legendary.

Juana is the second of six surviving children. Maria, her older sister, was born after three children died in infancy. Juana's mother came from a wealthy Indian family. Her maternal great-grandmother was a midwife. Juana's father, a shaman who specialized in curing insanity, came from a poor family. However, he strategically married Juana's mother and, by agreeing to uxorilocal residence, took over the management of his wife's estate.

When she was growing up, Juana was modest, obedient, and respectful, mastering the required feminine skills of grinding and weaving, in contrast to her older sister, who was recalcitrant, "lazy," and constantly at odds with her parents. Unlike Maria, who was "temperamental," Juana was quiet and would sometimes sit in the doorway just "gazing off into space" while she embroidered her father's pants. Her mother never disturbed her when she found her doing this. Daydreaming is generally discouraged, but children with special destinies are permitted, even expected, to show early signs of their presumed mystical tendencies. Nothing was ever said explicitly to Juana concerning her destiny, for to speak or boast of it might bring death to the girl from the supernaturals or from the *envidia* (envy) of other Pedranos. Furthermore, parents fear that if word got around their daughter might not get a husband. For what young man will court a girl who is to become a midwife?

On more than one occasion Juana, as a child of destiny, was taken to a shaman by her parents to have protective *costumbres* (rites) per-

---

*Of a total of 203 San Pedro births in 1973, Juana delivered 72, or 35%. Her closest rivals delivered 57 and 32 cases, respectively. The remaining 42 cases were delivered by four midwives.

formed for her. In the church, candles were burned and prayers were addressed to Santa Ana, chief of the "twelve Marias," the patron saints of childbirth. Under cover of darkness, the party would secretly go to native shrines on the outskirts of the village. Here candles, incense, and rum were offered by the shaman to the ancestral spirits of former San Pedro midwives, to other ancestor spirits, and to the supernatural lords of the many domains of nature and of calendric time.

Periodically, Juana observed the midwife who visited her own mother. Around this woman, called *iyom* in Zutuhil-Maya, there was an aura of awe and suppressed excitement. But Juana and the other children were told only that a new child had been "bought" from the *extranjeros* (foreigners). Whenever the *iyom* appeared everyone would kiss her hand respectfully, as they now kiss Juana's. One time the midwife put her hand on young Juana's head and told her she too would be an *iyom* one day, but it would be a long time before the child knew what meaning to attach to the word.

Juana repeatedly had enigmatic dreams around her twelfth and thirteenth years. One of these dreams resembled what Eliade (1964) calls the "ecstatic journey" characteristic of shamans. "In my dream an old man, all in white, with white hair and white beard, appeared," Juana recalls. "He tucked me under his arm like a bundle. He held me tight and we flew far far away, just like birds, over many towns and strange places. No, I wasn't afraid. It was very beautiful. I looked down from the sky and saw the houses like tiny toys down below. Everything looked so pretty. After a long time of flying, he brought me back."

Knowing nothing then of sex or reproduction, Juana says she felt both frightened and "strange" when she had a dream in which she saw a woman with her legs spread apart, her skirt up, and a "bloody" baby coming out of her. "A woman all in pure white from head to toe handed me a white cloth and showed me how to receive the baby." When she told her mother of the "funny sight—a baby emerging from its mother's anus," her mother only scolded her and sharply warned her never to reveal her dreams. "Being a child, I naturally told my cousins the next day and got a hard beating when the story got back to my mother. She warned me that I would die if I talked about it again." After that Juana kept her dreams to herself. Juana now interprets her early dreams as previsionary revelation of "primal" mysteries of creation, as early evidence of her mystical vocation. Juana's mother and her culture made clear to her that her dreams were sacred, that to reveal the forbidden mysteries she had seen could be fatal. She claims, as do all midwives, not to have understood the significance of her adolescent dreams until much later when she was to become a midwife.

Other midwives similarly report having had dreams of childbirth and of ecstatic journeys around the time of puberty. This time coincides with the period when courtship starts for most girls in San Pedro, a time of heightened sensitivity and self-awareness. But during the two decades or so of childbearing following marriage, the mystical identity seems to recede into latency while the young woman is preoccupied with the usual transitions to adult roles and with the pains and pleasures of every normal woman's life in San Pedro.

Unlike most other Pedrano girls of that period who chose to be "stolen" (Paul and Paul 1963), Juana did not run off with a suitor to his parent's house. Instead she agreed to marry him only if he would live with her parents. Her husband's family had less property than Juana's but he too came from a family of some distinction. His paternal grandfather and aunt were divinely chosen bonesetters, famous in distant towns as well as in San Pedro.

Juana's mother, on her deathbed in 1958, a year before Juana herself fell ill, revealed to Juana her own divine destiny, unfulfilled because of *vergüenza* and fear of her husband's violent temper. She entrusted Juana's birth sign, the treasured piece of amniotic sac, to Juana's father, to be revealed at the proper time. Juana says her mother died prematurely young because of her failure to exercise her own mandate to be a midwife.

Juana had already lost six of her ten children when her mother died. For over a year she suffered weakness, shortness of breath, "heavy heart," a variety of aches and pains—the classic symptoms of grief described by Lindemann (1944). Finally she was "forced to stay in bed," a rare event for stoically trained Indian women. She was unable to eat or drink, grew weak, and slept only fitfully. She did not respond to pills, herbs, or prescription medicines. She lost weight, grew "thin" (wasted), and began having strange dreams.

In her dreams Juana was visited by big, fat women, all in radiant white, who told her that she was sick and that her children had died because she was not going out to help the women in childbirth. These were the spirits of dead midwives. When she tried to sleep, the spirits would appear. They would grab her ears and scold her, tell her that she would die and her husband would die if she did not exercise her calling. They reminded her that she had already lost six children. You were punished, they said, because you did not pay attention to those who gave you the *virtud*. Now, if you continue to hesitate your other children will also die. Remember, they reminded her, that your mother died because you did not obey God's call.

When Juana protested that she was too ignorant and incompetent, that she knew nothing about the skills that a midwife must have, the spirits assured her they would instruct her. They showed her the signs of pregnancy, how to massage the pregnant woman, and to·palpate the abdomen to feel if the fetus was in correct position for delivery. They demonstrated "external version" (turning the fetus). In her dreams she saw graphically a woman delivering a baby. The spirits showed her how to hold the white cloth with which to receive the fetus and how to clean the newborn infant. They showed her how to cut the cord and interpret its markings. They instructed her not to cut the umbilical cord before the placenta was presented. They showed her how the umbilical cord must be followed back up to the placenta in case it does not come out, and the placenta removed manually if necessary. They showed her how to "smoke" a woman with embers from the fire in such cases. They told her they would always be present, though invisible, at deliveries to help her. The spirits instructed her how to bind the woman's abdomen after delivery to "hold the organs in place." "All these things I saw," Juana says, and in addition, they taught her prayers and ritual procedures.

When she related her disturbing dreams to her husband, he protested. He did not want her to go about the village as a midwife, neglecting the household and their children. Finally, he too fell ill and was visited in his dreams by the women in white. They scolded him, saying he must tell his wife to start practicing, or both would die. Juana's father, in his capacity as shaman, was finally consulted about their dreams. He lit candles in the house, burned incense, and performed divination rituals. He confirmed the warnings of the spirits and ceremoniously brought out the proof, the birth sign entrusted to him by her mother. Juana began to regain her strength.

Shortly thereafter, as Juana was returning from the lake, a curiously shaped white bone about nine inches long suddenly skipped down the road before her. She was frightened and dared not touch it. That night the women in white appeared again and instructed her to pick up the bone. They said, "This is your *virtud*, you must keep it always, never show it to anyone, guard it carefully." The next day the bone reappeared in her path. She obeyed the spirits, and picked it up. When she arrived home, the magic bone was no longer in her shawl but in her cabinet, already waiting for her. Soon afterward a small knife also appeared magically in her path. This time she did not hestitate, but picked it up and carried it home. This she uses to cut the umbilical cord.

Finding her objects was the final sign. Juana's father urged against further delay. He performed nightlong *costumbres* this time, keeping Juana and her husband on their knees for many hours. In the ritual rhetoric of shamans, he summoned and addressed the patron saints and the ancestral guardians of childbirth, the deities of hills, waters, rains, winds, the masters and spirit guardians of all domains. He begged forgiveness for all the sins of Juana and her relatives, both past and present, promising the supernaturals that Juana would fulfill their command willingly and with a good heart. He assured the spirits that her husband bowed to their mandate and would give his wholehearted support to the selfless sacrifice she was about to make for the sake of the women of San Pedro. On the following day the standard ritual gift for a shaman, a cooked chicken and a basket of tortillas, was sent to her father, now remarried and living again in his natal town.

On our return to San Pedro in 1962 we found that Juana, then 37, had been practicing midwifery for two years. Juana's reputation as a midwife was early enhanced by her successful delivery of twins in a breech presentation. The case had been given up as hopeless by another midwife. Her career was a frequent topic of conversation among Pedranos, both male and female. Her supernatural experiences and her "miraculous" obstetrical skills were already becoming legendary, recounted with dramatic effects and in the lowered tones Pedranos characteristically use when speaking of native supernatural phenomena, as opposed to Christian deities. Blending new elements with the traditional, Juana performs the special rituals for children born with divine destinies, as well as the rituals of purification that end the eight-day postpartum period (Paul and Paul 1975). The combination of faith in her supernatural power, confidence in her medicine and new methods, and a relationship based on trust seems to predispose her patients to experience relatively easy deliveries. Yet the concept of painless "natural childbirth" is unknown to her. When one of her patients laughed and talked throughout labor and the delivery, Juana worried that the patient might be crazy.

Because a midwife may not become pregnant, Juana began using birth control pills in 1962. Two years later she was using an I.U.D. But for the last decade she and her husband have not shared a bed. "How would it look" she says, if I, a midwife, went out pregnant to see my patients. A fine sight I would be! What a shame! And a sin!" Moreover it could be dangerous for her patients, she adds. Once her case load increased to sizable proportions, she announced to her husband that she could no longer sleep with him. "As a midwife, I must think first of my patients," she pointed out. Pedranos view sex as polluting, and therefore dangerous to the woman in childbirth. Juana told her husband she would not blame him even if he left and refused to provide food and clothing for her and their children, but that she had no choice. She even advised him to find someone else to satisfy his sexual needs. "Not an angry type of man," he agreed to her celibacy but pleaded with her for "just one more time," she recounted amidst gales of laughter.

In a sense Juana solved the problem of her relationship with her husband years in advance, by selecting the suitor who agreed to live on *her* home ground rather than his. This gave her preferential treatment in inheritance and enabled her to acquire her own house and a unique measure of independence. It also ensured for her a husband who was less concerned about his manliness than are the many Pedrano men who balk at uxorilocal marriage. But her husband's initial resistance to her career was real, the resistance of a normal Pedrano husband, just as Juana's illness and suffering prior to practicing were real.

Juana's economic independence, her husband's own familial background and his regard for the sacred professions, the mix of their temperaments, all facilitated Juana's final emergence as a full-fledged ritual specialist, but she was too successfully socialized as a normal woman to make the transition without a crisis of identity (her illness).

3. Maria, an Atypical Midwife

Thus far there are no instances of two sisters occupying the role of midwife concurrently in San Pedro, but one of the most popular midwives in a large neighboring town is Juana's older sister, Maria. Maria too suffered before becoming a midwife, but her suffering has not completely resolved her internal and interpersonal conflicts. Her life continues to be punctuated by crises of identity.

Maria was the first child to live after three who died in infancy. She was therefore given the ritual protection of *costumbres*, plus unusual care and attention as an infant. But at 15 months she was abruptly weaned to make way for her sister. At the age of two she was dethroned when Juana, who became the favorite, was born. For a year or so Maria was indulged as a typical "knee child" (B. Paul 1967:207). Her temper tantrums were characteristically indulged, ignored, or pacified with a fruit or sweet, but like most children of this category, she was relatively neglected until she became her father's constant *compañera*, as he fondly called her. He treated her like a son. She accompanied him wherever he went, to supervise his field hands or on trips to markets and fiestas. As her father's companion, Maria enjoyed unusual freedom and independence, traits normally encouraged only in boys.

However, when Maria was seven or eight years old and had therefore reached the age of responsibility, by Pedrano norms, she was expected to stay home and learn feminine tasks. But she resisted her

mother's efforts to train her. Her willfulness, wandering ways, and independence were intolerable and led to frequent conflict and punishment. She was soon defined as the "bad" child in contrast to Juana, her
"good" little sister.

Although she started school most unwillingly, Maria was one of the
few girls of that period who remained in school to complete all three
grades of primary school (there are now more grades in San Pedro). She
learned Spanish and some ingratiating ways to avoid "discipline" and to
win approval from the ladino (non-Indian) school teachers. Maria's
beauty attracted the attention of male teachers and she began to enter-
tain fantasies of escape from her family and into the ladino world.

Maria was more worldly than her sister, and assumed the prerogatives of a youthful male, experimenting with sexual liaisons before eloping with her first husband at 14. By the time she was 18, when we first
met her in 1941, she had had three husbands—nearly all unions were
then common-law marriages—and was nursing a nine-month-old girl,
child of her last marriage. Each of her marriages had ended abruptly as
the result of conflicts with her various mothers-in-law, as well as with
her husbands. Each of her mothers-in-law complained of Maria's laziness, her bossiness with the younger children of the household, her
long absences from home, and her brazen habit of stopping to talk with
men in the street.

Constantly seeking an escape from home and the confinement of
the woman's role, she had married young men from relatively wealthy
local Indian families, each time in the hope of escaping with her husband from San Pedro. Each of her husbands was literate and ladinoized;
two were educated in the capital—a rare event at the time—and qualified as rural school teachers. She realized her wish with one husband
who took her to live for a while in a ladino town on the coastal plain,
where she improved her Spanish and was exposed to ladino ways.

But Maria's life in the ladino town came to an end when she and her
husband were stricken with malaria and had to return to his parents'
home in San Pedro. The three youths she successively married were
unable to liberate themselves or Maria from their society. They were
among those early temporary migrants who became marginal men when
they returned to the village, no longer willing to work with hoe and
machete in their fathers' fields, turning to alcohol for consolation.

Maria's elopements were defined by her parents as defiant acts,
humiliating to their pride. Despite the fact that elopement was the popular mode of marriage at the time (Paul and Paul 1963), the girl's parents
but not the boy's were typically angered, often bringing suit against the

eloping couple in the local courthouse, if only to see the young offenders punished with the imposition of a fine, which was usually paid by the parents of the boy. Maria's family reluctantly accepted her back home after each separation, but the atmosphere grew increasingly strained, particularly when she returned with a baby, another mouth to feed.

Maria's knowledge of Spanish, her beauty, her poise among ladinos, and her talents as a performer led to her election on repeated occasions to represent the village in provincial or national folkloristic events such as displays of native weaving (other Pedrano women did the weaving) or demonstrations of "typical Indian dances." Maria was a good dancer and drew criticism from her parents and neighbors for the many hours she spent like a man, dancing in the *cofradías* (sodalities) to the marimba music during fiestas. It was at one such dance during Holy Week in 1941 that we observed Maria dancing coquettishly with José, who, she misleadingly assured us, was not a *novio* (sweetheart) since they were cousins. A week later she eloped with him from our house one evening, going to live in the house of his parents and abandoning her baby at the home of her own parents.

This time Maria's alienation was nearly total. Enraged, her father brought suit against her in the local court, demanding that she be sent to the local jail for abandoning her baby. Everyone knew that the baby, claimed by its paternal grandparents in the ensuing local court suit, had little chance of survival since it was under a year old and still nursing. Maria's desertion of the baby and the baby's subsequent demise were widely considered a heinous sin.

Maria could count on the help of her new husband and his parents—who paid the heavy fine imposed by the court—but not for long. Maria again found herself under the thumb of a mother-in-law who was a martinet. Condemned by her culture's rules of residence and lack of alternatives, Maria had acted out of desperation and impulse, grasping at improbable routes of escape. Again Maria's mother-in-law was promptly antagonized by Maria's absences and insolence.

One month after the elopement, Maria and her husband had a violent quarrel, each accusing the other of infidelity. José struck Maria, who fell into a faint that lasted for two hours. When she came to, she experienced a dissociated episode that lasted for several weeks. (This event is described and discussed in B. Paul 1967.) During this episode, Maria was in a state of fugue, oblivious to her ordinary surroundings. She was considered *loca* or insane (*chuj* in Zutuhil-Maya). She became alternately violent and morose. She paced, gestured, and talked to spirits who tried to take her with them to the other world. They said they needed her to help nurse the many dead babies in heaven. In her dissociated state, Maria chanted forbidden snatches of her father's shamanistic prayers.

The spirits who pleaded with Maria to join them in death symbolically represented the "social death" she had suffered by alienating every member of her human society. This illness, however, posed the threat of common jeopardy to all the relatives and set in motion "self-regulating processes" (B. Paul 1967), which reversed the process of social alienation. Maria's father, until then at odds with her in-laws, was called in as the expert in curing insanity. Maria, accompanied by her husband and both sets of parents, was taken by canoe to the shrine of *Maximón*, where her father and another shaman performed the appropriate rituals. Maria became the center of concern, sympathy, and attention; she recovered. By an abrupt change in her mode of deviance from argument and rebellion to psychological withdrawal, "Maria was able to trip the cultural lever that set restitutive processes in motion. Having no hospitals to hide her in, the culture provided Maria with a key to re-enter their own society" (B. Paul 1967:165). Maria's illness had the effect of temporarily reknitting her relations with her own family and with her husband, but it was not a prelude to becoming a ritual midwife, at least not immediately.

At the time (1941), we recorded the following observation in our field notes:

> Her society provided no feasible alternatives to the standard feminine role of home-maker. The specialized role of midwife might accommodate such a unique person but one may not merely elect to become a midwife. This role is assigned by fate and must be validated by certain supernatural insignia and by social confirmation. In any event she is not old enough to fill the position of midwife in this culture. The only realistic way she might escape the limitations of her society would be if she leaves the village. . . .

As it turned out, she did leave San Pedro at a later date; and she did become a midwife, but not for another 20 years.

In fact, Maria and José lived for several years in the capital of Guatemala, where we saw them briefly in 1946. The following year, after the birth of a baby girl, Maria and José separated and Maria returned again to her parents' home in San Pedro.

On our return in 1962, we learned that Maria was living in a large Indian town nearby. She was married to her fifth husband, a native of that town. Maria had not yet become a midwife but we found her ill and complaining about peculiar symptoms. Maria was sure she had been bewitched because of her "powers." She referred to her illness and its causes in hushed tones, to dramatize the mysterious implications of her innuendos. The town to which Maria had moved is known among its neighbors for the high prevalence of witches. At the time we recorded in our field notes that we would not be surprised if Maria emerged as a shaman or a midwife in the near future.

When we returned two years later in the summer of 1964, Maria had indeed already become one of the most respected and well-known midwives among a large group of midwives in her adopted town. We learned that a powerful shaman had counteracted her bewitchment by removing several foreign objects from her body. He also divined that she was being "called" to be a midwife.

Like the case of shamans described by Silverman (1967), Maria has had cognitive experiences that in our society might be labeled schizophrenic. But her culture has provided her with a socially acceptable role for the expression of her psychological peculiarities. Although Maria may not have been born with signs of her future role—it is not clear that midwives in her adopted town, like those in San Pedro la Laguna, are born with a distinctive sign—she plays the part so convincingly that Juana, her own sister in San Pedro, now asserts that Maria was born with the *virtud*, just as Juana herself was. Retrospectively, Maria's early episode of mental dissociation is now reinterpreted as premonitory evidence of her supernatural *virtud*.

But Maria has not entirely overcome her inner conflict, the envy of her neighbors, or the opposition of her husband. In varying degrees, all three problems still trouble Maria. Her present husband is a literate Indian who retains Indian dress and in other respects exhibits an Indian style of life. He works as a lawyer's assistant on Indian inheritance disputes and has political connections in the local and national ladino hierarchy. A man of property and entrepreneurial skills, he is economically well-off by local standards and has his own need to command and be important. He depends on Maria to help promote his own fortunes and those of their growing sons in the ladino world. One son has graduated from military college and the parents hope to see one of the other two sons become a full-fledged lawyer. When facing the outside world, Maria and her husband make a successful team. Her charm and fluent Spanish make her popular with visiting dignitaries and medical personnel. In 1967 Maria was chosen to act as interpreter in a ten-week course given by visiting public health nurses for local midwives, most of whom spoke no Spanish.

But Maria and her husband have equally strong characters, and within the privacy of the domestic sphere they frequently clash. When this happens Maria does not yield; her "manly" temper often flares. Unlike other females in her culture, she does not cry or go limp when her husband strikes her. To the amazement of her sisters, Maria "fights back like a man."

Maria's extraordinary need for ascendancy and power seems to have its roots in the discontinuities in her early socialization. After her father had encouraged "male traits" in his young daughter, her culture unsuccessfully attempted to impose narrowly defined female norms on the male templates.* Unable to express herself constructively, she alienated her society by her "manly" behavior. Defined as a deviant, she was made to feel unworthy as well as powerless. In any case her present problems are with her husband, whose need to dominate her is stronger than his pride in her accomplishments. Although the two are evenly matched in their drive for ascendancy and in their quick tempers, her husband is the stronger in physical combat. Moreover, Maria lacks the independent economic base that enabled Juana to successfully assert her terms of independence vis-à-vis her husband.

Maria and her husband have frequently quarreled over Maria's insistence on sexual abstinence in the name of her ritual requirements. In the asymmetrical context of sexual relations in her culture (L. Paul 1974:289) it is all too true, as De Beauvoir (1970:368) claims of women generally, that "to give oneself to someone is to abdicate one's will." In Maria's culture midwives gain in two ways by abstaining from sex. To her society and to herself, the midwife demonstrates her continuing sense of professional commitment and her right to the office. Moreover, freed from the necessity of submitting to her husband's sexual demands, she gains a positive sense of self-direction. While Juana is assertive without being aggressive, Maria characteristically challenges her husband by communicating defiance in her demands for sexual independence. He is not fully resigned to Maria's career, nor does Maria countenance his extramarital liaisons.

Thus Maria has not completely overcome the strains in her conflicting obligations as wife and midwife. Nor has she fully reduced the

---

*Other "Marias"—nonconforming girls—growing up in San Pedro at the present time have more alternatives: in the past two decades there have been significant changes in alternative roles available to females. A few, from families with means, have received higher education outside of the town and are now teaching in rural schools, earning the same relatively high salaries ($125 per month) that men in that job category earn. A few have been trained as paramedical personnel but are not yet accepted as midwives. One has become an injectionist and another has been stationed in another rural village as the public health nurse. Other less fortunate young women have escaped from broken marriages and their town by taking jobs as servants in the capital. Still others, out of desperation, have availed themselves of the questionable "opportunity" of entering the underpaid pool of temporary plantation laborers earning $1 or less a day—cash much needed as San Pedro grows more "modernized."

strains in her subjective identity. In moving to another Indian town, she left some of her history behind, but she carried with her the product of her upbringing, her overdetermined needs. Her commanding and dramatic style enhances her professional role, giving her a certain measure of charisma, but her aggressiveness and unbridled temper bring her into recurrent conflict with her husband and with other members of her society. In the eyes of their society, Juana and other Pedrano midwives ameliorate the social ascendance of their role by genuine displays of compassion and emphasis on the hardships of their office. Maria, in a sense, is too successful; she enjoys the power of her position too obviously. The very quality that adds to her success as a ritual specialist also incurs envy and occasional bewitchment. Periodically she is overwhelmed by feelings of powerlessness and vulnerability. At such times she withdraws into illness. Such withdrawal often is the desperate strategy of the powerless (Lewis 1971; Uzzell 1974).

However, Maria does not disintegrate into madness. Her culture provides the means for cloaking domestic conflicts and locating the hostility outside in envious neighbors. Local metaphysics and cosmology recognize "permeable body boundaries" (L. Paul 1974:299) and the intrusion of injurious objects by witchcraft. This same permeability makes possible miraculous curative acts. Following a recent conflict with her husband and his mistress, Maria became seriously ill once again. For weeks on end she lay in bed, virtually paralyzed. She scarcely ate, suffering severe weight loss. But she was cured by miraculous intervention. Winged women in white appeared in her dreams to perform a bloodless operation that removed a disabling foreign object from her side. Following the dream, she rose from the bed feeling hungry and strong. Both Maria and her husband marveled at her miraculous recovery.

Silverman (1967:28) points out that persons on the threshold of becoming shamans or schizophrenics face crises revolving around a severely damaged conception of the self and that their abnormalities may be regarded as the result of a desperate attempt to redefine a personally meaningful self-concept. Both redefine their self-image from one of being faulty and unworthy to one of being more than human, a person of momentous importance. The shaman is supported in his self-imagery by his culture's belief in his supernatural powers, while the schizophrenic in our society suffers for his. The role of midwife, like that of shaman, has made it possible for Maria to redefine her self-image from that of an unworthy and undesirable deviant to that of one who possesses some measure of supernatural power and is a person of momentous importance. But she remains dependent on an unwilling husband and lacks the full support she needs to stabilize herself completely in the midwife role or to feel secure in her new identity.

4. Social and Economic Characteristics of Midwives

The life histories of Juana and Maria suggest answers to two general questions about the recruitment of midwives. From a panel of potential midwives (those reputed to be born with the call) only a few actualize their destinies. The process of selection is not random. What are the salient characteristics of those women who make the grade? Those women like Juana who become successful sacred professionals share characteristics that relate to family background, parental expectation, economic situation, and personal character.

4.1. Family Background

Although inheritance is not explicitly acknowledged as an avenue to the role, most midwives come from families in which the mother and/or grandmother are midwives or the father is a shaman. In Juana's case her father was a shaman and her mother herself had the divine calling although she did not practice. Identification of a future midwife is made at her birth by the midwife who delivers her. The identifying symbol is a part of the caul attached to the head. Such identification is more likely to occur, to be taken seriously, and to be acted upon when the parents are themselves sacred professionals. Like Juana, children of ritual specialists are exposed to the private rituals and prayers of midwives and shamans. These children's early experiences are framed in the esoteric cultural symbols available within the particular family culture of the midwife or shaman.

4.2. Parental Expectation

As in Juana's case, mothers of midwives are strongly motivated to have a daughter become a midwife. If the mother is a midwife herself she serves as role model. In any case the mother's motivation is implemented through the close bond that is characteristic of the mother–daughter relationship in such instances. The mother's own affect and subliminal cues form the basis for implicit communication as the girl is growing up. The prophecy is fulfilled by the predictive behavior of the parents, particularly of the mother. Thus Juana was the subject of mysterious awe-inspiring rituals; her mystical experiences were encouraged.

Her mother's dire warnings and punishment gave heightened significance and a sense of fearful wonder to her early dreams. These became
templates for the mystical dreams during her divine illness, her identity
crisis.

4.3. Economic Situation

In San Pedro inheritance of land and wealth is theoretically bilateral
but residence of young couples is predominantly virilocal, although
there is an increasing tendency toward neolocal residence at an earlier
stage of marriage. Michaelson and Goldschmidt (1971) in their cross-
cultural study of female roles and male dominance among peasants find
that where inheritance is bilateral, the increased economic power of
women tends to create a *machismo* syndrome where male authoritarian
roles are expected and males feel threatened. This seems to fit the case of
San Pedro. However, although women's economic power often remains
a theory rather than a fact, male dominance *is* very important. Midwives
like Juana are generally women who not only have a claim to economic
means but have the means, in the form of houses or other property.
Lacking the tangible means, they may have instead the moral and potential economic support of parents as a base from which to assert an
independent stand vis-à-vis their husbands. All husbands balk at the
prospect of losing some control over their wives, of giving up a measure
of convenience, authority, and manliness in the name of community
welfare. To be a successful midwife requires a husband who accommo-
dates to the role of husband of midwife. Some men in this role prove
their manliness to themselves and others by discreet sexual liaisons,
which their celibate wives tend to overlook. The marriages of midwives
are characteristically more complementary and less asymmetrical than
most other Pedrano marriages (L. Paul 1974:289) because of the midwife's higher level of economic independence, the aura of her sacred
office, and the sexual independence that she enjoys.

In effect midwives constitute an unacknowledged professional elite
in San Pedro rather than the part-time category of older kinswomen or
poor widows typical in some other areas (Paul and Paul 1975). But to
attain this elite status, midwives in San Pedro suffer an initiatory illness,
the price they pay for prestige and power and for the agreement of their
husbands. The illness, like classical rituals of transition (Van Gennep
1960), separates the woman from ordinary roles and provides the liminal
ground on which the transcendent authorities intervene to resolve the
conflicts arising from competing role obligations. In a culminating ritual
performed by the shaman who validates her sacred office, the woman is

reincorporated into her family and her society in a new hierarchy of roles: the priority of her professional obligation to society is made explicit to her husband as well as to the new midwife herself. Divine election and intervention, at the same time, maintain the boundary between the role of ordinary women and the extraordinary role of midwife, keeping ordinary women in their place.

4.4. Personal Character

As stated at the outset, the midwife must also overcome her own inner resistance, a combination of fear, shame, and accustomed comfortable passivity. The woman typically has resources within herself to draw upon: an empathy based on her own experiences in giving birth, the suppressed knowledge of her own supernatural destiny, the wish to transcend her own passivity and enjoy the power and prestige of office.

The midwife has a reservoir of competence and command, heretofore exercised within the limited domestic domain, as well as a mastery of physical skills and craftwork. This gives the Pedrano woman a genuine sense of effectiveness. These domestic sources of inner competence are the resources that the midwife has only to transfer once she has redefined her identity.

The process of redefining herself, in a somewhat limited way, resembles the cognitive stages in the pattern of transformation which Silverman (1967) ascribes to shamans. During her long illness, the midwife-to-be legitimately withdraws her psychic energy from normal responsibilities and relationships and is turned inward. Her prolonged fasting and sleeplessness induce altered states of consciousness in which normal cognitive categories and affective controls give way to a flooding of released psychic materials from the various levels of the mind. In dreams and visions she confronts the repressed "mysteries" of early youth and traumas related to menstrual blood, the fear and masochism of sexual experience, and the fears of bodily disintegration in giving birth to children. Like the visions of the shaman, her visions take on cosmic proportions.

Graphically the sick woman sees female genitalia, scenes of birth, the bloody fetus, the placenta and organs out of place. She confronts chaos in the tabooed "primal scenes" of her childhood. These are the very things she will have to confront as a midwife and they strike terror into her. But having confronted them, she overcomes her terror. Through the culturally available iconic symbol—the transcendent maternal authority figure—cosmic mysteries are brought under control and reduced to the level of domestic tasks by the reassuring instructions, the lessons in obstetrics that the supernatural tutelaries give her. She is readied to assert herself and assume the mandate but she does not give up passivity completely, remaining the obedient child in fulfilling a supernatural command.

To the woman and her society the illness poses the threat of real death, despite the social and psychological functions it appears to the anthropologist to fulfill. Struggling in her own "rebirth" to overcome fear and passivity and to actualize her inner resources, the woman does for herself what the Cuna shaman does to facilitate a difficult childbirth. She expresses "otherwise inexpressible psychic states" in the symbolic forms of her culture (Levi-Strauss 1963:201). As her feelings and thoughts take shape in templates provided by her culture's cosmology, she is doing the "dream work" necessary to bring about the isomorphic coherence between the subjective woman and the objective role. The reality and gravity of the struggle are affirmed by the fact that some women destined to be midwives do succumb to death—the ultimate passivity. It is clear that in San Pedro the role of midwife demands women strong in body and mind. The case of Juana illustrates the process by which the successful transformation is made from ordinary woman to sacred professional.

Deficiency in any of the foregoing characteristics—presence of role models, a climate of expectation, economic advantage, and strength of character—accounts for the many failures among the women credited with supernatural birth signs.

The case of Maria constitutes an instructive exception to these rules of selection. Although given unusual attention as an infant, she was not defined by her parents as a potential midwife. Nor did she have a base of economic independence from which to assert her autonomy. She did, however, anomalously identify with her shaman father as a role model. And she did have an unusual amount of drive and talent, which made it possible for her to escape the role of deviant and redefine herself as a sacred professional, a person of momentous importance. However, it is unlikely that she could have become a midwife had she remained in San Pedro. That her situation is not as stable as Juana's is not surprising. That she was able despite family expectation and lack of economic support to become a capable and prestigious midwife is the more noteworthy. In another culture she might have been driven into madness. Although her role as wife is not altogether syntonic with her role as midwife, she is able to find structure and resonance in the role of midwife to fit her unique personality needs.

In the cases of both Juana and Maria, we have seen what belief in supernaturals *does*—how spirits of ancestor midwives as cultural symbols overcome strains and role conflicts and effect the resynthesis of the individual woman's ego, her transformation to a sacred professional.

But an equally interesting question is what supernaturalism *means*, what it communicates to Pedranos about the nature of reality and the relation of that reality to their view of the cosmos.

In the face of rapid modernization and rivalrous sectarian claims to represent the only true religion, a new phenomenon has arisen—the skeptic who questions the very existence of God, of ancestor spirits, and of nature deities. In San Pedro, shamans are diminishing in number, their office challenged by new religions and by medicines that can now be bought in local pharmacies. But pastors and pharmacists do not deliver babies, hospitals are far away, and nothing is locally available to take the place of native midwives. Midwives who are supernaturally selected and instructed are still preferred to the few who have recently learned their art from public health nurses. Belief in supernatural assistance at childbirth not only gives midwives and their patients an extra measure of assurance in the face of danger and uncertainty, but also provides evidence that a deeper layer of meaning lies beyond the seemingly capricious losses, suffering, and inequities of the existential world. The supernaturals may be punitive and arbitrary but they are not mad or disinterested in the affairs of humans. The midwife's mystical experiences are proof that the invisible supernaturals exist, and that the midwife herself is blessed with supernatural powers to assist other women in childbirth.

References

Colby, Benjamin J. 1967. Psychological orientations. In Robert Wauchope (ed.), *Handbook of Middle American Indians* (Vol. 6). Austin: University of Texas Press. 416–431.

De Beauvoir, Simone. 1970. *The Second Sex.* New York: Bantam Books.

Eliade, Mircea. 1964. *Shamanism: Archaic Techniques of Ecstasy.* Princeton: Princeton University Press.

Landy, David. 1974. Role adaptation: Traditional curers under the impact of Western medicine. *American Ethnologist* 1:103–127.

Levi-Strauss, Claude. 1963. The effectiveness of symbols. In *Structural Anthropology.* New York: Basic Books. 186–205.

Lewis, I. M. 1971. *Ecstatic Religion.* Harmondsworth, England: Penguin Books.

Lindemann, Erich. 1944. Symptomatology and management of acute grief. *American Journal of Psychiatry* 101:141–148.

Michaelson, Evalyn J. and W. Goldschmidt. 1971. Female roles and male dominance among peasants. *Southwestern Journal of Anthropology* 27:330–352.

Paul, Benjamin D. 1967. Mental disorder and self-regulating processes in culture: A Guatemalan illustration. In R. Hunt (ed.), *Personalities and Cultures.* New York: Natural History Press.

Paul, Lois. 1974. The mastery of work and the mystery of sex in a Guatemalan village. In M. Z. Rosaldo and L. Lamphere (eds.), *Woman, Culture and Society*. Stanford: Stanford University Press.

Paul, Lois. 1975. Recruitment to a ritual role: The midwife in a Maya community. *Ethos* 3:449–467.

Paul, Lois and Benjamin D. Paul. 1963. Changing marriage patterns in a highland Guatemalan community. *Southwestern Journal of Anthropology* 19:313–148.

Paul, Lois and Benjamin D. Paul. 1975. The Maya midwife as sacred professional. *American Ethnologist* 2(4):707–726.

Silverman, Julian. 1967. Shamans and acute schizophrenia. *American Anthropologist* 69:21–31.

Uzzell, Douglas. 1974. Susto revisited: Illness as strategic role. *American Ethnologist* 1:369–378.

Van Gennep, Arnold. 1960. *The Rites of Passage*. Chicago: University of Chicago Press. Phoenix paperback edition.

8

MOLLY C. DOUGHERTY

Southern Lay Midwives as Ritual Specialists

Midwifery in the southeastern United States is closely bound to the feminine reproductive–domestic role and requires specialized ritual, economic, and social behavior. Contemporary Southern lay midwives* are typically elderly black women; all of the midwives discussed here are black and live in rural areas or in towns having populations of less than 10,000 persons. Although the practices and events described here may reflect black–white relations in northern Florida, there is evidence that midwives throughout the United States shared similar experiences when local and state regulations affected their activities (Darlington 1911; Noyes 1912; Kobrin 1966). This presentation examines traditional birth ritual and changes in birth practices and midwifery initiated by state control.

There is scant information available on midwifery in the Southeast before the twentieth century. Prior to this century midwives were not considered specialists to be trained by a specialized agency but rather gained their expertise from immediate experience with women. The organization of lay midwives by local and state health departments in the Southeast between 1920 and 1940 (Hanlon 1964) resulted in midwifery becoming a status to which there was limited access. The intrusion of health officials into the practice of lay midwifery caused a sharp reduction in the numbers of midwives and a resultant increase in economic status, social prestige, and contact with modern medicine for those admitted to the profession. In 1970 there were over 100 licensed lay

*Lay midwives and nurse midwives are distinguished by differing educational and social backgrounds.

MOLLY C. DOUGHERTY · Associate Professor of Nursing, University of Florida, Gainsville, Florida.

midwives in six Southeastern states; the vast majority of them were black (Southeastern Council on Nurse Midwifery 1974). They represent a minute fraction of those who practiced earlier in the century. Midwives were organized in an effort to reduce infant and maternal mortality, and to improve the reporting of vital statistics compiled by state health departments. This effort resulted in lay midwives being trained in medical techniques.

With the regulation of midwives in the South, a period of rapid change regarding birth techniques ensued. The rituals associated with midwifery, which were based on long-standing tradition, were partially interrupted by official regulation. In the South elements of the traditional midwife system were incorporated by regulating bodies but many of the traditional rituals were branded as superstition. Health officials holding positions of status and authority were both emulated and feared, and birth ritual became an amalgam of traditional and modern medicine. Medical concepts, such as aseptic technique, were combined in midwifery with traditional rituals that were embedded in the Christianity practiced by the midwives and their clients. The extent to which divinity is important in midwifery becomes apparent in the recruitment and training of midwives.

1. Recruitment and Training

Recruitment and training take place within the community before apprentice midwives are presented to county health officials.* Central to the recruitment process is supernatural intervention directing the midwife to serve women in childbirth. Supernatural experiences validate the role and require that midwives accept the responsibilities and obligations of the position. Midwives report that they are called to service by God. For example, one woman, now over 80 years of age, recalls:

> I was plowing in the field, plowing cotton, when a voice within told me he wanted me to be a midwife, to take care of mothers and babies. The Lord showed me just how it was to be done. I seen I was [enclosed]† in a tall fence and my mother was standing on the outside with her arms folded.
> When the Lord talk to you, he talk to you so you can understand. These cows was young heifers and they was all expecting to deliver calves. I was in the pen, how I got in there I couldn't tell you. All at once the calf come [she demonstrates the way calves are born, front legs first] from the cow. All of a

---

*The material for this presentation is derived from discussions with local and state public health personnel in Florida, life histories of seven lay midwives in north Florida, and participation in the activities of other lay midwives in 1971-1972.
†Portions in brackets indicate author's clarification of tape transcriptions.

sudden a little boy, he was about that high [2½ feet], run to the calf and showed me just how to tie the cord [motioning] here, and then here, and cut in between. Then I woke up in the cotton field.

After this experience she knew her calling but did not reveal it to others. She heard a recurrent voice saying, "Why don't you tell it?" Eventually, when she was 55 years of age and a grandmother, she went into training. She states, "It was all in the plans of God, it was nothing on my part. No, it was something that I didn't have no control over." Something within guided her: "After I done got the call, I couldn't stay home; if I knowed a woman was in labor, I was gone. I just had to be there, just had to help."

Established midwives report mystical experiences identifying their trainees or replacements. Their independent supernatural experiences provide validation for the potential of the aspiring midwives. A midwife describes the calling of her teacher: " 'Mary Carter,' she told me, 'I'm getting old and I done been on this journey for 45 years. I am tired. I won't give it up until the Lord replace me with someone. When I asked the Lord, he showed me you.' " The midwife responded, "Uh, uh, Aunt Minnie, the Lord didn't show you me. She say, 'Yes Sir, you got to serve. You can't get from under it.' "

The woman served because, "Something come to me, within me, say, 'Go ahead and do the best you can.' " During her training she experienced fear and felt she could not go on, her inner conflict indicating the heavy responsibility midwives bear. They are hesitant to carry "the burden" of midwifery with its attendant power of supernaturally ordained office. However, repeated supernatural confirmation of their destiny forces them to serve. Women come to feel that they are motivated by forces beyond themselves and that it would be dangerous to them to ignore the signs they sense and feel.

The recruitment of midwife-trainees suggests that supernatural validation is a significant sign to both clients and community. The visions and experiences that emanate from within indicate a more direct relationship with supernatural powers among midwives than is customary for other women. Most midwives receive the call to serve after menopause although they usually have fewer pregnancies than their age-mates in the community. Of the 14 midwives in my study, none had more than four pregnancies, yet all of them had borne at least one child. All had established a conjugal relationship that endured for over ten years, although most of them were unmarried at the time of the study. Most of the midwives' children were not living in the community and the midwives were not responsible for young children. Other postmenopausal women who do not become midwives usually have children to care for, which continues their maternal–domestic role. Thus it is midwives who, unlike other women, are free to turn their attention from child care to care for birth, women, and children in general (see Figure 1).

Mongeau and colleagues (Mongeau 1973; Mongeau *et al.* 1961), who studied lay midwifery in rural North Carolina, found midwifery to be a role passed from mother to daughter and held within families over generations of time. In contrast, in this study none of the midwives' mothers were midwives; apprentices refer to their teachers as "aunt," connoting affection, respect, and social proximity. The term usually does not identify a blood relationship but rather indicates respect in reference to and in the address of women of one or two generations senior to the speaker. Midwives sometimes do not have daughters and necessarily select trainees outside of their immediate families. Midwife trainees are usually residents of their teachers' communities and are sometimes their kin. Close interpersonal relationships between apprentice and teacher usually exist prior to training and develop further while they work closely together.

Figure 1. A southern lay midwife maintains a close relationship with her own great-grandchild. (Photo by Ed Dougherty.)

Midwife-apprentices participate in their teachers' practices, by first observing and assisting, and then taking charge at birth. Although midwives' experiences and learning periods vary considerably, they usually observe seven or more births before managing a birth unassisted in the presence of an experienced midwife. Apprentices are not totally unknowledgeable at the beginning of their training; they are usually women who have an interest in childbirth and are present in homes during birth on many occasions throughout adulthood.

Initial training periods contain dramatic lessons concerning birth rituals; these remain part of midwives' repertoire long after their practice is sanctioned by health officials. A midwife describes the first delivery at which she assisted in which prayer played a major role in the delivery:

> My sister-in-law gave birth to her son. He came to the world, he was what you call, it's not a normal delivery, he come foot foremost. Aunt Susie had quite a time getting him to live. I was with her and she found that this baby was coming foot foremost so she taken it over. It was my first experience seeing a baby born that way. She was nervous herself. She had quite a lot of luck because she was a Christian woman. She believed in prayer. She said that was the only thing that was going to save that baby was prayer. So she prayed to the Lord that this baby might live. He was gasping for breath and he was so tired. The smaller parts of the body come and then the head came. The baby have a chance of losing his life on account of the fluids there, but somehow through the will of God she was prepared to take care of that baby. I just know it was the Lord's will because lots of time they die in that condition.

When prayer is not sufficient to produce the desired results, it is believed that the will of God is served in death. In the quotation above, there is reference to impending loss of life "on account of the fluids." The amniotic fluid is considered dangerous to the infant, it is described as "hot," and as preventing the baby from "getting air." Infants, therefore, are removed from the perineal area and have mucus and fluid wiped from their bodies immediately after birth. Part of midwifery training consists of realizing the significance of various physiological events during birth and acting on them. However, it is the relationship with and reliance on supernatural power that is considered most important to midwives' success. One midwife stated,

> I tell them [her clients], "It's nothing that we can do alone, we got to have the help of the almighty God." When they go carrying on I say, "Girl, trust God." I say, "The Lord will put no more on you than you can bear." I say, "He know that you can bear this baby. Trust in him and then everything will be all right." I always talk with the Lord first, before I ever do anything.

The training period sometimes produces fear and apprehension in apprentices. Teachers test their trainees' determination and skill, demon-

strating important lessons to them. Some unforgettable lessons are related with levity:

> While I was on the training she wanted to see how much I could stand. The
> girl was in bed. Auntie told me and she said "Mary, I'll tell you what you do.
> The girl wants you to press her some. See, sit on the foot of the bed and catch
> her arms. You pull her arms when she has a pain to press down." I thought I
> was doing something big and the girl's water burst and went all over my face.
> Boy talk about somebody near about broke. I say, "Don't you ask me to go
> nowhere else with you, Aunt Mary, I ain't going." And she fell over laugh-
> ing. She said, "I just done that cause I wanted you to know what you was in
> for." Boy that thing liked to have kill me, I'm telling you. I told her, I said,
> "Don't call me no more because I ain't going with you," and she say, "Oh
> yes, you going."

She continued in training and remembered the lessons learned at her
teacher's side more vividly than those learned later from nurses.

2. Symbolic Interactions—Nurses and Midwives

After established midwives recruit their apprentices, they inform
the nurses about the trainees. Midwives and nurses look for some of the
same qualities, which include determination, dedication, and depend-
ability. Midwives expect, in addition to these, faith in God, performance
of ritual, and amiable social relations with clients and community. Public
health personnel require another set of characteristics, principally cleanliness, literacy, and participation in the system of hierarchical social
relationships. Midwives encourage their trainees to relate appropriately
with health department personnel. The history of this relationship puts
the contemporary situation in perspective.

When standards of performance for midwives were established and
enforced, thousands of midwives were excluded from practice throughout the South. A fee schedule was provided by health departments and
granted midwives access to economic resources, independence, and
status unavailable to other women in their communities. Midwives' access to health department resources and acquaintance with health personnel further increased their community status. However, their clients'
emulation of higher-status middle-class women who had their babies in
hospitals eventually reduced the numbers of women attended by midwives. This coincided in most geographical areas with medical groups
enforcing physician attendance at birth, which resulted in fewer clients
requesting midwives' services. The identity of midwives as separate
from other community members yet similar to all other midwives in a
wide area was enhanced by periodic meetings in health departments

and by "midwives' clubs." When midwives were organized, midwives' clubs were formed and held meetings on the same days that midwives met at health departments with nurses. The clubs elected officers and collected monthly dues of about 25 cents which they used for sick benefits, death benefits, and other purposes. They also provided financial assistance and social support to midwives and their families. At present the midwives club is almost identical in structure to community-based voluntary associations that provide support during illness and at death. Unlike community organizations, the club draws members from a wide geographical area and functions to promote a sense of group identity and purpose among midwives.

The organization of midwives provides elevated status for midwives in their communities, gives them access to specialized knowledge and permits social networks incorporating women from dispersed communities. Midwives function autonomously but are drawn into the social structure of the health care hierarchy. While they are prestigious within their own communities, their status is low relative to the wider organization of health practitioners. They are controlled by the educated and powerful of the wider society, principally those having economic and social influence in public administration and medicine. Midwives successfully incorporate elements from the prestigious medical system while retaining the integrity of traditional rituals. The nurses require that midwives eliminate certain practices considered superstitious and dangerous and that they incorporate other practices.

The result of long-term contact is a set of social relations incorporating measured mutual respect, limited communication, and an articulation of medical ritual with lay midwifery. Ritual expresses cultural values and has meaning as part of a nonverbal system of communication (La Fontaine 1972), and in a midwives' meeting the ritual expression of values and the nonverbal meaning of relationships can be seen. Five of the seven midwives from two counties are present for the meeting. One midwife has called in to say that she has "a bad case of the flu" and another is at home with her infirm mother. A state public health nursing consultant, Mrs. Green, is the guest. Mrs. White, responsible for the supervision of the midwives, assumes leadership. She formally introduces Mrs. Green and each of the midwives is asked to identify herself. Mrs. White comments that they are "very happy" to have Mrs. Green at the meeting and states that she is sure Mrs. Green has many "interesting things" to tell them. The midwives nod, smile, and murmur an indication that they are pleased to see Mrs. Green again. The midwives, who command respect and are leaders in their own right, assume a submissive posture when the nurse speaks. The purpose of the meeting is to review medical ritual eminently important to the nurses. Although midwives have seen the demonstrations innumerable times, there have been two recent instances in which infants' eyes became infected, requiring medical treatment that might have been unneeded if the midwives followed health department procedures. Mrs. White suggests that Mrs. Green review the procedure for instillation of silver nitrate into infants' eyes.

A baby doll, silver nitrate ampule, sterile water, and the *Midwives Manual* are removed from storage. While Mrs. Green demonstrates on the lifeless doll, Mrs. White turns to the pages in the *Midwives Manual* where the procedure is described in four steps with accompanying drawings. The midwives are attentive and silent. Mrs. White solicits questions, but there are none. Mrs. White adds information: the silver nitrate is available at the health department, the instillation is required by law, no one would want to know that her "carelessness" resulted in an infant's blindness and so on. Her statement reflects the behaviors and attitudes the nurses desire to instill in midwives. The ceremony reinforces the authority of health officials, the presence of the legal code, the largesse of the health department in providing necessary objects, and the responsibility of midwives in serving their clients and the health department. The redundancy of the presentation symbolically affirms the midwives' autonomy in their realm and their legal obligation to integrate medical rituals into their repertoire.

The next topic is introduced by the nurse, who has a film on newborn infants. The film featuring an infant and a nurse in a clinic depicts the inspection, appraisal, and bathing of a newborn. Mrs. Green emphasizes important points in the film. Afterwards, questions are again solicited and none come forth. There are a few moments of silence, signaling the end of the formal presentation of material by the nurses. Then, one midwife quietly asks Mrs. White, seated next to her, about their fee schedule, an aspect of regulation that midwives accept. Mrs. White repeats the question for all to hear and then indicates that they may charge $65 for a delivery.* One midwife reveals that she has been charging $60 but that she will "go up." She states, "United we stand, divided we fall." The midwives begin talking to one another about the difficulty they have collecting their fees. Mrs. White recommends that they obtain payment in advance, taking the stance that the basis of a midwife–client relationship is structured, formal, and businesslike, likening it to the doctor–patient relationship. Speaking to a midwife, but

*The payment schedule is controlled by local health departments and is not uniform throughout Florida. In some counties midwives are permitted to charge $100 for a delivery.

not directly to the nurse, one midwife states that they are all "Christian women," obligated to serve women in need. It is God's will that they serve, whether women intend to pay them or not, pointing out the essential element of selfless service in traditional midwifery. Midwives are bound to serve and have status related to supernatural sanctions, yet they want and need the payments that organization and regulation by health departments have created. State regulations conflict with traditional practice in other ways.

Any woman who plans a midwife-attended home birth must be examined by a physician, who judges whether she can "safely" deliver at home. The physician provides the woman who may deliver at home with an "O.K. slip." The woman gives the O.K. slip to the midwife, who, in turn, submits it to the health department. The physician assumes responsibility for the woman's care should an emergency arise. Any woman who is not judged to be a "good risk" for a midwife-attended birth is directed to secure the services of a physician and deliver in a hospital. Many women do not submit to the examination until near term, or physicians may delay giving them O.K. slips, requiring them to return to the office several times. If a woman goes into labor and does not have an O.K. slip, the midwife is forbidden by law to deliver her. Again the regulations conflict with midwives' supernatural mandate to serve women in need. According to Mrs. White, if the O.K. slip is not in good order, the midwife must "turn the woman away" and refuse to serve her. In a very real sense, midwives provide services only when physicians and other health personnel permit them to do so.

When this problem is presented during the meeting, Mrs. White suggests that the midwife go to the physician's office and obtain the O.K. slip when the client is near term. One midwife relates her experience to the group. Complying with this regulation regarding physician approval, she awakened a physician at night and angered him. Mrs. White praises her behavior despite its consequences. She emphasizes the importance of the client bringing the O.K. slip to the midwife prior to her due date, although she recognizes that midwives are usually not in a position to force their clients to engage the services of physicians. The nurses recommend an ideal set of behaviors required by the state which are impractical. The ritualized interactions permit limited communication and allow the nurses to reiterate the regulations and their intent without actually addressing the midwives' concerns. The meeting becomes more informal and refreshments provided by the nurses are served. The midwives talk freely among themselves. Mrs. White moves into another room with Mrs. Green. The midwives gather their purses and move outside, talking as they wait for rides home. The purpose of the meeting has been to validate the regulations and reaffirm cultural values that underlie the relationships between the midwives and the health hierarchy.

The bridge between the two systems is Christian belief, which, in its local interpretation, emphasizes the sanctity of life, motherhood, and family. The *Midwives Manual*, prepared by the State Board of Health, incorporates a strong current of Christian compassion, duty, and reverence for life. It also contains information on the birth process and the ideal attitudes and behaviors of midwives (Graves 1960). Birth techniques and the events and difficulties that arise during pregnancy, delivery, and the postpartum period are also included. Alternative actions are listed for many situations but the final directives are almost always "Call a doctor," or "Take the woman to the hospital" (Graves 1960:50). There is a list of 13 "danger signals" relating to the mother and 18 baby-related "complications" (Graves 1960:21, 22, 98, 99).

Many traditional beliefs are rejected by nurses. Graves (1960:4) states, "Teach your parents what the nurses teach you; to be a good teacher you yourself must believe the modern way is better than the old superstitions." Such information is stressed at midwives' meetings. Midwives are very sensitive to the vehemence nurses hold for "superstitions." When they relate practices they know to be in disfavor they say, "Well, I know the nurses call it a superstition but I know it works." Although many traditional rituals are deprecated, a strong Christian theme prevails. The *Midwives Manual* contains "The Midwives Creed," and "Midwives Song." The "Midwives Prayer" includes themes drawing together the belief systems of the nurses and midwives:

> Almighty God, our heavenly Father, the Author and finisher of our lives, we give Thee thanks for health and strength and all the joys of life. We pray that Thou wouldst bless the mothers and fathers everywhere, make them more loving in hearts and more Christ-like in the things they say and do.
>
> Guide us in this meeting. And may it be the means of preparing midwives to render service more pleasing to Thee, and more acceptable to our fellow man.
>
> May Thy will be done and Thy kingdom come everywhere. And when our work on earth is done grant that we may enter the building of God the house no [sic] made with hands eternal in the heavens. In Jesus' Name— Amen. (Graves 1960:125)

The "Midwives Prayer" reflects the value of Christian love and parenthood, belief that events on earth are guided by the supernatural and responsibility invested in midwives by God and humankind. The Christian symbolism shared by nurses and midwives is probably the most important element binding them together. There is frequent conflict between nurses and midwives regarding the correct behavior and belief during birth events. Nurses, vocal in denouncing traditional practices and beliefs, are physically and socially separated from midwives' usual activities; at actual births midwives combine traditional ritual and modern medical techniques.

3. Birth Ceremonies and Rituals

Certain birth events are symbolically related to supernatural belief (and called rituals here) while others are more related to medical action (and designated as ceremonies). Rituals used during birth reveal an amalgam of the tradition, supernatural and medical, that characterizes the heritage of lay midwifery in the South. For example, a ritual related to the supernatural is considered efficacious in the treatment of postpartum hemorrhage. A midwife relates a ritual cure: "I had a hemorrhage case. I would always elevate the foot of the bed and read the Bible, Ezekiel 16:6.* Read it in her hearing and that would stop hemorrhaging."

Despite the reliance on supernatural forces there is reference to the medical practice of elevating the foot of the bed. Magical practices performed with a definite purpose abound. Placing an ax beneath the bed of a woman with postpartum pains without her knowledge is said to "cut the pain." Drinking a glass of water hastens the delivery of the placenta. Some practices have a weak connection with supernatural belief and are mentioned by informants almost as an afterthought.

In the past, women were confined to bed for seven or more days after delivery. On the first day they were permitted out of bed, they carried the baby outdoors, walked around the house in a counterclockwise direction, and stopped at four corners, which was said to symbolize the four directions of the wind. Another midwife stated that the purpose was to thank God for a safe delivery. Another, perhaps more anxious to offer a "medical" explanation, stated that it was to acclimatize the woman to the air, to close her pores so that she and the baby would not "catch a cold." The event, involving most household members, can be seen as a rite of incorporation of mother and infant into the family. If birth is conceptualized as a rite of passage (Van Gennep 1960), the isolation (or separation) of the woman during and after birth is significant, just as is the traditional rite through which mother and child were welcomed back to the family. Isolation included remaining in a room, bedfast for many days. Drafts and water were avoided because they cause colds and make women weak. This isolation was reinforced

---

*"And when I passed by thee and saw them polluted in thine own blood, I said unto thee when thou was in my blood live, yea, I say unto thee when they wash in thy blood live."

in earlier years by the darkening of the room, which was thought to prevent blindness in the infant.* A midwife reports her own childbirth experience:

> You didn't have no light after the baby come. You shut up in that room for weeks without light. I don't care how many holes was in the house, they found them holes and chinked them. When the lamp was on they go in there they'd put a cardboard in front of it. You was back in a room, you didn't go out, they squeezed in the door and they squeeze out the door, you ain't seen no daylight, that was a dreadful time. They say that was on account of the eyes, the baby would go blind, it couldn't have no light in it eyes. You didn't have to wait till they got sore eyes, that was took care of.

The midwife reports that after she was permitted out of the room, "I was a new person, when you seen the trees and daylight you was some kind of happy because you did not see no daylight for so long."

The midwife enacts her role with supernatural validation, a keen understanding of human needs, and a repertoire of techniques and applications. She carries a bag filled with lotions, creams, patent medicines, and household items, which she employs in treating her client and other family members. The midwife's bag symbolizes her power, creativity, and skill. When midwives were organized and aseptic technique was introduced as an aspect of medical ceremony, one component of traditional practice incorporated by health officials was the midwife's bag. But, by regulation, the official bag may contain only specified items. The midwives resist discontinuing the use of traditional items and often create one bag for health department inspection and another for actual use. The midwife's bag, symbolically bridging the traditional and medical system, is often a source of conflict and misunderstanding among midwives and nurses. The regulation midwife's bag contains only medical objects: it has seventeen pieces of equipment, including a sterile "O.B. Pack No. 1" containing twelve items (Graves 1960:6, 9). The bag symbolizes the midwife's social position, expert knowledge, and association with high-status medical practitioners. The importance of cleanliness, a symbolic touchstone in midwifery, is clearly understood by midwives, its purpose being to prevent infections and death among mothers and babies. The purpose of sterile technique is essentially the same but it is not understood by midwives as nurses and others intended. The destruction of germs on articles by autoclaving or dry heat and the almost "ritual" procedures attached to the use of sterile

---

*Gonorrheal ophthalmia neonatorum was a common cause of blindness among infants. Until the use of silver nitrate was established, from 25 to 30% of all children in schools for the blind suffered impaired sight as a result of a gonorrheal infection (Fitzpatrick and Eastman, 1960:480).

objects is not perceived in the same manner by midwives an
The destruction of microorganisms, never seen or actually belie
midwives, is not clearly understood. The ceremony intended t
a "sterile" delivery is followed to some extent but the rationale ....u
the actions is described only as "cleanliness." The practical actions of
nurses appear "magical" to midwives. In the perceptions of midwives,
the pragmatic end sought by the use of sterile objects at births does not
reduce disease or death. Midwives carry out the procedures enforced by
the health department, such as care of the umbilical cord, instillation of
silver nitrate into the infant's eyes, weighing the baby, and completing
birth certificates. All of these are significant in health officials' belief
system. The primary objectives of health personnel are to lower maternal and infant mortality rates and to obtain more accurate vital statistics.
Through time, the independence and stature of midwifery are reduced
as physicians and public health administrators insist that hospital delivery is universally safer than home birth.

4. Conclusion

◄ The role and function of lay midwives provide an example of ritual
and ceremonial specialists, of women relating to women in crisis. Birth-
related beliefs in the American South are changing, and control over
health services is becoming fully institutionalized and controlled by
professional groups. Public health nurses function as interpreters of the
medical belief system and adapt it, in some ways, to fit local conditions.
In their positions of authority emanating from the controlling institutions of society, they are placed in conflict with midwives and only
weakly comprehend the source of miscommunication. Midwives, holding positions at the lowest level of the health hierarchy, are deprecated,
their skills and abilities rarely appreciated by those above them. Within
their own communities they provide needed services, and their supernatural and technical abilities are respected. Lay midwifery in the South
exemplifies women in conflict, competition, and cooperation, often manipulated and controlled by institutions over which they have little
control.

ACKNOWLEDGMENT

The research on which the article is based was supported by Department of H.E.W. Special Nurse Fellowship numbers 1F04-NU-27,
257-01, 5F04-NU-27, 257-03, 4F04-NU-27, 257-04, 2F04-NU-27, 257-05,
and 4F04-NU-27, 257-06.

References

Darlington, Thomas. 1911. The present status of the midwife. *American Journal of Obstetrics and Gynecology* 63:870–876.

Fitzpatrick, Elise and Nicholas J. Eastman. 1960. *Zabriskie's Obstetrics for Nurses.* Philadelphia: J. B. Lippincott.

Graves, Jules O. 1960. *A Manual for Midwives.* Jacksonville, Florida: Florida State Board of Health.

Hanlon, John J. 1964. *Principles of Public Health Administration.* St. Louis: C. V. Mosby.

Kobrin, Frances E. 1966. The American midwife controversy: A crisis of professionalism. *Bulletin of the History of Medicine* 40:350–363.

La Fontaine, Joan (ed.). 1972. *The Interpretation of Ritual: Essays in Honour of A. I. Richards.* London: Tavistock Publications.

Mongeau, Beatrice. 1973. The "granny" midwives: A study of a folk institution in the process of social disintegration. Ph.D. dissertation, University of North Carolina.

Mongeau, Beatrice, H. L. Smith, and A. C. Maney. 1961. The "granny" midwife: Changing roles and functions of a folk practitioner. *American Journal of Sociology* 66:497–505.

Noyes, Clara D. 1912. The training of midwives in relation to the prevention of infant mortality. *American Journal of Obstetrics and Gynecology* 66:1051–59.

Southeastern Council on Nurse Midwifery. 1974. Mimeograph report on maternal–infant health. Jackson, Mississippi: University of Mississippi.

Van Gennep, Arnold. 1960. *The Rites of Passage.* Chicago: University of Chicago Press.

9

ANITA SPRING

Epidemiology of Spirit Possession Among the Luvale of Zambia

1. Introduction

In the past few years in the West, medical notions concerning the cause and nature of disease have been changing rapidly. Not only does a more organic and synergistic model of the human organism replace the Cartesian separation between mind and body, but we now recognize that environmental factors, especially conditions in society and culture, are integrally related to the well-being or harmony of the organism (Chesler 1973; Illich 1976). The Cartesian view of the world influenced anthropological studies of non-Western healing. This is implicit in most analyses of the phenomena, which often divide into the materialist concepts of "organic" and "psychosomatic," even though most non-Westerners make no such distinction themselves. Spirit possession studies in particular suffer from this Western idiosyncrasy in that many anthropologists who write about possession show that it was "only" a palliative for psychosomatic illness brought about by disharmonies in the social order, and that actual "physical" disease is not the "important" aspect of possession cults and rituals. Following Evans-Pritchard (1937), anthropologists have tried to look at people's answers to the moral question of "why me" in relationship to possession, but consistently neglect the physiological condition of persons that possession cures treat. Although possession rituals undoubtedly do treat both symbolic–social disorders and physical illnesses, the emphasis placed on the symbolism of participation in ritual possession cults means that we

ANITA SPRING · Assistant Professor of Behavioral Studies and Anthropology, University of Florida, Gainesville, Florida.

have a great deal of literature that illustrates the "symbolicity" of non-Westerners, but not much that demonstrates their empirical recognition of personal ill health, technical proficiency in treating disease, or the relationship between possession and individual cure. Thus we have a picture of possessed individuals who are not "really" sick, who use "mystical pressure" against their relatives (Turner 1966; Curley 1973), and who employ possession to "gain attention" from people (Lewis 1966, 1971). Nowhere do we find a study of the actual health of patients, of the curative role of the altered state of consciousness in possession, or of the health of the patients afterward.

This chapter empirically examines how physiological problems trigger the performance of spirit possession rituals and how survivors utilize these illnesses to achieve ritual prominence. Essentially this is a case study of one particular group, the Luvale of Zambia, but the people provide a particularly apt example because their neighbors, the Ndembu, are famous in the anthropological literature (see Turner 1957, 1967, 1968, 1969).* Among the Luvale spirit possession is a state that women deliberately utilize to cure illness. Most theories say women are sick because they want to disrupt society, that is, they are disorderly (see below). I suggest it is possible to study the incidence of spirit possession rituals epidemiologically—in terms of what disease patterns occur and whom they affect (cf. Rubel 1964). In this particular case, women are subject to certain fertility inhibitors, and children to certain morbidity conditions. Women are the primary participants in possession rituals for their own illnesses and on behalf of their children. Furthermore, these women participate in a system of curing that is run for women by women although the theory behind it connects at the larger, societal level. This chapter documents the social concomitants of illness and ritual participation in people's lives. I submit that through the common experience of repeated illness and problems in having children and keeping them alive, women come to form cooperative networks of ritual specialists who administer specialized knowledge of clients and aides.

---

*The Luvale and the Ndembu share many cultural patterns, including spirit possession rituals, as a means of treating ill people. Their adaptation to the environment and level of sociocultural integration are similar. Both are hoe-agriculturalists having cassava as a staple with millet and maize as supplements. Both are organized into chieftancies. Both have matrilineal descent and practice virilocal marriage (a woman joins her husband at marriage). I studied the Luvale between 1970 and 1972 and collected information on ritual and medicinal participation vis-à-vis illness, fertility, and morbidity. I am able to present only a small amount of documentation of the relationship between possession rituals and illness here, and the reader should refer to Spring (1976a, 1976b) for more complete information.

2. Theories about Female Possession

Many authors (Beattie and Middleton 1969; Lewis 1966, 1971; Turner 1968; Wilson 1967), having little access to and perhaps little interest in female affairs, repeatedly see possession as a legitimate way for women to voice their frustrations, fears, demands, and criticisms in male-dominated societies, both patrilineal and matrilineal. Frequently, when possession rituals occur for a woman experiencing "reproductive disorders," her problem is said by the anthropologist to be "social conflicts," which inhere in her status as a woman in male-controlled society. This male rationalization of female illness represents yet another way in which Western prejudices influence the interpretation of non-Western materials. Not only are woman's concerns seen as negative complaints, "reproductive disorders," rather than positive affirmations, "I want to have children," but women themselves also are viewed as "conflict producers" who disrupt the order of the male universe with fictitious complaints.

This point of view, unsupported by empirical ethnographic evidence, is strikingly similar to the nineteenth-century idea in the Western medical establishment that female reproductive organs controlled a woman's life. Her ovaries and uterus were "inherently defective" and since her energy was finite, she was advised to concentrate it "internally toward the womb" (Ehrenreich and English 1973:27). From a doctor's view, reproductive development was totally antagonistic to mental development. Therefore, uterine and ovarian "disorders" were "found behind almost every female complaint, from headaches to sore throats, to indigestion" (Ehrenreich and English 1973:29). Woman's body was polluting to her own existence, to the well-being of her family, and to the health of male society.

Curiously, when reading accounts of possession cults in Africa dedicated to female health (Beattie and Middleton 1969; Turner 1968, 1969), the same image of the woman's body appears. And not only are the analyses couched in negative female imagery but they ignore the legitimizing functions of female rituals and their usefulness to societies' structures in the inculcation of attitudes and beliefs. They never consider whether or not female cults constitute the basis for membership in a female community of specialists who have their own models of society, separate from the models used by men. Edwin Ardener, arguing that the ideological position of women in anthropology is more primitive than that of men, says:

> . . . when we come to that second or "meta" level of fieldwork, the vast body
> of debate, discussion, question and answer, that social anthropologists really

depend upon to give conviction to their interpretations, there is a real imbal-
ance. We are, for practical purposes, in a male world. The study of women is
on a level a little higher than the study of ducks and fowls they commonly
own—a mere bird-watching indeed (1972:136).

Lewis (1966, 1969) views possession as a means by which deprived,
frustrated, and insecure people air their grievances to their superiors
and seek attention and redress. Since women, especially married
women, are most frequently possessed, and their husbands are responsible for sponsoring the cure, his analysis focuses on the "war between the
sexes." Among the Islamic patrilineal Somali whom he studies, women
lack authority and other means of defense and are therefore treated like
"pawns" by men. "Aggrieved wives" use illness, in the form of possession, to exert "mystical pressure" upon their husbands, who apparently
are too "strong" to be approached by the "weak" women in any other
way.

Other data from African societies follow Lewis's views. Mary Smith
(1954) reports that Nigerian Hausa women turn to possession because
under Islam, women have little participation in ceremonial life. Women
do, however, have access to economic participation and essentially a
separate status hierarchy from men's. Curley (1973) shows that Ugandan
Lango women, who have in fact gained some independence from their
husbands, still use spirit possession in their battle for attention because
the traditional social system provides them with little mobility and freedom. This portrayal of spirit possession as a manifestation of the "war
between the sexes" is very popular, perhaps because in many male-
dominated societies women do indeed use backstage strategies such as
illness to gain attention and goods (cf. Lamphere 1974).

Although most of Lewis's material concerns patrilineal societies, he
cites Colson's (1969) analysis of the matrilineal Tonga of Zambia to demonstrate how his perspective easily incorporates economic deprivation
anywhere. The Tonga husbands, studied by Colson during the colonial
period, became increasingly involved in labor migration, leaving the
isolated Gwembe Valley to work in towns. The wives remained at home
and, relatively, became increasingly deprived of equal access to desired
goods available only in the urban areas. As this deprivation increased,
she argues, the women responded by being more frequently possessed,
and being possessed by different types of spirits, which needed offerings of much-sought-after town goods to be expiated. Undoubtedly the
frequence of possession increased, but no data are given on the public
health of these people, which also may have changed.

Wilson (1967) disagrees with the view that possession reflects inter-
sex conflict and the recognition by wives that they are deprived relative

to their husbands. He instead contends that the conflict is among individuals of the same sex, and generally among women, the most frequently possessed. He denies the importance of "the war between the sexes" in traditional male-dominated societies. It is precisely in these societies, he argues, that the sexual division of labor is well defined, and the possibility of any overlap between the sexes in the performance of tasks is minimal. Men and women do not compete for the same goals or in the same arenas. Rather, women compete with other women as men compete among themselves. (Only in societies such as ours, where men and women compete for the same goals and in the same arenas, is "the war between the sexes" a reality, based partially on a consciousness among women of their deprivation in relation to men.) In the traditional male-dominated societies that Lewis and Wilson focus on, whether spirit possession is a peripheral or a central institution, wives are structurally peripheral to the virilocal residential unit. The status of in-marrying wife is periodically rendered ambiguous or threatened by tensions among coresident women, or by the arrival of a co-wife. In Wilson's view spirit possession is a means by which the threatened woman restores, transforms, or improves her status.

A different interpretation is given by Turner (1957, 1967, 1968, 1969), who focuses on the matrilineal, virilocal Ndembu—neighbors of the Luvale. He writes that spirit possession rituals occur for "hunting misfortunes" of men, "reproductive disorders" of women, and general illness for both sexes. Women are most frequent victims of the last two groups of "afflictions." The ritual process includes social dramas that alleviate tensions within the patient's village. Women suffer "reproductive disorders," he argues, because they reside in their husband's villages. Turner writes:

> . . . women, through whom succession and inheritance are reckoned, go to their husband's villages after marriage, often far away from their own villages, and may in the course of time cease to remember their older kin on the mother's side who have died. Moreover, when they were young girls they would have spent most of their time in their father's villages where they would have been living with their mothers. Yet, in spite of spending so much of their lives away from their "own" villages, they are still expected to send their sons back in the course of time, and if they themselves are divorced or widowed their matrilineal villages are regarded as their sanctuaries until remarriage. It would seem . . . that being "caught" by a matrilineal shade serves as a sharp reminder that their own first loyalty is to their matrilineal villages and that they bear children not for their husbands, but for their mother's brothers and brothers "back home." We find that "forgetting" the shade is the usual cause of affliction (1967:12–13).

He sees these afflictions as part of the battle between husband and matrilineal kinsmen, that is, reflecting the principles of virilocality and matriliny. His view is similar to Lewis's and Wilson's in that he sees the scheduling of illness as a reflection of social tensions; he follows Wilson in that he sees the conflict as an intrasex one; however, it is between men (the husband and the matrilineal kinsmen) instead of women. These men compete for their sisters and sisters' sons as well as their own children. Once again women are "pawns" or "agents of conflict."

Turner (1957:201, 1967:12) questions whether or not there is in fact physiological basis for this scheduling of illness for the Ndembu:

> In a sample of nineteen women whose ritual histories I recorded, not one had failed to have such a ritual performed for her. . . . Is there any medical basis for these widespread cults connected with reproductive troubles? My evidence is slight but suggestive. Figures supplied to me by the lady doctor at Kalene Mission Hospital in August, 1951, revealed that out of ninety women accepted as normal pregnancy cases, . . . nearly 18% underwent abnormal deliveries. My wife was asked to assist at half a dozen cases of prolonged childbirth or miscarriages in the villages adjoining our camp in about three months. Many women showed clear signs of anemia and some revealed that they had frequent periodic troubles. It may well be that the modern prevalence of these disorders is associated on the one hand with the shortage of meat and fish in many areas . . . and on the other with the low protein value of the staple crop cassava. . . (1967:12).

He does not follow out the effects of diet and in fact rejected the evidence for organic dysfunction in favor of the conflict–resolution model. He asks an important question but does not answer it.

On the basis of the medical data collected among the Luvale (Spring 1976a, 1976b; White 1959) it is difficult to accept the anthropological conceit that spirit possession is precipitated solely by social tension. Spirit possession is a means of treating personal illness. It is true that illness and possession may be considered by the people concerned to have social causes and there are social rewards for its enactment. Similarly, the attribution of certain illnesses to possession by spirits may be a subjective recognition of specific social tensions. It is also true that the mobilization of personnel and resources involved in the possession ritual may have social consequences. The catharsis associated with the spirit possession also may have social consequences. However, for anthropologists to pursue only social/functional explanations for spirit possession is to flirt perilously close to suggesting that the illnesses treated by spirit possession are all psychosomatic or consciously induced. The fundamental patterns and scheduling of illness among a population and the selection of victims are the parameters of disease. A question to be asked in any specific case is what are the diseases or physiological conditions that underlie the scheduling of spirit possessions or any other ritual cures and the selection of specific victims?

3. Luvale Spirit Possession Ritual

Among the Luvale, spirit possession rituals treat illness for men and women. A spirit (ancestral shade) and its ritual exorcism or possession are called *lihamba* (singular) or *mahamba* (plural). The term *mahamba* also includes all the cults* surrounding spirit possession. The Luvale distinguish three varieties. Cults for general illness are simply *mahamba*. Those that center on bearing and rearing children are distinguished by adding *wakusema* (for giving birth). A recent type focusing on infections is *wapeho*, "from the air."

The performance of a spirit possession ritual for childbearing, for example, commences with a public all-night drumming, dancing, and singing session in front of the patient's home. A ritual "crew" (the cult members and relatives) assembles at this time to aid the patient by singing and teaching her the appropriate dances (see Figure 1). (Women feel

*The term *cult* refers to an informal group made up of people in the same or neighboring villages, which convenes for a particular performance.

Figure 1. A Luvale ritual expert (right) and her assistant conduct a spirit possession ritual. (Photo by Anita Spring.)

it is their obligation to help other women during these rituals so they
may expect future assistance.) The spirit possession doctor invokes the
ancestral shades, who people believe are within the patient's body and
cause the sickness. The shades appear by the patient being possessed—
as evidenced by dancing codified dance movements associated with
each cult. The doctor gives the patient medicines and exorcises the
shades through a combination of the inhalation of steam from the
medicines and by dancing. Each ancestral shade appears not as an individualized personality but as a representative of a particular cult that she
belonged to when alive. For example, one cult associated with a mythical female ancestor who bailed water out of small pools to collect fish has
a dance that consists of movements depicting bailing water. This sequence is repeated for each ancestral shade and cult that was specified
during the divination. Luvale spirit possession rituals typically include
possession of the individual by one ancestor who was a member of
many cults, or by several ancestors who belonged to one cult each.
Hence, medications and possession dances for as many as ten cults may
occur. The ritual lasts all night and ends with an early-morning ritual
bath. This completes the first phase and suspends public participation
until the closing ritual.* Then the patient privately takes medicines and
observes food restrictions and behavioral constraints for a period of time
from a few weeks to a year. Following recovery from illness or success at
childbearing, the final phase of the ritual sequence takes place. This
essentially consists of a repeat of the possessions, during which time the
patient is initiated into the cults. It is interesting to note that all patients
say they feel better physically after the possession ritual. However,
sometimes their condition worsens; other times, it stays the same or
improves.

Mothers undergo spirit possession rituals for their own illnesses
and on behalf of their sick children. People believe that ancestors may
send illness and death at any stage from gestation through childhood;
the retribution reflects upon the worldly conduct of the child's mother,
as on her lack of ancestral devotion. Children whose mothers have possession rituals for them are eligible for cult membership as adults. In this
way, the two are incorporated into the matrilineage as ritual initiates (see
below). The type of treatment recommended for sick children relates
closely with their mothers' natality profile.† If a mother bore living
children who are still alive, only herbals and minor (shrine) rituals are

---

*Spirit possession rituals, like rites of passage, follow the three-phase procedure of separa-
tion, liminality, and reintegration (Van Gennep 1960; Turner 1967).
†By *natality* I mean the total profile of a woman's childbearing and child rearing.

necessary when one of her children sickens. However, if she did not bear live children or if her live children died, spirit possession rituals are necessary.

Seclusion in the *chipango chachinene* ("big fence") is the most elaborate ritual for childbearing and rearing (see Figures 2 and 3). This may be carried out only if the child is *in utero* or under the age of a year. Depending on her past fertility and the mortality of her children, a diviner may recommend that the woman enter seclusion either before parturition, with her newborn child, or at her baby's first illness. She enters seclusion in a dramatic spirit possession ritual. Seclusion procedures include elaborate medications and minor rituals. Many foods are taboo. Interdictions on intercourse obtain as well. The woman may stay in the fence for a few months or up to a year and a half (if she were secluded during pregnancy). When the child is ready to crawl or walk out of the fence by itself, there is another and more elaborate coming-out spirit possession ritual for mother and child, during which time cult initiation for mother and child occurs. (Should anything happen to the child, the seclusion ends and no further possession ritual or initiation occurs.) From the

Figure 2. A Luvale doctor (the woman facing the circle, to the right) directs the women in various phases of the *chipango* (big fence) ritual. Men are in supporting roles as drum players. The *chipango* enclosure is on the left. (Photo by Anita Spring.)

Figure 3. In her efforts to become a mother or cure a sick child, a woman undergoes the *chipango* ritual, thus entering the most "chosen" Luvale sisterhood. The white clothes and unbraided hair symbolize her ritual status. The child on her back is covered for extra protection. (Photo by Anita Spring.)

Luvale point of view, the "big fence" ritual allows women to enter the most "effective" and "chosen" sisterhood of all. Women and their children who undergo this ritual acquire ritual names. On the basis of my statistical evidence their "luck" at keeping their children alive seems to improve (see Table 5 on child mortality). I suspect it is because of the seclusion/quarantine phase of the rituals* and the increased vigilance and attention toward the child's health and well-being.

Traditional spirit possession cults are multipurpose: performances take place for a woman's illness or her natality problems, for her ailing children, or prophylactically to prevent miscarriage, stillbirths, and illness or death of a child. For those who would consider that female possession cults reflect social tensions alone rather than physiological ailments, the following data concerning Luvale women's ailments show that this is not so. An examination of the histories concerning women's ritual participation in relation to their efforts to become pregnant, deliver safely, cure menstrual distresses, cure themselves, and cure sick children

---

*An epidemic of measles occurred during the fieldwork. The children in the "big fence" seclusion were unaffected, while many others died from respiratory complications.

shows about seven typical patterns. These patterns place the data on the epidemiology of illness and possession rituals in a social context. (1) A woman who is childless receives treatments for barrenness (see Spring 1976b). Subsequently, if she becomes pregnant, a performance of several *mahamba* cults will take place. After the birth of her baby, she may undergo possession rituals if her child becomes ill, or more commonly, she will have the possession ritual in conjunction with the ritual that secludes mother and child (the "big fence" ritual). (2) A pregnant woman has a miscarriage unexpectedly or delivers a stillborn child. As a result, the diviner will suggest the enactment of a possession ritual. If she becomes pregnant again and bears a live child, a possession ritual must be performed. (3) A woman has menstrual dysfunctions, usually long periods or dysmenorrhea. After using herbal treatments and failing to end this problem, a spirit possession ritual occurs. (4) A woman's child or children sicken and she undergoes a possession ritual to aid the sick child. This may or may not include the "big fence" ritual and depends on previous illness and successes at having children and the particular illness the child has. (5) A woman's child or children die. If she conceives again, she undergoes possession ritual both during the pregnancy and after parturition. Sometimes children's minor illnesses are cause enough for the spirit possession rituals, especially if the mother has lost other children. (6) A woman becomes ill with problems unrelated to childbearing or rearing. If she is young and still fertile, it is possible to include some possession cults for fertility, but usually she participates in cults for general illness that are either traditional or new (cf. White 1949). (7) There are particular cults for particular ailments such as madness and dizziness, and for any illnesses that recent widows suffer.

4. Epidemiology of Ritual Participation

These cures are in response to the actual physical problems Luvale women, men, and children have. This discussion focuses on women and children and, as such, I shall discuss their unique physical difficulties. Luvale women have few live births, many genital and urinary-tract diseases, much barrenness and reproductive wastage. The following data briefly document these. (The reader may refer to Spring 1976a, 1976b for further information.) Table 1 shows that Luvale women have few live births; women of completed family size have an average rate of 2.05 children per woman, which basically is a replacement population. This rate is particularly unusual in a country with a high average birth rate per woman (4.99), and many theories (e.g., therapeutic style, diet,

TABLE 1. AGE-SPECIFIC AVERAGE RATE OF LIVE BIRTHS PER WOMAN

	Age group (years)		
	15–29	30–44	45+
Number of live births	99	98	125
N of population	49	43	61
Rate of live births	2.02	2.28	2.05

TABLE 2. CHILDLESS WOMEN BY AGE GROUPS

Age group (years)	Number childless/N	Percentage
15–29	9/49	18.4
30–44	9/43	20.0
45+	13/16	21.3

TABLE 3. AGE SPECIFIC FECUNDITY OF WOMEN (AS PERCENTAGES OF THE TOTAL POPULATION)

Age group (years)	Subfecund	Infertile	Total
25–29	16.6	0	16.1
30–34	53.8	0	53.8
35–39	58.3	0	58.3
40–44	33.3	50.0	83.3
45–49	15.8	73.7	89.5
50–85	0	100.0	100.0

TABLE 4. WOMEN WITH DYSMENORRHEA AND THE RITUALS FOR THEM (AS PERCENTAGES OF THE TOTAL POPULATION)

	Age group (years)		
	15–29	30–44	45+
Women with dysmenorrhea	24.5	46.5	31.1
Ritual Performances			
Spirit possession			
Kula alone	33.3	10.0	15.8
Kula with other possession cults	25.0	60.0	57.9
No possession	41.7	30.0	26.3
	100.0	100.0	100.0
Shrine (alone or with *Kula*)	41.7	70.7	73.7

disease, marriage customs, promiscuity) try to account for this discrepancy (see Spring 1976b; Ohadike 1969; Mitchell 1965; White 1959).*

Luvale women, in fact, are ill frequently with abdominal pains, dysmenorrhea, and fevers probably caused by bilharziasis, gonorrhea, and nonspecific bacterial diseases, in addition to malaria, hookworm, and amebiasis, which are endemic. These diseases generally do not kill adults but can interfere with fertility and menstruation and cause feeble health. Luvale women are particularly susceptible to bilharziasis, a disease known to affect the female genitalia (Gelfand 1950), because they enter stagnant pools of water to catch fish with drag baskets. As an anthropologist I had to rely on self-reported diagnosis of illness rather than on confirmed laboratory tests. People reported the presence of various diseases, some of which correspond to standard etiology and others of which do not. Forty-six percent of women over 45, 49% of women 30 to 44, and 6% of women 15 to 29 years of age reported that they had or were suffering from *kalwena*. This illness includes the symptoms of pus or blood in the urine and may correspond with either gonorrhea or bilharziasis. Either of these might affect fertility and might be compounded by the traditional therapeutic style which employs genital administration of medicinals. Diseases such as *kalwena* (sometimes the Luvale are called the Kalwena) and the great multitude of named genital and other illnesses seem to have a great effect on the number of live births.

It is useful to consider several components of women having few live children. Childlessness, subfecundity, and infertility (caused by bilharziasis and gonorrhea), menstrual disease, miscarriages, and stillbirths all reduce the number of live births. Mortality of neonates, infants, and children reduces the number of living children. A brief consideration of each of these in relation to spirit possession rituals follows.

Many women undergo possessions for childlessness and large numbers of women are childless (Table 2 shows this by age groups); 21.3% of women who have completed their reproductive years are childless.† A careful scrutiny of women's fertility histories shows that some

*A fertility survey that correlated with ritual participation was administered to 300 women, half of whom were a "modern" subpopulation and the other a "traditional" subpopulation. The former were hospital parturients who used modern medicine, the latter were village parturients who relied on traditional therapies. The argument here uses data from the traditionalists only.

†Four additional women in the over-45-years category had one infant who lived only a short time. Since there is a taboo on mentioning the dead, particularly deceased infants, these women at first stated they were barren, as did some women whose children died within the first two years of life. Careful checking of these "childless" women revealed they were not barren but simply sorrowful mothers. In any case, the 21% figure is much less than the 31% and 38% given by Mitchell (1965) or White (1959). The lower numbers in these present data probably reflect increasing natality, a nationwide trend, and a careful check of women claiming they were childless.

women have not become pregnant recently, even though they use no contraception and enjoy intercourse. Women with no pregnancy within the past six years I call subfecund; those without a pregnancy in the last fifteen years I call infertile. By looking at the data in Table 3 given by five-year age groups, we see that more than half (53.8% of women between 30 and 34 and 58.8% of women between 35 and 39) are subfecund, and almost all women over 40 are subfecund or sterile. Most women have their children before 30, after which they are less likely to conceive. (They may undergo spirit possession rituals during this time, and as they approach 35 become apprentice doctors and eventually full-time specialists as discussed below.)

Many women reported excessively long and heavy menstruation. Table 4 shows the relationship between the illness and the traditional cures.* Women in the middle age group (30–44) have more dysmenorrhea than the other group (15–29, 45+). The table shows that a high proportion of women have treatments and the overwhelming majority have spirit possession rituals for this problem. Younger women (15–29) have fewer possession rituals than older women (30–45+); this is expected because they have fewer years in their "natality careers" to have had them performed. Younger women have more shrines erected than older women, probably because spirit possession rituals attract attention, and many young "modern" women disavow possession.

Other components of low natality and maternal ill health are the rates of spontaneous miscarriage and stillbirths (often difficult to distinguish in retrospective data). I call these "fetal wastages." Women report bleeding and fatigue after these events.

An important component of having few living children that is not related to maternal ill-health is infant and child mortality. The common illnesses and diseases for children are respiratory ailments (especially pneumonia as a complication following measles), gastrointestinal ailments (with diarrhea and dehydration), parasitic infections, malaria, and whooping cough. Table 5 shows that between 20% and 33.3% of all children die within the first year of life, with younger women losing more children than older women.

---

*Women rely on a variety of remedies for pain and heavy flows. All women know the common "home remedies" taught as part of the girl's puberty ritual; some women herbal doctors specialize in esoteric treatments. But if these procedures fail to stop the flow or recurrence of dysmenorrhea, people believe that the ancestors are implicated. A divination specifies whether a minor shrine ritual or a spirit possession ritual is necessary. In extreme cases, a possession ritual for the cult connected with menstruation (*Kula*) occurs by itself.

Table 5. Percentages of Fetal Wastage, Infant and Child Mortality (as Percentages of Total Pregnancies)

	Age group (years)		
	15–29	30–44	45+
Fetal wastage	16.1	26.5	20.1
Infant mortality to 1 year	33.3	23.5	20.0
Child mortality to 5 years	34.4	26.5	24.0

Table 6a. Women's Participation in Traditional Spirit Possession Rituals for Childbearing and General Illness (in Percentages[a])

	Age group (years)		
	15–29	30–44	45+
Spirit possession for childbearing (*mahamba wakusema*)	26.5	40.7	31.2
Spirit possession for general illness (*mahamba*)	12.2	24.4	34.4
Spirit possession for general illness (*mahamba wapeho*)	12.2	30.3	40.0

[a] A woman may participate in more than one type of ritual.

Table 6b. Women's Participation in Child-Rearing Rituals (in Percentages[a])

	Age group (years)		
	15–29	30–44	45+
Herbals and shrines	35.0	35.3	22.4
Spirit possession for sick child (*mahamba wakusema*)	20.0	33.3	33.8
Spirit possession and "big fence" for sick child (*chipango chachinene*)	30.0	41.2	42.9

[a] A woman may participate in more than one type of ritual.

Maternal and child ill-health symptoms and events have ritual treatments and require ritual action; all follow the sequence that first employs herbals and shrines and then spiritual possession rituals. Tables 6A and 6B give the frequency of ritual participation in possession rituals for childbearing and for child rearing, respectively. Forty percent of women in the age group 30–44 underwent at least one spirit possession ritual for childbearing. Women over 45 have more possession rituals for general illness and the frequency of traditional and air spirit rituals not connected with childbearing increases with increasing age. The participation in rituals for child rearing is extremely high. Over 40% of women over 30, for instance, had undergone the most elaborate spirit possession ritual for child rearing (*chipango chachinene*).

Divinations occur for all major illness. The majority of women follow diagnosis with treatment, which often includes a full performance of a possession ritual. Sometimes the diviner simply recommends that rituals be held if certain events occur. For example, if the woman conceives again, the spirit possession ritual must be performed; if she bears a live child, then *chipango chachinene* should occur; if she becomes ill again, then herbals need to be administered and/or possession cults performed. On some occasions a woman's relatives fulfill their obligations to seek advice and treatment, but the woman herself refuses to submit to it for several reasons: either they consider themselves modern, have become Christians, or lack resources. Table 7 gives an idea of the frequency with which full performances occur in response to a diviner's advice. Older women tend to follow the diagnosis. Some younger women may not have full performances, although it is likely that many will eventually if circumstances allow. The high amount (47–78%) of

TABLE 7. WOMEN'S PARTICIPATION IN RITUAL PERFORMANCES
(AS PERCENTAGES OF TOTAL POPULATION)

	Age group (years)		
	15–29	30–44	45+
Divination	16.3	14.0	1.6
Divination but woman refused	6.1	4.6	6.6
Full performance according to diagnosis includes minor and spirit possession rituals for childbearing and rearing	47.0	67.4	78.7
None	30.6	14.0	13.1
Total	100.0	100.0	100.0

participation in rituals including spirit possession rests on ill health in general. Participation was not optional in the past, but the presence of modern medicine available in the area means that young women may forego some traditional rituals and rely on hospital treatments instead.

5. Categories of Persons Possessed and Matrilineal Continuity

Mbiti (1969), an African theologian, argues that ancestor-centered religion requires the living to "keep in touch" with deceased relatives. Whereas living persons are in constant balancing interaction with each other, there is no direct monitoring of interaction with the "recently" departed" or long-dead ancestors. People should remember their ancestors and pay homage to them regularly. But devotion lapses. Therefore, the ancestors call attention to the need for devotion by sending illness. Why do the ancestors choose illness? Perhaps because ancestors and their descendants are in a personal relationship, and illness is personalized as well. Why do Luvale ancestors interfere with fertility? Partly because the Luvale view reproductive ailments and fertility dysfunctions as types of illnesses. In any case, both the ancestors and the living concern themselves with lineal continuity, which is based on women's fertility. Affliction is absolutely directed toward close, lineal relatives with mother, mother's mother, and mother's mother's sisters forming most of the shades responsible. At marriage, a woman joins her husband and becomes separated from the living members of her matrilineage. Yet it is this line for whom she produces children and to whom her children must return at puberty. Deceased matrilineal ancestors in the form of ancestral shades "float around" and afflict these matrilineal descendants who are away from the natal village. Turner writes that uterine female descendants are in peril of having their bodies "tied up" by these shades. As a result they miscarry or deliver a stillbirth. Alternately the shade "runs away" with the menstrual fluids (dysmenorrhea) so the woman does not conceive.* Many people worry about a woman becoming a mother. Her husband and his surrounding matrilineal relatives who live in the same village worry. They know a man should impregnate his wife and that they are responsible for a woman and her children under their jurisdiction. They will initiate a divination and engage a doctor. A husband who fails to impregnate his wife, or to seek treatment for a sick wife or child, is censured severely by the woman's relatives, who demand that the couple divorce.†

*People believe that dysmenorrhea prevents conception.
†This contrasts with the husband's right to divorce a healthy wife whenever he desires.

Although the husband and his matrilineal relatives assume the responsibility for the women's fertility and sick children, they are simply the expediting agents in any "conflict" between the woman and her own matrilineage. The woman's female ancestors are the cause—they send sickness to remind her of her proper allegiance and that she must rely on them for help. Consequently, they "instruct" her in the performance of cult rituals that are the guardians of fertility and health for mothers and children. Her living matrilineal relatives aid as much as possible. Often, they perform the rituals, act as doctors and helpers, and contribute ritual paraphernalia and funds.

Most rituals for childbearing and child rearing occur when women are young and when their children are growing up. At this time they reside with their husbands. Rituals for general illness for both sexes take place later. Depending on her marital status a woman may be living virilocally—in which case her husband is responsible for the cure.* More commonly, a woman over 50 prefers to be divorced and reside with her matrilineal kin—understandable since she is approaching her ancestors—who undertake the cure. Men may have general or air spirit possession rituals at any time during their adult lives but mostly tend to have them as they reach 50 or 60 years of age when they suffer body and limb pains. Fathers never undergo possessions on behalf of their sick children.

In essence, matrilineal ancestors afflict their female descendants to remind them of matrilineal obligations. But affliction and recovery pave the way for ritual specialization either simply as a cult member or as a cult doctor. Within her matrilineage she carries cult membership, which she will pass to her descendants. Through ritual each woman gains recognition and a place in the memory of the living. A woman who has children may one day be the "cause" of her daughter's participation. A childless woman may be "responsible" for many of her nieces' experiences. Women who have become dispersed through marriage become integrated through their participation, and in this sense spirit possession and ritual become the vehicle for bonding women of a matrilineage. Along with membership, ritual expertise is passed down through matrilineal lines and certain matrilineages have a preponderance of ritual experts. The nature and sequencing of ritual cures correlate specifically with success and failure in having children, on the one hand, and having the proper matrilineal ancestors who are cult members, on the other.

A 22-year-old woman's natality profile provides a classic example of the multiple rituals a woman may undergo in her efforts to become a

---

*The husband may not divorce a sick wife and is caught in a "zero-sum game," for he pays a very large death forfeit if she dies at his house.

mother. Linda miscarried her first pregnancy. She carried her second pregnancy to term and delivered in the village. However, this baby girl died within a month. After consulting diviners, her relatives discovered that she was afflicted by many ancestral spirits. A public possession ritual was held to identify and placate these spirits. The patient's mother, maternal grandmother, and father's sister are all medical and ritual specialists, and they assisted her in the ritual. She had many deceased female relatives who had belonged to a variety of cults, so it was not surprising that many cults were suggested. Seven *mahamba* possessed her in this single ritual. Subsequently, Linda became pregnant again and also had severe abdominal pains. Her relatives immediately consulted two diviners, who recommended another type of spirit possession performance (called *Tuta*). They suggested that, if the delivery were a success, mother and child should later be placed in the elaborate "big fence" ritual *(chipango chachinene)*. The diviners also ordered that the rituals be supervised by a specialist who had a large repertoire of ritual cures and was not a relative. In fact this spirit possession ritual was performed in the eighth month of Linda's third pregnancy. Leaving nothing to chance, Linda, accompanied by her mother, subsequently went to the Mission Hospital, where she delivered a baby girl and received treatment for a pelvic infection.

Once home, the patient's mother, her matrikin, and her father and his matrikin were all anxious that mother and baby be placed in the "big fence" ritual as quickly as possible. Linda's mother herself was not only a spirit possession doctor for illness, she specialized in the "big fence" ritual and had been placed in it with her baby Linda. The maternal grandmother was an important local spirit possession doctor. Linda's mother-in-law underwent the "big fence" ritual with one of her young children years before. Only Linda's husband and his father were hesitant about performing the ritual with seclusion in the fenced enclosure. They worried that Linda and her husband always argued about sharing food, and they feared that the restrictions on food and activities would exacerbate the already existing tensions. Linda's matrikin were adamant, however, and the ritual was performed when the child was two months old and had colic and diarrhea. Linda was possessed by the same seven cults, all of which her mother and mother's mother belonged to. Both mother and child terminated their ritual experience in good health. All the relatives were pleased about their good health and Linda's relatives were delighted to have another ritual adept and potential ritual expert in the family.

Linda's husband and his father tried to discourage the plans of the women (Linda's mother and mother-in-law) because they saw a difficult husband–wife relationship being exacerbated through the enactment of the ritual, but they knew a divorce would occur anyway if the husband did not sponsor the ritual. Usually, a husband desires to sponsor a ritual and give things to a wife he loves or placate an estranged one because it improves his status and prevents divorce. Hence the sponsorship of any spirit possession ritual *prevents* conflict between husband and wife, and husband's and wife's brothers. Further, it is easy to see how observers could see the spirit possession rituals as only a palliative for social problems rather than as something based on actual disease and illness. Although the conflict model is tempting for analyzing the in-marrying wives vying for attention, the empirical evidence shows that non-related women who belong to curative women's cults cooperate in curing and initiating new members as discussed below.

It is useful to summarize the types of ritual participants and the social consequences of their participation. Healthy adult women fall into two groups. Some have no problems and therefore no need for ritual cures. As such they are bypassed for cult membership and ritual careers. But their children may become sick and die, so they participate in possession rituals for child rearing. Unless subject to excessive losses, they may undergo relatively few rituals because their good health and fertility preclude the elaborate rituals. On the other hand, many Luvale women have much illness and reduced fertility. In their efforts to become mothers or cure their own or their children's illnesses, they may have undergone many rituals. To be sick and recover is the way a person becomes a ritual expert, and hence these women are candidates for ritual careers. For the survivors of these ailments the fertility news is not all bad. In a sense, failure to become a mother in one part of the life cycle may be translated into successful ritual participation at another time.* The next section explores the ways in which women become ritual experts and what this means.

6. Doctors and Adepts: A Cooperative System

Both men and women participate in rituals and become specialists. Men run the boys' puberty camps and a men's funerary society, and are herbal and spirit possession doctors. Women run the girls' puberty camps, a women's funerary society (now defunct), and birth rituals, and are herbal and possession doctors. These practitioners have high status

---

*I discuss only spirit possession doctoring here, but there are other roles, such as midwife (this career often attracts barren women), herbalist, and leader in the women's funerary society, that may be undertaken simultaneously or separately.

in their society—some people have noted that the curers of any society represent its hope for well-being—and consequently these people are at the top of the social structure and well compensated for their work. Male spirit possession doctors perform possession cults for general illness and the hunters' cults, which can affect both men and women in reproductive and nonreproductive ways. Female doctors focus on cults connected with childbearing and child rearing, but they also perform cures for general illnesses that affect both sexes. Because herbal treatments and possession rituals require long periods of time to complete, much time and effort by the doctor, and substantial payment by the patient, it is not surprising that doctor and patient build up a relationship during the cure. This may set the stage for an apprenticeship, which may follow. Doctors also keep track of their patients and tally their cures. Survivors provide the best advertising; doctors are popular and in demand if their patients recover.

In general, an individual progresses from outsider-uninitiated to novice-participant and then to instructor-expert. At each ritual, be it rite of passage or life crisis ritual, people learn more of the ritual procedure and of the underlying cosmological–symbolic system. Men and women experts always have helpers, and it is useful to view these people and the way in which they acquire ritual expertise as adepts who are serving their ritual apprenticeship. This forms a system, a regular program that may have disparate steps but ultimately forms a coherent whole. The "curriculum" produces pupils and teachers, adepts and doctors. The apprenticeship system is necessary for the transference of ritual knowledge. It also serves to create relational and mutual aid systems that enhance and crosscut kinship ties.

The prerequisites for learning curative treatments are to have been a patient and to have recovered. Access to spirit possession doctoring rests on (1) being ill, (2) being diagnosed (by divination) as being possessed by ancestors as members of particular cults, and (3) being confirmed for nomination for cult membership through possession during the ritual performance. After recovery, the individual participates as adept in the cult performances of others. A man or woman may then express the desire to formally apprentice himself or herself by paying a fee to the person who did the curing. It may be said that illness outlines and channels careers, for one may become an adept only in those traditional spirit cults one has personally experienced. Persons who eventually become ritual practitioners do not have to learn all the songs, dances, invocations, and sequencing of events because they are already familiar with these through attending rituals. They may have to learn the esoteric medications and their methods of application. During the apprenticeship, which may last a matter of days, months, or years, the doctor teaches these things, but the actual conferment of ritual status hinges on the payment of a large fee to the doctor. All healers stress that if the learner did not pay a fee, the medicines would be valueless and would not work. Medicines and rituals work, according to informants, because of their "inherent worth" and because the practitioner transfers the knowledge to the apprentice correctly and for a fee.

The relationship between doctor and adept may be close or distant. People attempt to engage related people for cures because they know the payment will be less. But sometimes divination forbids that a relative conduct the cure, and a "specialist" is engaged. Sometimes a woman learns doctoring from her kinspeople, her mother, her grandmother, or a matrilineally related person; other times she learns from someone unrelated to her. Men learn from their kinspeople and from nonrelated persons. In any case, election to cult membership is through matrilineal ancestors, and cult members and cult doctors tend to come from certain matrilineages. On the other hand, people without the necessary matrilineal antecedents may be hindered if they desire to become ritualists. They can, however, specialize in midwifery, herbal remedies, or the new air spirit possession cults which do not require that the patient be selected by a deceased cult member.

To specialize in women's cures is tedious and time-consuming, and women actively involved with the day-to-day tasks of child care and pregnancy are not able to do this. Generally, women ritual experts are mature but vigorous people (often married a second or third time) in their 40s and 50s; they have the stamina for the long curing procedures (see Figure 2). They become apprentices (cult adepts) in their 30s after they have completed active reproduction and child care. Women specialists over sixty or prematurely infirm act as "retired consultants" who give advice at performances but no longer are the principal curers. As a result, it is common to find that women have spirit possession rituals for themselves and for their children's illness—with concomitant successes and failures—in their 20s and 30s. Then women spend the time after their own fertility is completed taking up the calling and undergoing apprenticeships.

The apprenticeship system facilitates the learning of ritual esoterica and roles through constant and continued participation of people both formally and informally. Ordinary persons thereby transform themselves into ritual officials with supernatural legitimacy to conduct others through the required procedures. As a result of continual renewal of ritual personnel, two single-sexed ritual traditions, a men's and a women's, coexist.

Women cooperate with each other during curing rituals, sharing their expertise or simply their participation in the dancing and singing. Wherever a woman may go (at marriage or on visits) she will find other women who can rally to her aid and who require her help through the idiom of ritual and through common membership in cult groups. Women feel it is their obligation to help other women with whatever knowledge they have during sickness and ritual cures so that they may expect reciprocity (a good insurance policy when sickness abounds). Even where social interactions may be less than harmonious, illness and ritual will generate this expectation of aid and good will. As a result of this cooperative policy of ritual participation, nonrelated women build up ties with each other. Women in close residential proximity, who are often affinally related, may participate together in rituals. The junior aids the senior and eventually apprentices herself and becomes a specialist as well. Women form a "community of sufferers," and the participation in cults crosscuts kinship ties (Turner 1957, 1969). Hence, women are linked in groups wider than their matrilineages and for purposes other than domestic (cf. Leis 1974). They help the entire society attain more cohesion through this cooperative mechanism.

7. Conclusion

All the conflict models that discuss spirit possession turn on the notion that ritual action dispels conflict and by so doing helps people to recover from illnesses largely "psychosomatic." Women are the inciters and the objects of conflict, and thus are always implicated. Recently, anthropologists have begun to see that we need not view women in this way, for women use strategies that are either the same as (Hoffer 1972) or different from men's (Collier 1974; Leis 1974), depending upon the situation. Further, they may not be conflict producers at all, often are not "in competition" with each other or with men, and may not be objects over which men in societies fight. Lamphere (1974) sets up a model in which women cooperate when it is in their interests to do so, usually when they are in autonomous positions domestically (vis-à-vis males in the family unit), and compete with each other when they are in very dependent situations. Thus the models presented above may in fact be operative for some societies but are certainly not generalizable for all. Rather than seeing women in "special situations which regularly though not necessarily give rise to conflict, competition, tension, rivalry, or jealousy between members of the same sex" (Wilson 1967:366), it is possible to view spirit possession rituals as one of the bonding mechanisms that enable women to form ritual groups and enter arenas other than the domestic one. A curative system that is woman-controlled may operate to link and bind living women to their deceased ancestors, and living kinswomen to each other as well as to nonrelated women.

Illness prevents Luvale women from achieving the goals of motherhood. But in their efforts to achieve physiological well-being for themselves and their children, they undergo spirit possession rituals. Men see this as absolutely essential—after all, women are childbearers and women attend to their own bodily functions just as men attend to theirs. Not surprisingly, women with actual reduced fertility become symbolic mothers to cure and nurture their clients (patients) with possession rituals. Luvale women are able to translate the reproductive potential into alternative pursuits. Women generally have a long period of time when they theoretically should be fertile and engaged in child rearing but are not. People cope with these situations with ritual and medicinal techniques through individual participation in curing rituals and through subsequent specialization in doctoring during the nonreproductive period. Because of the prevalence of physiological "disorders," women band together to provide symbolic "order" through the enactment of a coordinated and elaborate set of rituals.

Although female models of interrelatedness are found in many societies, they may be intensified in matrilineal ones. Turner notes for Ndembu boys' and girls' rituals that "there is a masculine ideal of a community of male kin, consisting of full brothers, their wives, and sons. But matriliny, strongly ritualized in the girls' puberty ceremony and in many cults connected with female fertility, prevents the full realization of this ideal" (1968:12). Undoubtedly, there is a feminine ideal of community among both the Luvale and the Ndembu whose realization is prevented by virilocal residence. However, female rituals that transcend residential separation involve all women in a community of concern for themselves, their children, their mothers and grandmothers, and the whole body of female members of Luvale society, both alive and departed. Women require female ancestors to direct their fertility and channel their ritual careers. A priest among the patrilineal Nyakyusa once said, "The shade and the semen are brothers" (Wilson 1971:31). For the Luvale, the equivalent statement would be that the shade and the womb are one, and that matrilineal kinswomen control fertility within a lineage. A Luvale woman's reproductive power is ritually and physically channeled and transformed through membership in possession cults, to prepare her to become specialist, expert, and priestess serving and preserving the wider community.

References

Ardener, Edwin. 1972. Belief and the Problem of Women. In J. La Fontaine (ed.), *The Interpretation of Ritual: Essays in Honour of A. I. Richards.* London: Tavistock. 135–158.

Beattie, John and John Middleton (eds.). 1969. *Spirit Mediumship and Society in Africa.* New York: Africana Publishing Corp.

Chesler, Phyllis. 1973. *Women and Madness.* New York: Avon Books.

Collier, Jane F. 1974. Women in politics. In M. Z. Rosaldo and L. Lamphere (eds.), *Women, Culture and Society.* Stanford: Stanford University Press. 89–96.

Colson, Elizabeth. 1969. Spirit possession among the Tonga of Zambia. In J. Beattie and J. Middleton (eds.), *Spirit Mediumship and Society in Africa.* New York: Africana Publishing Corp. 69–103.

Curley, Richard T. 1973. *Elders, Shades, and Women: Ceremonial Change in Lango Uganda.* Berkeley: University of California Press.

Ehrenreich, Barbara and Deirdre English. 1973. *Complaints and Disorders: The Sexual Politics of Sickness.* Old Westbury: Feminist Press.

Evans-Pritchard, E. E. 1937. *Witchcraft, Oracles, and Magic Among the Azande.* Oxford: Clarendon Press.

Friedl, Ernestine. 1975. *Women and Men: An Anthropologist's View.* New York: Holt, Rinehart & Winston.

Hoffer, Carol. 1972. Mende and Sherbro women in high office. *Canadian Journal of African Studies* 6(2):151–164.

Illich, Ivan. 1976. *Medical Nemesis: The Expropriation of Health.* New York: Pantheon.

Lamphere, Louise. 1974. Strategies, cooperation, conflict and women in domestic groups. In M. Z. Rosaldo and L. Lamphere (eds.), *Women, Culture and Society.* Stanford: Stanford University Press. 223–242.

Leis, Nancy B. 1974. Women in groups: Ijaw women's association. In M. Z. Rosaldo and L. Lamphere (eds.), *Woman, Culture and Society.* Stanford: Stanford University Press. 223–242.

Lewis, Ian. 1966. Spirit possession and deprivation cults. *Man* (ns) 1:307–309.

Lewis, Ian. 1971. *Ecstatic Religion.* Middlesex: Penguin Books.

Martin, M. Kay and Barbara Voorhies. 1975. *Female of the Species.* New York: Columbia University Press.

Mbiti, John. 1970. *African Religions and Philosophy.* New York: Anchor Books.

Mitchell, J. Clyde. 1965. Differential fertility amongst Africans in Zambia. *Rhodes-Livingstone Journal* 37:1–25. Manchester University Press.

Ohadike, Patrick O. 1969. Some demographic measurements for Africans in Zambia. *Institute for Social Research Communication:* No. 5. Lusaka.

Romaniuk, A. 1968. Infertility in tropical Africa. In J. Caldwell and C. Okonjo (eds.), *The Population of Tropical Africa.* New York: Columbia University Press. 214–224.

Rubel, Arthur. 1964. The epidemiology of a folk illness: Susto in Hispanic America. *Ethnology* 3:268–284.

Schlegel, Alice. 1972. *Male Dominance and Female Autonomy: Domestic Authority in Matrilineal Societies.* New Haven: HRAF Press.

Smith, Mary. 1954. *Baba of Kano.* London: Faber and Faber.

Spring, Anita. 1975. Apprenticed not oppressed: Luvale women as ritual leaders and learners. Unpublished paper presented at the Southern Anthropological Society, Clearwater Beach, Florida.

Spring, Anita. 1976a. An indigenous therapeutic style and its consequences for natality: The Luvale of Zambia. In J. Marshall and S. Polgar (eds.), *Culture, Natality, and Family Planning*. Chapel Hill: Carolina Population Center. 99–125.

Spring, Anita. 1976b. *Women's rituals and natality among the Luvale of Zambia*. Ph.D. dissertation, Cornell University.

Turner, Victor W. 1957. *Schism and Continuity in an African Society*. Manchester: Manchester University Press.

Turner, Victor W. 1966. Ritual aspects of conflict control in African micropolitics. In M. Swartz, V. Turner, and A. Tuden (eds.), *Political Anthropology*. Chicago: Aldine. 239–246.

Turner, Victor W. 1967. *The Forest of Symbols:* Aspects of Ndembu Ritual. Ithaca and London: Cornell University Press.

Turner, Victor W. 1968. *The Drums of Affliction*. Oxford: Clarendon Press.

Turner, Victor W. 1969. *The Ritual Process*. Chicago: Aldine Publishing Co.

Van Gennep, Arnold. 1960. *The Rites of Passage*. Chicago: University of Chicago Press.

White, C. M. N. 1949. Stratification and modern changes in an ancestral cult, *Africa* 18:324–331.

White, C. M. N. 1953. Conservatism and modern adaptation in Luvale female puberty ritual. *Africa* 23(1):1–23.

White, C. M. N. 1959. A preliminary survey of Luvale rural economy. *Rhodes-Livingstone Papers*: No. 23. Manchester: Manchester University Press.

White, C. M. N. 1961. Elements in Luvale beliefs and rituals. *Rhodes-Livingstone Papers*: No. 32. Manchester: Manchester University Press.

Wilson, Peter J. 1967. Status ambiguity and spirit possession. *Man* (ns) 3:366–378.

10

SUSAN MIDDLETON-KEIRN

Convivial Sisterhood

Spirit Mediumship and Client-Core Network among Black South African Women

Divination through spirit mediumship is one essential means by which the urban black South African* can order experience, gain some measure of control in a daily life fraught with uncertainties in a context of apartheid, and despite these external and seemingly uncontrollable forces feel fortified, renewed, and refreshed. This chapter examines the process of recruitment to the role of *isangoma* diviner (plural *izangoma*) and emphasizes the reinterpretive and reintegrative aspects of this mediumship. I suggest that the position of the African woman in the social, political, and legal system is one of structural inferiority and liminality.

Referring to the liminal state in rites of passage, Turner points out that "the attributes of 'threshold people' are necessarily ambiguous, since this condition and these persons elude or slip through the network of classifications that normally locate states and positions in cultural space" (Turner 1969:95). Black South Africans, both male and female, in South Africa's white-dominated color-caste society stand in an ambiguous structural position. Their statuses and roles are primarily established in relation to the expectations of the dominant white minority. These expectations include a subservient demeanor and general pleasant acquiescence when dealing with whites. In this situation a dynamic per-

*Following the preferred usage of the majority of urban African township residents, the term *black South African* will be used often in this discussion in preference to *Bantu* or *African*.

SUSAN MIDDLETON-KEIRN · Associate Professor of Sociology and Anthropology, Jacksonville State University, Jacksonville, Alabama.

sonality, forceful statement of a specific belief, special training and professional expertise, or other similar aspects are not generally congruent with the "racial" mythology perpetuated within the white-controlled political, legal, economic, and social system.

Within the black South African color-caste the social relationships of male and female are to a large extent characterized by superordination–subordination. The nature of this male–female relationship should be understood as an aspect of cultural continuity from the traditional rural patrilineal system. Analogously, the expectations of an African husband regarding his wife are structurally similar to those generally met by any African in dealing with whites. Wives are subordinate in relation to husbands, blacks are subordinate in relation to whites. Black women, therefore, occupy a dual position of structural inferiority. Women who occupy positions incongruent with law, custom, and convention may be further considered ambiguous. The ambiguities, which inhere in the statuses and roles of the urban African woman, can in many instances place her in what could be likened to the liminal state in a rite of passage. "There is a certain homology between the 'weakness' and 'passivity' of liminality in diachronic transitions between states and statuses, and the 'structural' or synchronic inferiority of certain personae, groups and social categories in political, legal, and economic systems" (Turner 1969:99).

1. Recruitment: Liminality and Structural Inferiority

Turner argues that such liminality is often associated with ritual powers (1969:100). Often liminality is characterized by a modality of social relationship termed community or *communitas* (Turner 1969:69). The social relationships of the *isangoma* and her long-standing core of clients may be characterized as representing *communitas*. The character of these relationships includes: a powerful communion of equality among marginal and structurally inferior individuals, an expressed feeling of euphoria as well as an expressed reluctance to depart from a prayer session, and intense one-to-one interaction. The generation of spontaneous *communitas* will be viewed as one mechanism for recruitment of new potential *izangoma* from such a core group. Once recruited, the *isangoma*, who is often, though not always, a married woman (Lee 1969:140), carries out her instrumental and expressive communication with the ancestral spirits, relays their wishes, and for her regular clientele becomes a dynamic intermediary figure in decision making, in

Figure 1. In one of the largest black townships in South Africa the typical matchbox houses stretch to the horizon.

township* gossip, and in ongoing local events. (A portion of a typical apartheid-created township is shown in Figure 1.) That the *isangoma* is viewed as an auspicious member of her society is reflected in the fact that she gains a good deal of prestige and respect not only from the immediate client group with whom she enters into intense and frequent interaction, but also from members of the African community at large. Vilakazi (1965:103) indicates that among clients consulting these ritual specialists, secrecy of their visits is important. However, I noted throughout my research a contradictory tendency. Those persons freely and openly consulting *izangoma* represent a wide spectrum that includes the ordinary "masses,"† as well as university students, ministers of religion with their

*African urban residential areas (townships) are usually located on the outskirts of major cities in South Africa. One of the townships where research was conducted has an approximate population of 125,000 persons and is located near Durban, Natal. The other township, with a population of at least one million inhabitants, is located near Johannesburg, Transvaal.

† *The masses* is a term popularly used by township residents to categorize the greater majority of fellow Africans who are not of the educational or occupational level of the speaker.

wives and children, qualified nurses, graduate professional social workers, and wives of medical doctors. Most of these people are in varying degrees adherents of the "established" churches—Anglican, Presbyterian, Methodist—or offshoots of these churches. This free and open consultation is only partially the result of the new and alternative styles of being a diviner.

In Zulu society the ancestors are viewed in an intermediary capacity between God and living human beings. Communication with the ancestral spirits takes place in order to determine the cause of misfortune, as well as to give thanks for good fortune. Such communication is facilitated by slaughtering certain animals as requested by the ancestors. The role of healer and intermediary between the human and the spirit world involves, as it has always done, the drawing together of these various elements.

The role of spirit medium is congruent with, and at the same time not mutually exclusive of, the procreative role or an additional occupational role. For example, of the numerous *izangoma* whom I knew, two were employed full time as qualified nurses and one was a graduate social worker (who was just completing her period of initiation as an *isangoma*). Another *isangoma* had just left her post as a high school teacher. Nomusa (shown in Figure 2), whose recruitment, mediumship, and client network provide illustrative material in this article, has been following full time her calling of prophecy, healing, guidance, counseling, and preaching since 1968.* None of these women who are *izangoma* are childless; indeed one very successful diviner has eleven children, while others, younger women, have at least one or two children.

Nomusa, like most other *izangoma*, has gone through a form of *ukuthwasa* possession (literally, to become possessed by a spirit), a state from which she has emerged as a "new" person, and has become a full-fledged *isangoma* serving as spirit medium as well as diviner. This emphasis on mediumship aspects rather than on possession itself follows the usage of Firth (quoted in Middleton and Beattie 1969:xvii), who states that in mediumship the accent is on communication, i.e., the person is conceived as an intermediary between spirits and human beings. This communication and intermediary position are of primary importance in the case of *izangoma* because possession is a phase in the process of becoming a full-fledged *isangoma*. Since possession does not always result in the development of such a full-fledged diviner, this distinction is especially critical here. Some of the women provide the personnel from whom are drawn the initiates (those "called") who after

*It is likely that as any individual woman's practice of divination grows, she will gradually leave aside additional occupations to become a full-time specialist in her calling.

Figure 2. Nomusa, a spirit medium, attired in colorful African beadwork at home.

a period of *ukuthwasa* may become full-fledged *izangoma* of a new type more congruent with the communities of which they are a part. Lee (1969) has noted that women who were undergoing *ukuthwasa* in rural Zululand were "shrewd, intelligent, morally responsible, dynamic members" of their particular community. My information on two black South African urban areas supports his observation. From this very fact stems the seeming paradox of the urban African woman's position. More highly educated than the average African woman, more professionally oriented, more highly visible than the "masses," she is at the same time female in a traditionally male-dominated society, and African in a traditionally white-dominated society outside the township. From such a dual position of structural inferiority she gains the "power of the weak."

Like the other *izangoma* whose case histories I gathered, Nomusa's recruitment follows fairly closely a stereotypic pattern outlined by Lee (1969:134–135). In most cases *ukuthwasa* possession has three distinct stages: initial symptoms of considerable change in both physical and mental functioning; treatment, either to "seal off" or to "bar" the spirits (Krige 1936:304), or alternately to "open the ways" of the victim for the ancestors; and finally, if the "opening of the way" does take place, emergence of the person possessed as a fully qualified member of the *isangoma* cult.

In 1962, after Nomusa gave birth to her first child by cesarean section, she began to experience rheumatic pains all over her body when she returned from work each afternoon. At this time, and in fact until 1967, Nomusa (who had begun but subsequently left off training as a nurse) was employed as a radio announcer. She had become quite well known for her acting ability in several plays, as well as broadcasting several programs such as the women's program, the children's program, the hospital requests program, and the young listener's program. During this first of the three stages of *ukuthwasa* possession an old woman whom Nomusa had never met before came to her home in the township and prophesied to her that she had psychic powers. In addition to this prophecy the old lady prayed over water, which, when Nomusa took it, relieved the rheumatic pains. Subsequently Nomusa was baptized by complete immersion under the supervision of the old lady and of an old man who had later come to Nomusa's residence in a similar manner. During this baptism, Nomusa did not fear water as usual, and in addition she came out speaking in tongues.* Her baptism by immersion served the purpose of "opening the way" for continued communication with the ancestral spirits. However, after the baptism and subsequent feast, Nomusa's husband and mother expressed intense dislike of those events. For the next five years Nomusa felt a desperate need to withdraw from normal society and felt completely unhappy with her radio work. Gradually, in this liminal period, her friends and neighbors turned against her.† Her visions during this time included a recurrent one in which she was beside a river hearing a voice say, "You are the chosen one—you will liberate the nations."

During these five years of "torture" Nomusa was "reluctant and

---

*Here it is important to note that certain Zionist aspects (Sundkler 1961) have been incorporated. The prophet or diviner stresses baptismal rites and cleansing as opposed to the more traditional "barring" or "sealing off" the ancestral spirits; or alternately "opening the way" for the spirits (Krige 1936:304–305). It is essential to note that for the individual actor the "opening of the way" is being accomplished through a different means.
†While an altered mental functioning and altered interaction patterns may have been the reason for this loss of friends, I was unable to obtain substantial information on this point.

afraid to give in to the spirits." Nevertheless, people came daily to her house to ask for guidance, prayers, healing, or help with their various problems. Finally Nomusa "gave [herself] up to God completely, and vowed to work for Him all the days of [her] life." She then left her job as a radio announcer and concentrated on her "heavenly assignment." Thereafter, her friends and neighbors returned one by one for reconciliation. Thus, accepted once again by her society (with the exception of one neighbor with whom Nomusa remains at odds, and who is, not coincidentally, a competing *isangoma*), Nomusa continues to receive and assist those who are troubled by illness, bad dreams, visitations from the dead, and various kinds of misfortune. Her reputation as an *isangoma* spreads rapidly.

2. Mediumship: Reinterpretive Methods and Materials

Nomusa's house and its fenced yard (see Figure 3) in the African township provide the spatial boundaries of what she and her clients consistently refer to as the *isigodlo* (the royal enclosure used by the king and his wives in traditional Zulu society), yet her "heavenly assignment" has no confines in social space or time. Her mediumship is between those who have passed to "the other side," i.e., the spirit world

Figure 3. A fenced house similar to that where Nomusa's *isigodlo* is located.

of the ancestors (*amadlozi*) and those still living. The ancestral spirits link the living and their God. This link is stressed when Nomusa prays using the praise songs of the various people involved in any consultation, her husband's clan, her own clan, and the praises of some of the Zulu kings such as Shaka, Dingane, and Mpande.

While anyone may consult Nomusa with no fee involved for such consultation, those who have afterward had good fortune, have been healed, or have been helped offer contributions. Clients may feel, or in some cases Nomusa may reveal to them, that they should be cleansed; on or around the time of the cleansing ceremony a fixed fee is contributed. This cleansing ceremony "opens the way for the will of 'God' and 'the angels' " (*amakhosi*)* to be done and protects those who are members no matter where they may be. In this way members are "channeled" into whatever the ancestors and the spirit world may want them to do. Death for those who have been so cleansed is viewed as a passing "to the other side," where as members of the spirit world they will definitely be able to pass on to those still living further revelations and miracles. Prayers on any occasion at the *isigodlo* are punctuated by Nomusa repeating in a semiecstatic trancelike manner, "yes, Lord, yes, wonderful father," as she receives the revelations and wishes of those on the other side. In other words the neophyte must be cleansed of the past, must be *tabula rasa,* a blank slate (Turner 1969:103) on which is to be inscribed the knowledge and wisdom of the group under the ritual elder.

Against the far wall of Nomusa's fashionably furnished living room stands the *iladi* (used by participants to mean "altar"), which is about twelve inches high, glass-covered, with perpetually lit candles at each end. Under the glass are pictures of the late Zulu Chief Albert Luthuli, Chief Gatsha Butelezi, the Pope, and Bishop Zulu of Zululand. On the floor in front of the *iladi* is a small square of carpet on which Nomusa kneels. When prayers are taking place no one wears shoes and everyone participating kneels with head nearly touching the floor in a darkened room. Contributions that are not monetary are also placed on this small carpet, while surrounding the *iladi* are small baskets and a clay pot with a grass lid and white beads of purity around its exterior. The clay pot holds monetary contributions made by clients. Standing beside them are Nomusa's walking sticks, which during the pitch of the prayers she usually picks up, handles, and holds until the prayers end. Sometimes during the course of prayers a medicinal herb (*imphepo*) is burned in

---

*Nomusa uses the word *amakhosi* to refer to the ancestral spirits (also, *amadlozi*), and she uses the same word *amakhosi* as equivalent to the English *angels*.

order to open the way for clear understanding and communication with the ancestors. During this period, no matter how she is otherwise attired—dressing gown, street dress, or traditional skin skirt and beads—Nomusa wears a shawl covering her shoulders, as is customary for a married Zulu woman to show respect.

From this brief description several points are clear. Members of the "established" churches are not excluded and are in fact encouraged to supplement their faith with regular visits, participation, and contributions to the *isigodlo*. There are representations of modern political movements, old established religious movements, traditional Zulu material culture, and aspects more closely associated with either independent churches or "established" churches. The heritage of the African in South Africa has been literally washed away, according to Nomusa, and Africans have been misled into believing that all their traditional beliefs in the powers of the ancestors are not only wrong but downright "heathen." In order to emphasize the importance of the ancestral spirits, Nomusa draws on the Bible to show how genealogies of important figures are recorded. Nomusa teaches that the elements of a worldwide ecumenical movement as well as a blueprint for living can be drawn from a firm belief in the ancestors. These spirit beings are in a position to guide, channel, and direct the lives and destinies of those in this phase of life. In addition to dealing with the problems already alluded to, Nomusa blesses new possessions, such as cars and houses. This may be done by prayer only, with holy water, or with *intelezi* (medicinal charms) as the spirits direct in each case. However, because clients, having heard of her effectiveness but not her methods or materials, move in and out of her house all day long and in many cases far into the night, some clients meet with rather a different diviner/prophet from the one they had expected.

One such case provides an illustration of the reintegration and interpretation involved in Nomusa's mediumship. Clients frequently arrive for an initial consultation expecting an emphasis on divination by more traditional methods using more traditional materials; instead they find a different style. In one such case* three people who entered Nomusa's living room on this particular day were introduced to Nomusa as Mr. Ngidi, Mr. Shozi, and Miss Shozi. Nomusa asked them to please have faith in God because her prayers would not help them if they did not. Having noticed that they seemed very worried, Nomusa said that before doing anything else she would pray for them. During the course

---

*During the events described, the researcher (who happened to be in Nomusa's kitchen when the clients arrived) remained unseen by them.

of her prayer, she said,

> I see a house burning, great smoke, and a woman present at home. Here is
> this house burning down completely, but there is no one inside and thank
> God for that. What is the cause? The couple who stays there is not on good
> terms at all, the man is stubborn and the woman has visitations of the dead.
> Why is it that I see this woman married to this man? You are very recently
> married, why then is there this misunderstanding? If you don't allow your
> wife to *thwasa,* you are faced with still greater danger. This place you have
> come to is the fountain *(umthombo)* of the *izangoma,* and if you want your wife
> to *thwasa* in the form of praying I can do that here, but if you want her to go
> somewhere else and *thwasa* in another form you can, but *thwasa* she must!

The prayers carried on for a time and when Nomusa finished, she asked
the three people consulting her to testify that what she was telling them
was true, but they said not a word. She continued to ask, "Whose wife is
this woman here who was introduced as a Miss?" Mr. Shozi finally
responded that the young woman was married to Mr. Ngidi. At this
point Nomusa reprimanded Mr. Ngidi for "sending his wife away"
because he had referred to her by her maiden surname (Shozi). The
fact that Ngidi had not fully accepted his wife, Nomusa said, was the
cause of most of these misfortunes. Nomusa asked again if what she had
said about them was true or not, and again there was silence from
everyone. Finally Mr. Shozi said to Ngidi, "Why don't you talk, isn't
this just what you came for?" Ngidi responded that he was very
perplexed and lapsed into determined silence again.

Mrs. Ngidi (Miss Shozi) began to relate that their house had burned
to the ground but that they did not know how it happened. That day she
had seen smoke and when she ran to locate its source, their house was
already burning so that no one could get inside to save any of their
possessions. Hence the woman was confirming what Nomusa had revealed during the prayer. Nomusa suggested that the couple should
come again for holy water, which they could use as an emetic and
enema, and told Ngidi that his "hardheartedness" was dangerous
to him. As for Mr. Ngidi, he was dumbfounded and still could not
utter a word. Nomusa (who later said she felt that their faith needed
strengthening) began quoting for the three clients instances of others
who had come to her on the verge of death, but because of their faith in
God, *not* in her powers, had been cured. She told the Ngidis that if they
relied on her powers they could not be helped since she has no powers
herself—she has only what God gives and shows her. Hence she advised them to trust in God. Nomusa offered them a cold drink and
cookies, which they ate before departing.

Cases I collected, concerning not only Nomusa, but other *izangoma*,
indicate that some clients expect to be healed or treated by laying on of
hands, or by the diviner throwing bones or asking for standardized

responses from the assembled people. New clients have heard of their reputations, their effectiveness, but not their materials and methods. When Nomusa does none of the expected things for clients, she feels she must "strengthen their faith," not in her psychic powers, but in the powers of those through whom she is gifted with powers of seeing and communication. She views these powers as ultimately originating with God, and views the ancestors as the "channel of communication" through mediums like herself.

3. Client-Core Network and Communitas

Nomusa's spirit mediumship cannot be viewed in isolation since she stands not only in a relationship with the ancestral spirits and God but also in relationship to a core group of her most faithful clients. This client-core now forms a friendship network based on several years' intense sharing of sacred revelations and miracles. The experiences shared by the client-core network have grown out of shared difficulties and problems.

Often liminality is characterized by a modality of social relationship termed *communitas* (Turner 1969:96 *et passim*). The *communitas* modality tends to characterize the social relationships of the *isangoma* and her long-standing client-core during their impromptu meetings. The character of these relationships includes: a powerful communion of equality among marginal and structurally inferior individuals; an expressed feeling of euphoria as well as an expressed reluctance to depart from a prayer session; and marked empathy and intense one-to-one interaction. The generation of spontaneous *communitas* will be viewed as one mechanism for recruitment of new potential *izangoma* from such a core group.

Within the client-core centering around Nomusa are a graduate social worker married to a local high school principal, a medical doctor's wife who is a nurse, a graduate social worker separated from her husband and currently employed full time in a town about 50 miles away (while at the same time pursuing her master's degree in social work and currently completing her *thwasa* phase), and the latter's younger sister, a qualified nurse employed locally and married to a medical doctor based in a city some 400 miles away. In comparision with the average woman in the African townships of South Africa, women in the core group associated with Nomusa are of unusual standing in the African community due to their spouses' endeavors, to their own, or to both. Still, despite their position of preeminence within the African color-caste, they are black in a white-minority-dominated larger society, and they are female in a strongly male-dominated African society. Limited outlets do exist for their personal talents and achievements, but at the same time the women are marginal to both their own and the larger society.

The women of this group share status characteristics and ambiguities that accentuate the importance of the quality of *communitas* shared within the core group. Within this convivial sisterhood is a communion of equal individuals, who outside the group are inferior and marginal. Within the group they share an intense one-to-one interaction based on shared trials and tribulations overcome through sacred intervention, or made more bearable by the empathy of the others. This basis lends the feeling of a sisterhood of fellow sufferers and makes this place (the *isigodlo*) a "fountain of renewal, refreshment, hope" and indeed life. The expressed sense of euphoria and confidence gained from the total experience, coupled with an expressed reluctance to leave the confines of the *isigodlo*, indicates the intensity of many of the sessions and the feelings engendered by them. The members are reluctant to return to the outside world of uncertainties, real dangers, jealousies, competition, and evaluations. But return they do—feeling revitalized by their experience—yet they are drawn back frequently to the sisterhood and communion of equality. In an average week members of the core group visit the *isigodlo* three times, usually spending at least three to four hours per visit.

Despite the fact that client-core members live as much as 20 miles apart, they often drive to the *isigodlo* together in their personal cars. In many instances they intend to depart from the *isigodlo* to a later meeting of one of the voluntary organizations of which they are members. If the women who constitute the client-core network wish to contact one another they may send a message with another network member who will be seeing Nomusa earlier than they. In fact they know each other's daily routines so well that they can often plan without previous discussion to meet at the *isigodlo*. This writer could on a given day be more certain of finding a client-core member in the sprawling townships by going to the *isigodlo* than by looking in any other place.

Nomusa greets client-core members arriving at the *isigodlo* like the old friends and confidantes that they are. And the client-core women greet each other in a similar way. A warm embrace at the door followed by a flood of greetings, questions, and nearly simultaneous conversation is a familiar scene in the *isigodlo*. All of the client-core members had undergone or were undergoing stresses and strains in their personal lives. These include unfaithful, violent, or alcoholic husbands; suicidal family members; recurrent interpersonal difficulties with superiors at work, neighbors, or fellow members of various voluntary associations.

In serving as a personal counselor for her clients, Nomusa always emphasized that *isigodlo* members are charitable, open-minded, and secure in themselves through God's powers. She urged them through her group sessions to be ever aware that others had problems too. "Being in this phase of life we must simply cope up as best we can."

Clients often testified spontaneously to the miraculous ways they had been helped since their cleansing. These testimonies occurred either during the initial stage of conversation and informal reporting of experiences or during the final stage of winding back to the world. Testimonies were never part of the main session in which Nomusa, client-core members, other clients, and her housekeeper-apprentice knelt facing the *iladi* in the darkened living room for communication with "those on the other side." These prayer sessions are superbly detailed with Nomusa mentioning each person present by name and problem. Those present then utter aloud their own prayer as they feel so moved, i.e., in no regularly prescribed order. Finally Nomusa interweaves all these into an emotionally charged prayer meeting in which she calls upon "our Lord Jesus and his wonderful Father, and the ancestral spirits of all those who have passed to the other side." She also sings portions of the praise songs of some of the Zulu kings such as Shaka, Dingane, and Mpande. The praise songs of clients involved in the prayer session are included if they are known, and Nomusa includes mention of her husband's clan as well as her own. In these impromptu prayer sessions Nomusa's dynamic personality, her prodigious memory, and her wealth of dramatic skills come to the fore.

Following this main prayer session a communal meal is usually served. Nomusa nearly always has food and various refreshments carefully prepared with the help of an apprentice diviner (a former client who was miraculously healed through Nomusa's powers). This communal meal seals the occasion as one that is unique in its removal from the competitions, evaluations, and ambiguities of the world outside.* At the same time the sharing of a meal facilitates a return to that world through free, wide-ranging discussion of topics as diverse as black liberation and current fashion. Here at Nomusa's carefully laid table the members of the client-core gossip, touching on several archrivals. The rivalry discussed by the women occurs in the context of voluntary associations. This gossip restates and reinforces the solidarity of the core group members and occurs despite Nomusa's attempts to minimize it. With regard to a few individuals widely recognized as "extremely dif-

---

*Of course, this core group does not form the total clientele of Nomusa's *isigodlo*. Neither are all her clients female, although the ratio of female to male clients is at least five to one.

ficult," Nomusa concurs in the group's opinions. After relaxing over their meal, members begin to drift reluctantly away as they feel they must.

In marked contrast, other groups of women in the urban townships (Keirn 1970) lack this powerful compelling communion of equality. It must be noted that members of this core group also participate as individuals (and many participate actively) in these other voluntary associations. From this participation they gain a heightened awareness of the hierarchical and competitive aspects of human relations associated with the role-playing required of them. These voluntary associations offer an outlet for the women, but such associations are ultimately linked with the very factors producing status ambiguity. Hence the women are not often eager to attend meetings that are in many cases characterized by undercurrents of tension and sometimes by open hostility between members who are also competitors.

In the *isigodlo* the women form and reaffirm social bonds out of or removed from the general structural ambiguities and inequalities of their lives; they find a place where for a time they form a communion of individuals who submit together to the general authority of Nomusa as the ritual elder. They share in their equal submission to the powerful beings of the spirit world and in so doing share a cathartic experience. From the *isigodlo* they move to their respective homes, and to the world outside revitalized by their shared experience of *communitas*. As Turner points out (1969:95–128), social life for individuals and groups is a dialectical process that involves successive experience of *communitas* and structure, homogeneity and differentiation, equality and inequality:

> There are two "models" for human interrelatedness, juxtaposed and alternating. The first is of society as a structured differentiated and often hierarchical system of political-legal-economic positions with many types of evaluation, separating people in terms of "more" and "less." The second model, which emerges recognizably in the liminal period, is of society as an unstructured or rudimentarily structured and relatively undifferentiated *communitas* (Turner 1969:96).

It is this feeling of community of the *isigodlo* (an enclosure also in the symbolic aspect of a place of safety, security, respite, or retreat) that helps to bind the core group, enables them to feel catharsis during and after participation in a prayer session, and draws them back again and again.

Communitas, such as that to be found at Nomusa's fountain of the *izangoma*, is of central importance in any discussion of catharsis and in any consideration of why certain people become possessed. There are at least three potential *izangoma* diviners emerging from this one *isigodlo*.

The first is the social worker just completing her *thwasa* phase; the second is Mrs. Ngidi (Miss Shozi), who was called to *thwasa* by her experience of visitations from the dead; and the third is the apprentice diviner, who has lived with Nomusa for over a year learning her ritual specialty, while at the same time serving as housekeeper and domestic helper. The generation of the feelings of community within the lives of structurally inferior African women may be not only an important mechanism of adaptation but also a mechanism central to the continuing recruitment and growth of the *isangoma* cult in urban areas.

ACKNOWLEDGMENTS

Field research on which this chapter is based was carried out in two apartheid-created black South African townships located near two major cities in the Republic of South Africa from January 1973 to September 1974. This research was supported by NIMH grant 1 FoloMH 54601-01 (CUAN). The support is gratefully acknowledged.

References

Doke, C. M. and B. W. Vilakazi. 1953. *Zulu–English Dictionary* (2nd ed.). Johannesburg: Witwatersrand University Press.

du Toit, Brian M. 1971. The Isangoma: An adaptive agent among urban Zulu. *Anthropological Quarterly* 44(2):51–66.

Keirn, Susan Middleton. 1970. Voluntary associations among urban African women. In B. M. du Toit (ed.), *Culture Change in Contemporary Africa*. Gainesville: University of Florida, Center for African Studies. 25–41.

Krige, Eileen J. 1936. *The Social System of the Zulu*. Pietermaritzburg: Shuter and Shooter.

Lee, S. G. 1969. Spirit possession among the Zulu. In J. Middleton and J. Beattie (eds.), *Spirit Mediumship and Society in Africa*. New York: Africana Publishing Corp. 128–156.

Middleton, J. and J. Beattie (eds.) 1969. *Spirit Mediumship and Society in Africa*. New York: Africana Publishing Corp.

Sundkler, Bengt. 1961. *Bantu Prophets in South Africa*. London: Oxford University Press.

Turner, Victor W. 1969. *The Ritual Process: Structure and Anti-Structure*. Chicago: Aldine.

Vilakazi, A. 1965. *Zulu Transformations*. Pietermaritzburg: University of Natal Press.

11

BARBARA MYERHOFF

Bobbes and Zeydes

Old and New Roles for Elderly Jews

1. Introduction

When I received a grant three years ago to study the cultural characteristics of an aged, ethnic group living in an urban setting, my first inclination was to examine Chicanos. I had previously worked in Mexico and the comparative basis thus provided would be useful. But the political climate was not hospitable, and American ethnic minorities were not welcoming outside investigators at that time. "Why don't you study your own people?" I was frequently asked. The idea had never occurred to me, since anthropologists are conventionally trained to study remote, often simpler cultures, or, when they work in urban, complex settings, they do not usually do fieldwork within ethnic or subcultural groups to which they belong. Of course, there would be hazards in such a study, particularly that of overidentification with people about whom one was supposed to be objective and detached, but there might be advantages too. The idea was intriguing. And there was no alternative.

I would work among elderly Eastern European Jewish immigrants, then. I was raised by my Ukrainian grandmother, and luckily, I admired her greatly. Sofie Mann had always been old, it seemed to me as a child. She liked being old, liked her "drapes," as she called her wrinkles, liked being stout, and thought her long hair made her look dignified. She was a *bobbe*, a grandmother, and a *baleboste*, a matron or householder. Only *bobbes* could tell folk stories well and make proper traditional foods, she

BARBARA MYERHOFF · Professor of Anthropology, University of Southern California, Los Angeles, California.

Figure 1. Barbara Myerhoff as a child, with her grandmother, Sofie Mann.

thought. Wisdom, humor, and certain slowly acquired skills were the natural rewards of aging for her. Sofie felt her innate qualities were standing her in good stead as she grew older. Her common sense, her great, comfortable strength, her good health, and her inner poise were sources of pride. Somewhere in her background, one of her Jewish forebears must have mated with a peasant, she said jokingly, and this accounted for her endurance. She was born in a cabbage field; "that's Jewish fruit," she said. Her mother delivered her in the field, wrapped her in her shawl, rested awhile, then finished the hoeing. "This was a good start," said Sofie. She was raised in one of the small, exclusively Jewish villages known as *shtetls*, within the Pale of Settlement of the Russian empire to which half of the world's Jewish population was confined in the nineteenth century. Desperately poor, regularly terrorized by outbreaks of anti-Semitism initiated by government officials and surrounding peasants, *shtetl* folk found life precarious. Yet a vital and complex culture flourished in these provincial, encapsulated semirural settlements, based on a shared sacred history, religious customs and beliefs, a common secular language, Yiddish, and a folk culture, *Yiddishkeit*. The worse things became externally, it seemed, the more the internal community ties deepened, and people drew sustenance and courage from each other, their religion, and their traditions, to a point. For many, life became unbearable with the reactionary regime of Czar Alexander II. The pogroms of 1881–1882, accompanied by severe economic and legal restrictions, soon began to drive out the more adventurous *shtetl* people. The great surge of Eastern European Jews swelled rapidly until by the turn of the century hundreds of thousands were leaving for the New World.

Sofie left her childhood home in the early 1880s, a young bride, married to a determined, taciturn man, Jacob, a stranger to her since it was the custom for orthodox Jews to arrange their children's marriages. Without relatives or friends in the New World, without skills, education, or knowledge of English, they managed to survive, then succeed in their life goals. Jacob at first was a peddler, eventually owned a small grocery store. They had many children. Five lived to maturity; two received a college education. All the children had considerable musical training; all understood Yiddish when spoken to but replied in English. None learned Hebrew or received any religious education. It was a time, as one scholar has remarked, when assimilation into American life was thought to require the jettisoning of all cultural baggage from the Old World, and religion was the first bundle to go.

During the American depression, Jacob and Sofie's house was filled with people. Their children worked and their grandchildren were cared for by Sofie. It was probably the happiest time of her life. She loved the full, noisy house. She found time during this period to go to night school to learn to read and write English. More educated than many of her childhood girl friends, Sofie had been taught to read and write Yiddish. She learned to speak and read English herself but never mastered writing. She knew America and foresaw that one day her grandchildren would be moving away; she would have to write to them in English. The grandchildren enjoyed helping her with English; the children were less patient. They always wanted her to be modern and urged her to wear stylish clothes and cut her hair so she would not look like a "greenhorn."

As the years passed, Jacob grew even more silent and morose and less certain of himself. We had always thought of him as the absolute head of the house. On Sabbaths and holidays, he was referred to as the King. Only he knew Hebrew; only he could pray. Little by little, we grew to feel less afraid of his stern looks, more sorry for him, especially after he retired. He was physically around the house more but he was not a presence. He had nothing to do but pray, and he was not a deeply religious or learned man. He had no friends. He was not needed.

Sofie was doing what she had always done, taking care of people and the house. In contrast to Jacob, she expanded with time. She grew stouter, jollier, cried and laughed more, talked freely about her childhood. It was hard to account for the differences between them. But I remember feeling that Jacob, whose life was now confined to the house, watched us enviously, not knowing how to get "in" to the family. He hung about and read the paper as Sofie cleaned, cooked, sewed, knitted, sang, baked, visited sick neighbors, and taught the grandchildren her skills and stories. On Friday mornings she was fairly feverish with excitement, plucking the chickens and baking the braided Sabbath loaves, dancing to "The Russian Hour" on the radio, whirling a laughing child or two across the kitchen floor covered with feathers, blood, and flour. She never sat down, and she thrived.

Now, 30 years later, I think I understand a bit about the role reversal that occurred sometimes among the elderly men and women of this culture. I have seen a similar pattern in the old people among whom I have been working recently, and whatever the problems of objectivity I have encountered, I wonder if, without the earlier experience of living with Sofie and Jacob, I would have noticed.

Before describing the present lives of these elderly folk, additional comments about their early, common *shtetl* culture are helpful in understanding their contemporary situation.

2. Male and Female Roles in the Shtetl

The dominant force in the *shtetl* was religion. The strongly patriarchal character of the religion was replicated in family and community organization with perfect consistency. Religion was the concern of everyone but was the specific responsibility and privilege of the men. Women were extremely important, absolutely essential, and highly regarded, but primarily as facilitators of the men's religious activities. The woman was to bear children and train them to carry on the faith. She was to provide a harmonious home, conducive to men's prayer and study. She had the task of carrying out the exacting dietary laws, according to the men's instructions and interpretations. Whenever possible, women worked outside the home, enabling their brothers, sons, and husbands to spend more time in religious study (Baum 1973). The woman provided the support system, the mundane base for the primary undertakings of the men.

In her own right, woman was nothing. Her prayers were not necessary except for her own pleasure. They did not benefit the community; therefore, it was a waste to educate women. But to the extent that a woman fulfilled her supportive role, she could achieve great esteem. Folklore extols a woman who sold her hair for money, which gave her husband economic freedom that permitted him to study. Another tale tells of a woman who sold her soul for her husband. (But this story may be apocryphal since there was debate as to whether women actually had souls [Zborowski and Herzog 1962:136].)

The *shtetl* woman fulfilled herself through others—children and men. She had to obey only three positive religious commandments. (She observed the same negative commandments as men.) Their substance illuminates the role of woman's nature and place. She must purify herself in a ritual bath after menstruation, so as not to pollute her husband and her community. She brings her household a taste of Paradise by lighting the Sabbath candles. She must burn a bit of dough when she bakes bread, "taking *hallah*," which represents a sacrifice to God, made in the household oven ever since the destruction of the Temple. All these commandments pertain to her biology and her position of homemaker and keeper (Hyman 1973:67).

It would be a mistake to assume that this explanation exhausts the question of woman's life in the *shtetl*. In all societies, women and men transcend, change, distort, enlarge, and otherwise make habitable restrictive roles. But it would also be a mistake to overlook the consequences of the stereotypes provided for by roles. Roles specify the norms against which behaviors are measured, and self-evaluation often follows these norms more closely than actual conduct.

The social role of the woman in the *shtetl*—performing her household and religious duties in a quiet and self-effacing manner—was the ideal. It specified not only her duties but the manner in which they were to be performed, that is, the kind of person she was supposed to be. She was expected to be submissive, docile, decorous, retiring, modest, patient, and utterly devoted to her family, without ambitions or aspirations of her own. In fact, a separate sexual stereotype was available to women, generated not by design and not according to ideals. It grew out of the practical necessities of her work outside the home, primarily in the marketplace. This role, less overt and not formally extolled, was nevertheless accepted and admired. It was a *contingent* sexual role, arising in response to and maintained because of its situational appropriateness. What were the attributes of this role, the *baleboste* in the marketplace?

Figure 2. A young *shtetl* woman wearing a *sheytl,* or wig, under her babushka. Notice that in the painting of Adam and Eve in Figure 10, Eve is also wearing a wig; Jewish matrons were required to shear their hair at marriage.

First, the *shtetl* housewife was required by circumstance to be a pragmatist. And she needed business acumen and great energy. She needed to know how to deal with government officials and peasants, and as a result often had a superior command over the vernacular languages—Russian and Polish—superior to that of her pious male relatives. She was the intermediary, more often than men, navigating the conflicting waters between home, *shtetl,* and the outside world. She had to manage the household, earn and budget money, regulate time, funds, and attention within the family, make the decisions, allocate the labor, organize and integrate family schedules and internal and external demands.

In addition to her activities in marketplace and household, the *shtetl* woman devoted herself with intensity to community work. She attended to the sick, shared home duties and child care with other needy women, collected money for brides without dowries, fed visitors and strangers, raised money for orphans, made clothes for Palestinian refugees, and worked on behalf of poor and needy Jews all over the world.

It was clear that the *baleboste* had to be purposive, robust, intrepid, and efficient. Jokes and stories about this stereotype abound, deriding her as fishwife, the shrew. No doubt some of these women were domineering, shrill, and implacable. But this was forgiven, since it was felt that woman's nature inclined her to great vigor and volatility. Naturally, she was seen as given to outbursts of emotion and was expected to be more expressive than her male counterpart. She was, after all, closer to natural forces, while men were regarded as more naturally spiritual.

Figure 3. A *bobbe* from the Center, her head still covered after lighting the Sabbath candles.

And because women were viewed as weak and imperfect, their complaints were acceptable. She was fortunate in having at hand explanations for her failures not available to men: after all, what could be expected from a poor, uneducated, sinful woman?

If there was a contingent role available to *shtetl* men, I have not come across it, in literature or ethnographic descriptions. It seems that men were more limited by the religious obligations that constituted the core of their sexually stereotyped role; and this is not surprising since their religious activities were of more public concern than the conduct of women. The ideal Jewish *shtetl* male, in physical type and demeanor, could not have been more different from the contingent role of his wife. He was expected to be dignified, soft-spoken, poised, reflective, and gentle; his hands were soft, his eyes weak, his brow furrowed, his skin pale—indicating the many hours devoted to spiritual questions and religious study. With an ideal and a contingent role available, women, it seems, had more options than men, more flexibility, more opportunity to express their individuality and adapt to circumstances. And it was the contingent female role, as we shall see, that years later provided some of the most adaptive features of these women's responses to old age, prefiguring their future accomodation, equipping them with the flexibility and pragmatism that ultimately serve them so well.

Sexual stereotypes aside, there were other consequences of the *shtetl*'s radical separation of the responsibilities of men and women. The domination of the home and marketplace by women is certainly not unique to this society. Wherever it occurs, it offers to women the possibility of considerable accumulation of power and influence. When men withdraw from the mundane world and leave to the women those presumably lesser duties of "running things," they lose all but titular control. Ultimately, everyday decisions shape everyday life and these are made in terms of situational needs by women. The men make the important decisions: when the Messiah will come, what the Torah means, and what the attributes of God are. The wife decides how much money to spend on clothes, whether or not to pawn the family candlesticks to apprentice the son, when the daughter shall marry, and whether it is better to buy fish or chicken for the Sabbath meal. None of this alters the basically patriarchal form of the society, all would agree. This common development (called a cryptomatriarchy by one anthropologist) is often the butt of jokes, but the laughter is aroused by the embarrassment of instant recognition.

The world of the *shtetl* shaped the men and women among whom I am presently working. Their childhoods there provided them with the basic materials on which they drew in formulating responses to the New World. They encountered some radical changes; among the most significant was the substitution of a different set of sacred duties assigned to men and women. In the New World, religion quickly gave way as the center of life. Work and money were the ultimately serious affairs and, as before, the most important concerns were assigned to men. As soon as possible, women were pulled out of the labor market, since in America a man did not want his wife to work. In America, immigrant women were soon confined to the home. They became more dependent on their husbands, more isolated from public life. In the absence of family, community, and economic activities, they contacted the outside world indirectly, through husbands and children. The *baleboste*'s qualities of strength and competence, energy and autonomy, were not to find adequate outlet during her middle years, and only in old age do these women rally and demonstrate once more some of the features associated with their roles in the *shtetl*.

3. The Present Population

The present world of the senior citizens is predominately female, since they are very old—nearly all in the middle 80s to middle 90s—and have outlived most of the men. The Center to which they belong, housed in a small dilapidated hall facing the ocean, is the hub of a stable but rapidly diminishing population, homogeneous for age, education, occupation, cultural background, religion, and social history. Many people have lived in the area for two and three decades, settling there soon after retirement. The present community is small and territorially bounded, and, though coexisting with other ethnic groups, constitutes a culturally intense and distinctive enclave. The old people all live far from children and family and, due to their long-shared residence, have established primary ties with each other; relations among them are ambivalent but stable and intense.

All these people are on small, fixed incomes—pieced together from pensions, savings, children's contributions, occasionally welfare—and the great majority are considerably below the national standards for official poverty. Every part of their lives is lived with great care, so as to conserve waning resources in terms of health, strength, and money. Virtually all live in substandard housing, even those few with savings. These senior citizens rarely venture out of the area and, in turn, their children rarely visit them here. Externally, they are cut off, poor, immobile, impotent, bereft. In fact they are, but they are also vigorous, resourceful, engaged, and independent. Often they are bitter and cynical but they are not defeated people.

The majority of the people in this group, perhaps 150, are widows living alone in a rented room or rooms, with meager cooking facilities or kitchen privileges. There are about a dozen couples, all of whom run their own households, and two of whom own their own homes. About 40 women and men live in boarding houses and the rest, perhaps 60, are single men living alone in rented rooms.

3.1. Sex Roles among the Elderly Men and Women

It would be reasonable to assume that men would dominate and lead the life of this group. Culture and belief, combined with scarcity of men, on logical grounds should give rise to male supremacy. The picture is not this simple, although everyone says that men, of course, are more important than women. Women with men, whether long-term spouses or newly acquired boyfriends, are regarded as enormously fortunate and viewed with envy and pain by the single women. Men exert a drawing power on the women. It is not unusual for a single woman to seek to insinuate herself with an amenable couple, forming a stable triad. Competition among women for men's favors and company is fierce, and many outbursts of jealousy occur, sometimes breaking up female friendships of long standing. The men are closely watched and fussed over. However, it cannot be said that they are leaders or even consistently significant in all the Center's activities.

In group discussions, men are not deferred to, and since they do not usually talk as loud or as much as women, they exert little influence on the flow of talk, though serious discussion was one of the exclusively male activities in the *shtetl*. It has become clear to the men and women, after years of association, that the men are no brighter, no better educated, no more perceptive than the women. Except for occasional pieces of specialized religious knowledge, or statements made by the two men who are rabbis' sons (wise, by definition), it is not assumed that the men have anything particularly worthwhile to contribute merely because they are men. Women are more outspoken and assertive in other verbal activities, abundantly producing essays, stories, poetry, and songs. Only one man in the group writes regularly, this though literacy was a totally male endeavor and of the highest value among Old World Jews.

Center events that require physical endurance are likewise female-dominated. Only a couple of men attend the exercise class. Men come with women to dances but are usually left to themselves, since they tire more quickly than their female partners. Men are passed around somewhat, since every woman wants to have a male partner for at least one dance. But the woman often appears inhibited by her male partner,

Figure 4. A dance at the Center.

dances with him slowly, then becomes more animated after depositing him on one of the benches lining the hall, where he sits smiling, clapping to the music, nodding his head, tapping his feet, and waiting for the next woman to sweep him away for a dance. Meanwhile, with undiminished enjoyment, women alternate "being the man" in dances that call for a male partner.

In governance, where one would certainly predict male domination, the pattern is repeated. The real work is done by the women—the organizational tasks, keeping of records, arranging for speakers and programs, planning agendas, collecting fees and dues, and performing those maintenance and administrative jobs that amount to running things. Several men are officials—officers and board members. The president is always a man and the president emeritus and the Center director are men. But, with one exception, they are allied with or married to important women whose direction and influence are unmistakable. Another of the most important activities in the Center, charity in the form of raising funds and gathering food and used clothing for Israel, is entirely female-dominated.

Men are used symbolically by women for various purposes. It is a common sight to see a woman entering the hall, marching across it

Figure 5. One of the *zeydes* at the Center.

accompanied by her male companion, bearing herself proudly, almost with disdain, asserting publicly her superiority in being "attached," then leaving her male companion on the benches while she enters the fray, unwilling to be encumbered or slowed down. On leaving, she stops for the man and departs as she entered, on his arm, grandly, donning him as she might her gloves. The men often appear as passive tokens manipulated in the more significant interpersonal exchanges between women.

As a group, the men appear more worn-out and demoralized than the women. It is impossible to do more than speculate as to why this might be so. Perhaps the same biological factors that cause men to die sooner than women contribute to earlier debilitation. At any event, there seems to be a definite difference between the sexes in terms of energy level, and this probably reflects some complex combination of physiology and culture. One may speculate also about the part contributed by different social roles of men and women, and here I refer to the sexual stereotypes that informed these people's earliest experiences with the sexes: their parents. These old men appear to be enacting the part of the idealized *shtetl* male—dignified, remote, self-absorbed, given to thought more than action. The women emerge in terms of the contingent *baleboste* sexual stereotypes for *shtetl* women, that which I described as issuing from their circumstances as custodians of the mundane realm. For the women are vigorous, resourceful, indomitable, often rude and brazen, antiauthoritarian, outspoken, and submissive to no one. They exude a presence, a sharp-tongued dynamism expressive of their determination

Figure 6. A young couple—the parents of the man shown in Figure 5—before their emigration from Russia.

to get by and make do, regardless of harsh external realities. In their present lives, men and women are cut loose from all the usual ties and obligations—economic, kinship, and ritual. They have a certain negative freedom as a result of the social vacuum in which they now live, and it constitutes an opportunity to do things in their own way; for the women it is usually the first such chance in their lives. None of them would choose this detachment, but since it is an unalterable fact, they must deal with it; the men do so by resting and waiting; the women by shaping their lives, exerting themselves, and molding their world. Nevertheless, there are two specific circumstances in which Old World role stereotypes of men and women reappear. In these two situations, male and female roles are once again complementary and unequal, genuinely reciprocal, and expressive of mutual need and service. In the two situations that I shall now describe, the interaction between the sexes is short-lived but intense, in contrast to the shallower and less comfortable associations characteristic of their usual relations. It is not surprising that these two circumstances revolve around matters thoroughly basic: ritual and food.

3.2. Men and Women in Ritual: The Sabbath

Elderly women, without their own households, have no access to the most important religious duties enjoined upon them, the ritual bath, making the Sabbath loaf, and lighting Sabbath candles. Post-menopausal, they do not attend the ritual bath. They no longer bake, so do not prepare or sacrifice the Sabbath loaf. And having neither home nor family, they do not light the Sabbath candles; though it would be technically possible for them to do so alone in their rooms or boarding house, it is probably too painful a reminder of their isolation from family and community. The women's only access to the three positive religious commandments pertaining to them is provided by the Center, which each Friday conducts an *Oneg Shabbat* ceremony to welcome the Sabbath.

The *Oneg Shabbat* is the climax of the week's activities. It is always well attended. People bring guests, wear their best clothes, and come to it in high spirits. There are scoffers and cynics who claim it is not *Shabbat* at all. It is held much too early in the day. But old people cannot be out in the streets of their deteriorating neighborhood after dark, so they cannot wait for twilight. Neither is there a Sabbath meal; for economic and mechanical reasons this is not possible at the Center. Thus the entire ceremony consists of what properly would be a ritual prologue to the meal. Nevertheless, the *Oneg Shabbat* is unfailingly effective and genuinely sacred.

People assemble in the early afternoon. A table, covered with a white linen cloth by the women, is placed before the audience facing it. The important men are seated there, the Center director, the president, the president emeritus, a young rabbinical student assigned to the Center for this occasion, and two or three honored guests. The latter may include women, but they are outsiders, never members. For this event, the men at the table wear head coverings, usually richly decorated velvet *yarmulkes*. Before them on the table is the ritual equipment: wine, glasses, prayer book, candles, matches, and two covered twisted Sabbath loaves. The ceremony opens with a greeting from the director, who welcomes guests and makes announcements concerning the activities for the coming week. The president then takes over and leads the rest of the program. The content varies little. The rabbinical student makes a short speech in English and leads the people in Hebrew Sabbath songs. The president emeritus, a venerated man of 95, reads the Yiddish poems he has written during the week. Then Bessie or Pauline is invited to sing, tell a story or folktale, or recite a poem that she has prepared in advance, concerning some aspect of the meaning of the Sabbath, usually in the *shtetl*. Some reference to the shared past, the childhood world of *Yiddishkeit*, is always brought in. More songs follow, and then there is a speech or discourse by one of the guests. Frequently young people attend, bringing guitars and accordions, leading the members in Israeli folk songs and dances. This program lasts about two hours, and people frequently grow restive. In uncharacteristically loud and authoritative voices, the men at the table admonish the audience to be more restrained. "What's the matter with you? Is this any way to act on Sabbath?" shouts Jake and pounds on the table. But to little avail. The women continue to engage in side conversations with each other and burst out in response to that which interests them when they are supposed to be listening.

Their excitement builds and the ceremony seems to be degenerating into complete confusion just before the climax, which occurs at the very end. The president indicates that it is time to light the candles, that a woman will be asked to *bentsh likht*, bringing the holiness of the Sabbath into their midst. This was the highlight of the week for all the *shtetl*, an event more sacred than the high holidays, the foretaste of Paradise on earth, the source of meaning for everyday life. And it is the moment of supreme significance for the woman, when her mundane activities are bent toward bringing Paradise to the home. Literally and figuratively, her kitchen becomes a sacred place and her most trivial, repetitive tasks of maintenance and sustenance are sanctified. Appropriately, the Sabbath is female, the Bride who comes to the people of Israel, and it is the woman, now Queen of the home, who brings this blessing to her family.

Figure 7. The *baleboste* (matron of the house) covers her eyes as she prays before the candles, welcoming in the Sabbath.

When she "takes *ḥallah*," her ordinary oven serves as high altar, and she is a priestess offering a sacrifice. For all the old women at the Center, the earliest memories of childhood are bound up in *bentshing likht*. Everyone remembers watching her mother perform this blessed obligation. It is a moment of the deepest personal as well as religious significance.

The *Oneg Shabbat* at the Center is predictable in every detail, except in the designation of the woman who shall light the candles. This is not established ahead of time. The tension before a woman is called, therefore, is acute and palpable. Who will be so honored this week? In the silence before one is named, there is a subtle fluttering of those women who know the prayers and wish to be called to the candles. They flutter their scarves quietly in their laps, wordlessly signaling their readiness. One is named. It is Sadie. She approaches the candles slowly, turns her back to the assembled group, and drapes her head. Barely audibly, she says the short Hebrew prayer, blessing "the Lord who has commanded us to kindle the Sabbath light." She lights the candles, bows her body forward over the flames, then circles her hands over them three times, drawing their holiness toward her face. She finishes this gesture by covering her eyes with her hands as she silently and privately prays to herself in Yiddish. Tears course through her fingers and she elongates the moment. When she removes her hands, she looks about with transformed visage, smiles at the assembled people, and bids them *Gut Shabbos*. She circulates among the people, kissing her special friends, shaking hands, wishing everyone *shavua tov*, a good week, while the men at the table exhort her to be seated and allow the ritual to continue. Reluctantly she does so, but smilingly reaches to clasp the hands of her neighbors, who thank and compliment her. Her characteristically strong, assertive personal style is nowhere in evidence. She is gentle, subdued, nearly wordless, submitting reluctantly to the president's annoyance at her disruptive behavior. Uncharacteristically, she does not make a sharp retort to his admonitions that she sit down and be quiet.

The ritual resumes with difficulty, since the women feel the important part of it has been completed and the Sabbath has entered. The men

Figure 8. A woman blessing the assembled guests after lighting the candles.

feel the most important part, the blessing and drinking of the wine, has not yet taken place. At last, the president restores order, says the prayers, and passes the glass of wine to those at the table. Then he concludes by taking up the Sabbath loaves and, blessing them, tears off a piece and hands it to the men beside him, who do the same. Finally, the women in the audience receive a piece of the bread and serve paper cups of wine to the guests.

Always it is a good ritual. The Sabbath never fails to come, and while the afternoon lasts, the people treat each other with uncharacteristic generosity, respect, and even tenderness. The atheists and the Orthodox purists complain about one thing or another but come again the following week. The event is a hierophany that lasts but a couple of hours, for when they meet again the next morning, it has fled without a trace. Normality reasserts itself. Outside of the ritual setting, the men resume their characteristic quiet and repose. As they walk out, Sadie spots a friend whom she presses to come to the *Kahal* luncheon next week, to raise money for Israel. An argument begins among the women as to who will bring what dish. The men shuffle toward the benches and sit facing the ocean, quietly enjoying the lingering light of the afternoon.

4. Men, Women, and Food: The Kahal Luncheon

Food never exists in its own right. It comes in a context—social and cultural. It is always a matter of ritual and symbol, in some cases richer than others but never absent. Food among these people is heavy with significance, part ritual, historical, part as a result of being poor, old, and alone. The ritual meaning of Jewish food is a subject of enormus complexity. The people described here were all raised in kosher homes; none of them observes the dietary laws at present. Nevertheless, they have very strong ideas about Jewish food (clean, more nourishing) and *goyishe* food (without nutritive value and dirty). Over and under their overt, stated beliefs are their associations of Jewish food with the women who prepared and served it, their wives and mothers. Here the sexual division of labor was absolute and unchanging throughout their lifetime. When men and women came together, the women cooked and served, the men received and enjoyed. Both sexes shared a verbal and nonverbal vocabulary based on food, expressive and satisfying to giver and receiver alike.

As always in such matters, personal statements and interpersonal manipulations took place in terms of this vocabulary. At table, a woman bestowed or withheld good feelings, read her worth and standing from the man's reception or rejection of her offerings, manifested her various moods and talents. For men food was never neutral; it did not exist apart from a profoundly social and emotional setting. The folklore surrounding the *Yiddishe mama* and her preoccupation with food, urging children to eat, interpreting their refusal as a rejection of love, is abundant. Like much folklore, it is an overstatement of a partially accurate observation.

Boys were especially favored with food. One man put it this way: "My mother on Friday, when she made the *ḥallah*, always made me a little loaf of my own. Just for me she would do that. She loved my sisters, naturally, but only I got my own special loaf."

Food had significance beyond the family. It was an expression of nurturance and responsibility for all who were in need, and anyone who came within the ambit of the Jewish householder in the *shtetl* was treated as one deserving of care. Food was the symbol of membership in the Jewish community, a gesture of household acceptance and hospitality, and in terms of the woman's role, it evoked her dominant function as a caretaker. Denial of this function was equivalent to denying her the major source of identity and self-esteem. Sadie explained that many older women would rather not live in their relatives' homes because they would not be able to cook for the family. And of course food was manipulated in these terms by husband and children, just as the *baleboste* manipulated them with food. Hannah remembered her mother this way:

> My mother, you had to admire her. No matter how poor we were—and believe me we were poor—my mother had the samovar going and a little piece of herring hidden away. When someone came to our house she would never let them go away without taking a glass of tea and a little herring, maybe some bread. To this day, when I go to someone's house, if they don't at least offer me, I don't feel like I'm welcome.

Meals were the focus of daily and religious life. Each holiday had its special dishes and stylistic variations. Regional identities were given in terms of the variations, and the strong antagonism between Litvaks and Galitzianers, for example, was stated in terms of the propriety of the soft matzah ball of the one versus the harder matzah ball of the other. Girls and young married women were considered incapable of making certain dishes; a lifetime of experience was necessary for concocting a proper *tsholent*. Only grandmothers made the *kreplakh* for major events.

Compounding these cultural and social levels of meaning are the special requirements for food among the aged and poor. Poor teeth and uncomfortable dentures, digestive difficulties, special diets for diabetics and those with high blood pressure mean attention must be given to every bite. The combination of "modern science" and ethnic dishes is considered both Jewish and healthy, as awareness grows of nutritional losses due to chemicals and processing. Organic squash is preferred for making latkes and brown sugar for making coffee cake, "to avoid modern poisons." But eating properly is harder and harder for them.

Most troubled by the need to eat properly are the single men, who are appalled at the necessity for obtaining their own meals. They find it difficult to get to restaurants and, when there, consider the food un-Jewish and expensive. Even worse is the prospect of cooking for themselves. "It isn't right for a man to do. It isn't natural. Who knows from cooking?" asked Abe when he talked about how unhappy he was. "It's the worst part of living alone." Mealtimes, unceremonial and lonely affairs, are reminders for everyone of their losses, physical and social.

Food is probably the single most important of their concerns, more charged with meanings, emotions, and associations, and more capable of giving pleasure as well as pain. For all these reasons, the luncheons at the Center are important occasions, presenting the opportunity for eating in a suitably social and Jewish fashion. In view of the deep significance of food, it is not surprising that at meals, the old *shtetl* models of male–female roles and relations reappear at these times. There are three charitable organizations of Jewish women which hold the luncheons. The one described here, *Kahal*, is strictly kosher, hence more traditional, but all are very similar in form and purpose. All raise funds and support for various projects in Israel. Many of the Center women have belonged to one of the groups for 10 to 20 years. Organizations provide opportunities for contact with non-Center people and with younger women and thus constitute an important extension of social ties. Among the three organizations at least one luncheon a month is held. Anyone who buys a ticket may attend. The meals are regarded as exceptionally good and good bargains, "a three-dollar meal for a dollar fifty, plus entertainment."

A recent, typical *Kahal* luncheon began at 11:30 A.M. on a Sunday—the hour and day chosen to maximize attendance. About 20 Center women belong to the local chapter of *Kahal*. They sponsor, attend, and participate in the affairs, and they are the luncheon hostesses. Another six to eight dignitaries from the national organization attend, as well as occasional guests and family members on whom Center women have pressed tickets. Altogether, about 80 people are served. The tables are carefully set by the hostesses, covered with bright oilcloth and fresh flowers. Everyone wears his or her best clothes—women wear gloves and men *yarmulkes*. The proportion of men attending is quite high, relative to other events. Seating is always a source of argument. The official hostesses attempt to distribute the guests as they see fit, and the guests insist on following their own preferences. Tables near the kitchen are much desired for quickest service, and tables with two or more men are also much sought after.

Seating at these luncheons does not reflect the social structure revealed in the seating arrangements at other events. Hostesses who are generally not among the leaders can sit wherever they like for their luncheons. The few non-Zionists present—otherwise accepted—are shunned at these affairs, since it is assumed "they only came to eat, not to help Israel." Those with pleasant table manners and "dignity" are preferred company; more than a matter of etiquette, this reflects physical condition. No one is eager to sit near the very old or sick people, some of whom wear bibs because their hands are too shaky to manage the food without spilling. Others need to have their food cut up for them. (Since the "silverware" is the flimsiest plastic, cutting is difficult for everyone, but for the really weak it is impossible.) Members who are known to be wealthy are also not preferred company for the luncheons. It is considered inappropriate for them to take advantage of these inexpensive meals; they should give their money to the organization or buy a ticket for someone else, people feel. And the *shnorrers* ("beggars") who pocket extra rolls or pieces of cake are likely to sit alone. For other events or when eating at a restaurant, pocketing extra food is viewed as sensible. But here, they are cheating Israel. Thus the seating at luncheons held to raise money for Israel is an indication of a set of social and psychological factors specific to a particular event. Indeed, one of the important functions served by these affairs is its offering of an additional arena in which people can receive honor and display abilities and attitudes not provided for in the usual Center calendar of activities.

The assembled guests are welcomed by one of the Center hostesses, and the food is brought out by the other hostesses, two plates at a time. They distribute dishes in order of their friendship ties, with a few exceptions. Naturally, this causes considerable commotion and women object loudly when they are passed by in favor of another, but no one contests that the men are served first, and a little struggle may develop as to which woman will be the last to handle a man's plate. If a woman sitting next to a man can take it from the serving hostess's hands so as to be the one to put it down in front of him, she will do so. It seems as though the one who actually places it on the table before him is regarded as the real giver of the food. It is understood that women with male escorts will be served before the single women. The latter are served last, the order of service reflecting the social networks of the hostesses.

Throughout the meal, women seated near men watch over the latter's plates, sometimes giving them morsels off their own, reminding a man that the back of the chicken is the best, that bread crust is healthy and he should eat it, that he must not eat salt because of his heart, that he likes lemon in his tea, and so forth. Occasionally, a woman will take something from the plate of another woman and give it to a man, behavior that would never be tolerated if the food were taken for a woman. Throughout, the hostesses in aprons and scarves bustle happily, importantly overseeing everyone and checking to be sure that the dishes they have prepared are appreciated and identified. "Don't tell me you already had Jell-O, Jake. Sofie's Jell-O you couldn't eat—it's like rubber. Mine is made with pure fruit juice. No water. Taste." Though the menu varies little, women's expertise in cooking is asserted in finely differentiated terms. When luncheons fall on holidays, festivity is more intense, and the ethnic character of the dishes is more evident. The effervescence is palpable when the women bring out *gefilte* fish, *matzah brei, tsimis*, potato *latkes* and *kugel*. Special diets are ignored and the hall is redolent with the scents and flavors that originated in people's shared childhood culture.

Throughout the luncheon the nurturant role of the women is divided into the joint tasks of raising money for Israel and serving food. While people are eating, one of the hostesses circulates, selling raffle tickets. Then, when the main course is finished the program begins. This is always a troublesome moment, since the program is the main reason for assembling for the organizers but not for the majority of those attending. If the meal is completed before the program, people leave, so dessert and coffee are not brought out until after the program. This annoys them, and they express their irritation loudly, until they are reprimanded sharply by one of the hostesses. "I talk to you about Israel and you talk to me about coffee. You should be ashamed." After her exhortations about Israel's need for their help, the "entertainment" section begins. Bessie's son-in-law, newly returned from Israel, describes his and his wife's recent trip, circulating pictures of the children on the *kibbutz* being supported by the organization. Though he refers to "my wife and I" throughout his presentation, and his wife, seated beside him, is a member of the organization and daughter of a Center member, yet there is no doubt that he and not his wife should give the talk. In other circumstances, the woman would be the lecturer. But it would be inconsistent to follow that norm at a luncheon covertly oriented to serving food and deferring to men.

Throughout the program, the hostesses circulate among the guests, collecting coins in little boxes called, in Yiddish, *pushkes*. These containers were a staple fixture in the kitchen of *shtetl* women, used to collect pennies for charity. Before lighting the candles on Friday, she, the *baleboste*, would put in a few coins, and whenever a bit of extra money was brought into the house, she would skim some off for the *puskhe*. Collectors regularly visited housewives, redistributing the funds to the needy. Many collectors had stable relations with certain women, and some of these ties were passed on between housewife and collector for several generations. The *pushke* was referred to by the women at the Center as "hungry little mouths," and as *pishke*, which also means "little pisser," an affectionate term for a small child, who requires care but is much loved. The use of terms such as these reflects the sentiments about Israel as needing the women's nurturance, requiring food and care; these are the areas of pride and expertise for the Jewish housewife in the Old Country and no less, in the New World.

Bessie's son-in-law passes around his photographs taken in Israel, telling the guests, "You see this *kibbutz*? You see these beautiful children, happy and well-fed? You built this *kibbutz*, you are feeding them, with your little *pishkes*, with your little nickels and dimes. Without you, there would be no Israel." His tribute is a very successful conclusion to the gathering, an affair in which the women found an opportunity to exercise their traditional skills and enact their traditional female role, as givers and caretakers, and at which men likewise fulfilled their traditional male role, as the cared-for and as appreciators of women. It was reassuring, familiar, and satisfying, full of nostalgia for all involved.

5. Ritual and Food: Integration and Continuity

Ritual and food provide the occasions for resuming the original *shtetl* complementary sex roles for men and women. Both are, in this as in many cultures, completely associated with household life, embedded in the matrix of family ties, and evocative of most formative and enduring experiences in the first home. Through ritual and food, the old people momentarily retrieve their past, as individuals and as a culture. A sense of continuity with the past is vital to all integrated adults, especially for the elderly, for immigrants, and for people whose society has been dispersed and whose original culture all but obliterated. Ritual is a common means used for creating experiential access to the past. It is a form that is usually deeply familiar to the people in a culture, often going back to their earliest memories. And it is, by its very nature, a form that interferes with ordinary perceptions of time and change. By its repetitiveness and formality, it is an assertion of order and predictability, an expression of the "tradition," *per se*, whatever its content. Whatever else it communicates, ritual is always a statement about continuity.*

In religious and domestic rituals, Jews are able to experience pro-

---

*For a more detailed discussion of the capacity of ritual to alter time and communicate order, see Moore and Myerhoff (1977).

Figure 9. A woman from the Center with a portrait of her mother, from Russia.

foundly meaningful connections, on many levels: with their ancient forebears, with their biological parents, with fellow Jews, and with themselves at other points in their individual histories, particularly as children. Ritual may be an occasion of personal integration, in which one is aware that he/she is the same person now that he/she was long ago, despite so much change, in one's body and one's world. Ritual takes up the task of allowing for an experience of continuity, for it provides the opportunities for the most basic, cherished symbols to become vivified, active, and transformative.

Bertha provided a particularly articulate statement about the personal integration made available to her in the course of the Sabbath ceremony of lighting candles:

> Do you know what it means to me when I am called to the candles? I'll tell you. When I was a little girl, every Friday I would stand this way, beside my mother when she would light the candles. She cried and I cried. We would be alone in the house, everything warm and clean with all the good smells of

the food around us. We were poor but we always had something special. We were fresh from the *mikvah*,* and I would save my best ribbons for Fridays. Mama would braid my hair very tight, to last through the Sabbath without being combed. We always wore our best clothes, whatever we had. To this day, when I feel the heat of the candles on my face and I cover my eyes and begin the prayer, I feel my mother's hands on my cheeks. Then we are reunited again.

It is in the context of two domestic events—the Sabbath meal and preparing and serving food—that the childhood *shtetl* sex roles reappear. At these times, the contemporary adaptations of men and women are suspended and the old forms, practiced by the peoples' parents and grandparents, are observed. The men are in power on Fridays, control-

*Much Jewish ritual takes up the need to provide opportunities for experiencing a sense of being One People, despite geographical and temporal separations. For further discussion, see R.-E. Prell-Foldes (1973).

Figure 10. A painter known as "Tatte Moshe" ("Father Moses"—a play on "Grandma Moses") with his iconographic depiction of Adam and Eve, the first parents.

ling the participation of women in the religious ritual of the *Oneg Shab-bat*, and in turn, the women dominate and control the men in the luncheons. Both men and women recognize that power is sometimes abused, but that this does not necessarily lead to questions of legitimacy of the roles and of the rights and obligations associated with them. Abe's statement after the *Kahal* luncheon is illustrative: "Those women think that they can do what they want with us. They bring out a bowl of *tsimis* and expect us to fall over dead. And why not? Where else can a man get real *tsimis* these days? Not for a dollar fifty, not for a hundred and fifty!" This is the woman's opportunity to give and withhold, for who can do without her cooking? The men, like the women, vibrate with excitement during the meals. They are animated and bold. They encourage the women to rush about perspiring, carrying the heavy, steaming bowls. They demand their due portion imperiously, inflame the competition between women, and acknowledge their physicality with a kiss or a pinch, or an amiable slap on the bottom. Their pleasure has a boyish tone, and one can imagine their feelings when the aroma and taste of a

Figure 11. Two men and a woman seated on a bench, slightly separated from each other, almost as they would be if seated in a synagogue; they are awaiting the beginning of a funeral ceremony.

rarely available, familiar, cherished morsel fill nostrils and mouths. Surely it brings them their past, a recollection of all the women in their homes who cared for them and bossed them around, blandishing them with food and love. Proust long ago demonstrated beyond all doubt that food—like ritual—has the capacity to take one back to the past, unfolding an entire lost world, not only referred to but relived.

The original sex roles, retrieved from their childhood culture, are available for certain occasions. It is not unlikely that both men and women continue to value those old roles and would choose to follow them on a regular basis if given the choice. The old women have developed alternative roles now, as they did in the *shtetls* of Eastern Europe, in response to the circumstances in which they have found themselves. There is no consistent ideological support for the women's new roles; they do not seem to regard their autonomy and competence with particular pride. As always, they are merely "making do." But it seems that "making do" is a very suitable means for adapting to their status and situation as marginal, old, and poor. Inevitably, one contrasts them with the men, who seem to have more difficulty with many matters that the women take for granted. The question may be asked of these people and perhaps of others in similar circumstances: Are old women better off than old men, and, if so, why?

6. Men and Women: Present Roles in Present Circumstances

Formerly, in *shtetl* culture, male and female roles were reciprocal and men and women interdependent, though men were more esteemed and ideally, at least, more powerful. In the present circumstances, it seems that the old woman's role has enlarged while the old man's has shrunk. The old woman has taken over many tasks and prerogatives previously belonging to the male world, particularly leadership functions. With the exception of a few religious rituals, the women are quite independent and have no need of the men, except in the token, rather superficial way described earlier. The women seem to thrive compared to the men, who grow quieter as the females become more energetic, robust, and self-directed, more engaged in the life around them and more involved with others. In discussion both men and women complain a great deal about their fates. Men are more often bitter, lonely, and depressed, whereas the women are more angry, but stoical and resigned to their difficulties. It does seem as though the women have made a better adjustment in old age than the men.

Women in the *shtetl* (and some would say women in all cultures) were emotional or expressive leaders *par excellence.** They were responsible for nurturance, for interpersonal relations, and for what might be called, in contemporary parlance, quality-of-life concerns. The women's specialty was maintenance of others, the emotional ambience in the home, the general and diffuse work of attending to the well-being of intimates, responding to the totality of their human needs. Men had the responsibility of providing for the family's worldly and spiritual state. In the middle years, women were withdrawn from public and economic affairs and the men became the exclusive link between family and society. The man's family leadership, psychology, and cognitive approach to life were more problem-oriented, more goal-directed, focused, and emotionally neutral than those of his wife. His responsibilities were instrumental where his wife's were expressive.†

Retired people generally have most of their difficulties with instrumental roles. Their essential link to the public sector, the job, has been severed. They lose all that goes with being identified with a job—money, of course, but also a sense of self-worth, social contacts, a schedule, location, and membership in the social structure. The life allocated to the retired in our society, for men and women, is expressive. Their entire time is expected to be spent in recreation, taking care of themselves, and socializing. These activities are often demeaned by men who regard them as trivial—women's work—and they rarely have had occasions for acquiring skills at such activities. The instrumental role of the husband/father in our society is completely demolished for the retired male. But the expressive role, regularly occupied by women, not only continues to be viable in old age but becomes *the* full-time role for both sexes in many communities of American retired persons. It is no wonder that women are better than men at being old.

There are other factors that account for women's seeming advantage over men. That these old women are marginal people thrice over could be important. All the people are marginal at present, being poor and old. And they have always been ethnically marginal, as Jews, in the Old Country, where anti-Semitism was official, relentless, and overt, and in this country as "greenhorns." The men, however, were uniformly regarded as superior to the women of their own society and thus

---

*Zelditch, Parsons, and other American sociologists believe that the expressive–instrumental dichotomy is a universal arrangement for allocating family roles to women and men, respectively. It is found in many cultures though several scholars question its universality.

†Some psychologists, Bakan (1966) and Chodorow (1974) among them, describe male–female differences of cognitive style in a fashion that corroborates and reflects the Zelditch–Parsons instrumental–expressive distinction. Whether universal or not, innate or learned, the cluster of characteristics suggested for men's and women's roles in the family are certainly stable and widespread.

Figure 12. A strong grandmother.

were caught in a conflicting set of hierarchies. They were exalted within their immediate group but disdained outside of it. In contrast, the status of the women was unambiguous: they were on the bottom, on all counts. Perhaps the simplicity and consistency of this made it easier for women to work out personal solutions. And certainly, it gave those who failed to do so every excuse necessary, all in terms of social definitions rather than individual shortcomings.

Compared to the women, the old men in this group are less connected, less needed, by each other, by women, by children. Moreover, they have not been prepared for recognizing their need for others, except in economic terms that are no longer applicable. The men are less enmeshed in social and kinship networks, less engaged in all kinds of interpersonal relations than the women. Indeed, the allotment to women of responsibility for expressive leadership has made them experts at relationships. Roles based on nurturant functions are durable and expandable. They can last a lifetime, and there is always someone around who needs taking care of. The nurturance role has two added advantages: putting the caretaker one-up in terms of never being the worst-off person in the world, and arousing obligations and sentiments in the cared-for which may develop into deep and long-lasting associations. By definition, expressive roles take account of the quality of people's emotions, and are more likely to expand than are narrowly construed instrumental transactions.

Another part of the nurturant role advantageous to old women is their experience in self-maintenance. If one's basic biological requirements have been provided by others, it comes as a shock to have to do these things for oneself. For the women, getting rid of their garbage, doing their laundry, mending, shopping, cleaning, cooking are not troublesome. On the contrary, this work is a steady source of satisfaction. (Bessie, for example, mentioned that her arthritis was growing worse. She did not mind too much that she was no longer able to carry heavy objects or hold a paint brush, even though she loved her art classes. But when she realized that she could no longer make her own bed, she said, that was when she wept.) The adage "A woman's work is never done" calls attention to the continuity of woman's tasks on a daily basis, but it applies no less to the continuity over a lifetime. In those instances where the old men have needed to perform maintenance tasks for others, usually their ailing or incapacitated wives, they are revolted and inept. But incontinent or invalid husbands present no surprises to the women. Changing diapers is not a shocking affair to these women, whether for a child or an old person.

Since childhood, the women have always been *bricoleurs*, as Lévi-Strauss (1970) calls the constructors of systems who use leftover materials, as does a handyman. These women have long known how to devise entire though miniature worlds out of their peripheral status and tasks. They were made of smaller and homelier materials but built in proportion, as complex and compelling as the external, male-dominated realm. In her own miniature world, the woman was in charge, using time and energy according to her own lights. Within the structured points of her day in the household, she did a great many highly diverse tasks, all at the same time, always expecting to be interrupted, never finding full closure, but hastening from one activity to the next, watching her work come undone as soon as it was completed. The standards for performance had to be more flexible and individually administered.*

Men did not usually work in isolation and thus were not as self-

---

*Some men who are taking over women's nurturant roles evidently find the lack of clear-cut "performance standards" in child care among the more troubling parts of the job. A young American psychiatrist recently delivered a paper in which he detailed his experiences as a "house-husband" when his wife went back to school. He described the continual interruptions in his work (or the expectation of being about to be interrupted) combined with never being sure when he had "done a good job" as being harder to bear than anything he had had to deal with in his years of medical practice. (American Psychiatric Association, Miami, 1976.)

regulating as the women. The loss of the world of work for men meant they lost the arena that dictated their use of time and energy in an absolute and external manner. Within the household, it was true that women were often tightly tied to biological rhythms of small children and had to repond also to the outside scheduling of other adult family members. But within this framework there was considerable choice and discretion, and a gradual lifting of nonpersonally generated limits took place as the children matured. The nearest equivalent to male retirement is the mother's "empty nest." But this phenomenon is less abrupt and irreversible than is retirement from a job. Her children need her less in small increments. And even after they have physically left the home, they return for her services, favors, meals, advice, baby-sitting, care of clothing, and the like. Before and after "the empty nest" she has more time to adjust, to establish her independence, and then accommodate to the changes.

Let us consider biology too. Perhaps women are more prepared for the inevitable infirmities of old age by a lifetime of acceptance of their bodily limits and changes. Initially, in this culture the little girl observes herself to be physically weaker than her brothers and nothing she does can alter the fact. With the onset of menstruation, again she finds that her body intrudes itself on her wishes and must be taken into account in her plans. Soon after, the cycle of childbirth and nursing begins, and once more her projects perforce take her bodily limits into account. Finally, menopause interrupts her activities and her fantasies; she must always make choices, decisions, and self-interpretation with her physiological base.

All this is good schooling for what lies ahead. The old men in this group have been able to indulge in more independent self-conceptions. Among the most agonizing of the difficulties they face is their daily awareness of being physically limited and, ultimately, dominated by "forces outside themselves," beyond their control. Old age is a brutal check on omnipotence fantasies. The discovery of their mortality, late in life, it seems, shocks the male ego far more severely than the female. The women have always known their bodies have a life of their own. Women always knew about needing others (especially men) but often the men (generously assisted by wives and mothers) have been able to overlook the forms and frequencies of their corresponding dependencies. It appears that for a woman to accept help from others has entirely different meanings than for men. An old woman in this community is more patient and grateful in allowing someone else to cut up her food, help her rise from a chair, or take her arm over a rough spot in the sidewalk. The men accept help when they must, but it is apparent that it costs them dearly to do so.

One of the tasks and pleasures for the elderly is life review (see Butler 1964), during which they take stock of their histories, estimating what went well, what could have been better, what remains, and what counts in the end. The men have devoted most of their lives primarily to two concerns, which "do not count" in their present reference group: making money and religious study. The meaning of the latter has been lost along with their religious community; life in America is a secular affair. The money they made has been long gone. Some still have savings, but the norms of the subculture prevent them from conspicuous demonstrations of wealth. Money brings the well-off no rewards in superior standards of living or recognition in this community; indeed, they are often suspect and resented for not being poor. And they are not permitted to engage in one of the most enjoyable and prestigious activities of the group: bargain hunting. The person who appears well turned out in a thrift shop purchase is much admired, more for his/her acumen than for appearance. The well-off man who gives a large amount of money to charity is awarded less admiration than the poor one who, by discovering a day-old bakery within walking distance, benefits the whole group. The former is only doing what is expected.

What does count for these people, in reviewing the merits of a life? Above all, rearing children who are well educated and well married, good citizens, good parents in their own right, children who consider themselves as Jews and raise their children to be Jews, and who respect their aged parents. Again the old women have the deck stacked in their favor. They have maintained closer ties with their children than have the men; moreover, the women are considered more responsible than the men for "how the children turned out." The men paid the bills, the women raised the children, and to them goes praise or blame. Since few women consider their children as complete washouts, they almost always gain more satisfaction than grief from considering their children as the important work of their lives.

There is a final comment to be made concerning the different bases for evaluation of one's lifework, comparing men and women. It is often said that the contingent nature of woman's work makes it intrinsically less satisfying, and that this is why it is consistently and permanently devalued by societies all over the world. Women are identified as responsible for the work of nature, and culture is officially the work of men. Women, it is felt, concur with men in viewing cultural projects as the move valuable enterprise. This opposition between nature and culture has been much discussed, by Lévi-Strauss (1969), by Simone de Beauvoir (1953), and recently by Sherry Ortner (1974). Women's projects are immanent compared with the lasting, transforming projects of men.

Her works are concrete as opposed to male abstractness. Hers involve subjectivity, personalism, and particularism. Says de Beauvoir:

> ... in her heart of hearts [a woman] finds confirmation of the masculine pretensions. She joins the men in the festivals that celebrate the successes and victories of the males. Her misfortune is to have been biologically destined for the repetition of Life, when even her own life does not carry within itself reasons for being, reasons that are more important than life itself (1953:59).

Is it surely true that women consider their work lesser "in their heart of hearts"? Woman's work is very complex and subtle, not made of the kinds of victories and successes celebrated in war dances and hunting parties. The work is not clear-cut; unequivocal successes and failures are relatively rare. Every mother is continually reminded as to how much of her "product" is beyond her control. She is facilitator, mediator, not maker. *Outcome* is not an accurate term in reference to people, who as long as they live offer surprises and are full of potentiality.

Women are kept humble by the nature of their everyday activities. They are immersed in unglamorous stuff—the mess of life itself, bodily excretions and necessities, transient and trivial details that vanish and

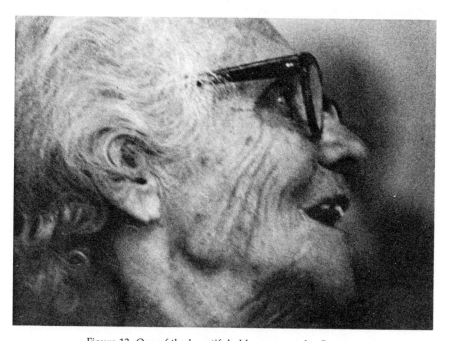

Figure 13. One of the beautiful old women at the Center.

reappear every moment. But this does not mean that a woman is not fully aware of the enormous importance of offering food, producing and raising children. Why, then, do we not hear about it? Why is there no public, general female statement vaunting these tasks? I would claim that there is a set of understandings, regularly stated and shared among women, concerning the meaning and value of their conventional functions. These are communicated but in a form not easy to recognize. They are enacted nonverbally in the quiet acknowledgments that pass between women in their work.

Because their tasks are particularized, concrete, embedded, and subjective, there is no natural desire (not to mention opportunity) to make them into platforms, public festivals, ideological treatises. They are known as part of living rather than discussions about living, and it would be inconsistent to formulate them as enduring, collective principles. These understandings are a kind of underground culture, quietly transmitted in situations, no less treasured than the starkly evident, grandiose cultural productions we customarily attend. They are real but rather easy to overlook. They continue through the life cycle, and it may be that they reemerge as essential aids in later life. These old women I have described communicate a quiet conviction and satisfaction with themselves. Perhaps because they did what had to be done, and knew that without what they did there would be nothing and no one. This is no scant comfort in looking back at one's lifework. Woman's work provided them with an end and a means. Perhaps this is the secret shared by these old women, who expected little and found more than did the men, who expected everything and are left now with much less.

ACKNOWLEDGMENTS

The research on which this chapter is based took place between 1972 and 1975. Information reported here is drawn in part from the University of Southern California Social and Cultural Contexts of Aging research project (V.L. Bengtson, principal investigator; B. Myerhoff, project director). This program is supported by grants from the National Science Foundation's RANN program (# APR 21178) and by the 1907 Foundation of the United Parcel Service. Conclusions are those of the author and do not necessarily reflect the views of NSF or the 1907 Foundation. All proper names of individuals and organizations are fictitious.

References

Adler, Rachel. 1973. The Jew who wasn't there: *Halacha* and the Jewish woman. *Response: A Contemporary Jewish Review 8* (18):77–83.

Bakan, David. 1966. The quality of human existence: Isolation and communication in Western man. In M. Z. Rosaldo and L. Lamphere (eds.), *Women, Culture, and Society*. Stanford: Stanford University Press.

Baum, Charlotte. 1973. What made Yetta work? The economic role of Eastern European Jewish women in the family. *Response: A Contemporary Jewish Review 8*(18):32–38.

Baum, Charlotte, Paula Hyman, and Sonya Michel. 1975. *The Jewish Woman in America*. New York: Dial.

de Beauvoir, Simone. 1953. *The Second Sex*. New York: Alred A. Knopf.

Butler, Robert, 1964. The life review: An interpretation of reminiscence in the aged. In B. L. Neugarten (ed.), *Middle Age and Aging*. Chicago: University of Chicago Press.

Chodorow, Nancy. 1974. Family structure and feminine personality. In M. Z. Rosaldo and L. Lamphere (eds.), *Women, Culture, and Society*. Stanford: Stanford University Press. 43–66.

Eliade, Mircea. 1969. *The Two and the One*. J. M. Cohen (trans.). New York and Evanston: Harper Torchbooks.

Herberg, Will. 1955. *Protestant-Catholic-Jew: An Essay in American Religious Sociology*. New York: Anchor.

Hyman, Paula. 1973. The other half: Women in Jewish tradition. *Response: A Contemporary Jewish Review 8*(18):67–76.

Lévi Strauss, Claude. 1969. *The Elementary Structures of Kinship*. J. H. Bell and J. R. von Sturmer (trans.), Rodney Needham (ed.). Boston: Beacon Press.

Lévi-Strauss, Claude. 1970. *The Savage Mind*. Chicago: University of Chicago Press.

Moore, Sally and Barbara Myerhoff. 1977. *Secular Ritual: Forms and Meanings*. Assen: Von Gorcum Press.

Myerhoff, Barbara and Deena Metzger. 1977. At the beck and call of life: Women's roles in a changing society. *American Journal of Psychiatry*. Forthcoming.

Ortner, Sherry B. 1974. Is female to male as nature is to culture? In M. Z. Rosaldo and L. Lamphere (eds.), *Woman, Culture, and Society*. Stanford: Stanford University Press. 67–87.

Prell-Foldes, Riv-Ellen. 1973. The unity of oneness: Unification and opposition in Jewish ritual. Master's thesis, University of Chicago.

Sontag, Susan. 1975. The double standard of aging. In *No Longer Young: The Older Woman in America*. Occasional Papers in Gerontology, No. 1. University of Michigan Institute of Gerontology. 31–39.

Zborowski, Mark and Elizabeth Herzog. 1962. *Life Is with People: The Culture of the Shtetl*. New York: Schocken Books.

Zelditch, Morris. 1955. Role differentiation in the nuclear family: A comparative study. In T. Parsons and R. F. Bales (eds,), *Family, Socialization and Interpretation Process*. Glencoe: Free Press. 307–351.

Part III
Dual Aspects of Women

Archetypic Destruction

12

JUDITH HOCH-SMITH

Radical Yoruba Female Sexuality

The Witch and the Prostitute

> In the beginning, God gave the world to the witches.
> YORUBA GELEDE DANCER

> The horseleach hath two daughters, crying, Give, give. There are
> three things that are never satisfied. Yea, four things say not, It is
> enough: The grave; and the barren womb; the earth that is not filled
> with water; and the fire that saith not, It is enough.
> PROVERBS XXX:15–16

> All witchcraft comes from carnal lust, which is in women insatiable.
> THE MALLEUS MALEFICARUM

1. Introduction

Ritual and symbolic representations of women in many cultures are
metaphorically grounded in feminine reproductive processes, processes
that have been universally designated as both mystical and carnal. In her
mystical aspect, woman is represented as an active medium or vehicle of
creative energy who transforms that energy into life-forms; in her carnal
aspect she is represented as being capable of transforming life-forms
into malevolent energy directed toward the destruction, rather than creation, of the universe. This latter image is focused particularly in beliefs
surrounding the witch, about whom—whether in medieval Britain and
Europe, contemporary Africa, or Freudian psychology—it is thought
that the witch threatens, exhausts, or steals the genitals or semen, or

JUDITH HOCH-SMITH · Assistant Professor of Anthropology, Florida International
University, Miami, Florida.

partakes of living flesh and blood, in order to increase her malevolent power. The image of witch depicted in many male-dominated societies is a blatant condemnation of female sexuality. Such condemnation is related to the threat to male-dominated society posed by the independence and authority of women.

1.1. European Witchcraft

Although the punishment of female witches did not originate in the European Middle Ages, it was perhaps there that it became elevated to the level of sexual genocide. During those centuries some writers estimate that millions of women were sadistically tortured, deceived, and executed by an educated male organization working for the Catholic church under the direction of a manual entitled *The Malleus Maleficarum* (the *Witch Hammer*). Written by two distinguished Dominican friars at the behest of a papal bull issued in 1484 by Innocent VIII, the *Maleficarum*—quoting, among others, St. Jerome, Cicero, Socrates, Seneca, Verterius Maximus, and the Bible—constructed the most defamatory indictment of the female character ever written. Among its scathing libels appear declarations that woman is more carnal than man, more deceitful, credulous, light-minded, impressionable, and slippery-tongued (Kramer and Sprenger 1971:43–44). Witches are blamed for a multitude of crimes: for bewitching men into inordinate love or hatred; for freezing up the generative forces in both man and woman; for purloining the penises of their lovers and enemies; for causing hailstorms, killing cattle, flying through the air devouring infant children, and consuming the purses and strengths of men while causing them to forsake God (1971:46–47, 66, 106). Speaking of sexual desire, the two friars exclaim, "If the world could be rid of women, we should not be without God in our intercourse" (1971:46). The *Witch Hammer* was used by witch-finders, inquisitors, and judges throughout Western Europe and England passing through 30 editions between 1487 and 1669 on the leading German, French, and Italian presses.

The Middle Ages were to leave a taint on the female character which is still perceptible today. Some authors have become unwitting apologists for female libel by arguing that the practical significance of witch persecution was to "shift responsibility for the crisis of late medieval society from both church and state to imaginary demons in human form" (Harris 1974:238). Others view witchcraft as a "fantasy" phenomenon produced solely through the application of hallucinatory herbal unguents, which carried a woman into imaginary realms of flight, sexual orgies, and cannibalism (Harner 1973; Harris 1974; Baroja 1965). One popular view describes the women who would use these unguents in order to experience witchcraft as "insignificant people in their normal environment, who wanted to be far superior to, and very different from, what they really were" (Baroja 1965:156), a description not unlike that given of the ambitious, light-minded, impressionable woman of the *Witch Hammer*.

Although witches may have utilized hallucinogens, that fact in no way dismisses witchcraft as a mere "mental projection" or emotional fantasy, but simply points out that altered states of consciousness may have been ritually utilized by women in the practice of their craft, as they have been by other shamans, healers, and sorcerers throughout the world. More to the point, as two authors argue, women in the Middle Ages were skilled healers, herbalists, and midwives who were systematically suppressed by the male establishment in their monopolization of health care (Ehrenreich and English 1973:2). Ehrenreich and English see the women of the Middle Ages as people's doctors who cured with herbs and ritual, attended at births, and in general helped a populace with no doctors and no hospitals, but who were made the object of a male ruling class campaign of terror which ended in the debasement of female status and the institutional monopolization of medicine (1973:2–8). They point out that women were "accused of female sexuality" and that all power derived from their sexuality (1973:9) This sexuality was related to the power of the devil and was in direct opposition to the church. According to the *Witch Hammer*, woman's power could also result in extreme goodness when used in the service of male desires. Thus women who could mold themselves to man's needs stayed alive (Savramis 1974) as long as they separated themselves completely from the rich tradition of feminine medicine. In 1527 Paracelsus, the "father of modern medicine," burned his text on pharmaceuticals, confessing that he "had learned from the Sorceress all he knew" (Ehrenreich and English 1973:15).

Art, folklore, literature, religion, and mythology continued to bear the characterizations of the nagging, wrathful, ugly witch—who was the darker side of the good mother and wife—long after the last European witch trial in the eighteenth century. Inevitably this view was again institutionalized and sanctified in the early twentieth century by Freud, who considered that most female neurosis was caused by pathological envy of the male organ, rather than something untenable in the social position and treatment of woman (Chesler 1972:75–85). Woman was viewed as inherently inferior to man, more emotional, hysterical, weak, just as her sisters in the Middle Ages had been. She was exhorted to adjust and accept her inferior role in life and often sadistically treated by male therapies that sought to bring her under their control.

1.2. Witchcraft in Africa

Where females gain authority in male-dominated societies in Africa, male suspicion and resentment are focused in the concept of witchcraft, with attitudes, practices, and roles that are strikingly similar to those of the European Middle Ages. In Africa, also, women are "accused" of "female sexuality" by men, and female power is believed to be derived from this sexuality. In Nigeria, Nupe witches are believed to practice cannibalism, fly to nocturnal gatherings, cause illness, make men impotent, and physically weaken men through their active evil wills. Some few men are connected to the female witch cults but their role is merely passive (Nadel 1970:167–169). Nupe women are skilled professional traders who often work at long distances from their homes, during which times they freely take lovers and opt for "voluntary barrenness" through the use of contraceptives. Tradition dictates that men should be the financial heads of households, but in fact many are in debt to their trader wives. The leader of the witches is identified with the titled head of Nupe women in every town, and Nadel concludes that "the whole market organization of the women is in a sense identified with the fantasy organization of witches" (1970:169). Feminine economic independence connotes the inadequacy of men who fear further loss in intercourse with their powerful wives, and thus men belong to a secret society, *ndako gboya*, which punishes witches and threatens female society in general.

Similarly, Zulu wives have a debilitative influence on the health of their husband's patrilineal kinsmen and, as witches, have animal and sexual familiars and take the lives of members of the group. Menstrual blood is a sign of woman's ambivalent fertility: dangerous to all things male, yet highly regarded as a source of mystical prosperity. Gluckman says that the tendency for witches to be women is so widely distributed that it must arise from conditions common to many societies, and he suggests that perhaps it is because women bear and influence the children who will be the competitive heirs for property, prestige, and status formally held by men (1965a:223–225, 1965b:97–100).

In modern West African literature written in English by African males, sexually aggressive prostitutes who are enormously powerful, who leach the strength of men, and who are filled with mystical evil influence are common. Such women are based on stereotypes carried forth from traditional village life. In *Jagua Nana* by the novelist Cyprian Ekwensi, Jagua, a middle-aged "high-life" prostitute, brings about the downfall and eventual death of Freddie, a "young, studious, honest" man. Freddie feels he is being held in "sexual bondage" by Jagua, who can easily make him believe the most capricious lies. Jagua is constantly likened to a witch and Freddie feels she is "weakening" him with medicine. He claims she is his "daily dose of anguish, lust, degradation, and weakness of will" (1969:47), but a few pages later he sinks into the "soft abyss" of the erotic woman (1969:51). Jagua, however, thinks of herself as a mature, independent woman, well-groomed and happy, who after Freddie's death goes to Onitsha to open a shop and become a "market princess" (1969: 105, 207). Jagua is childless and seems unable to bear a child, which contributes to her "witchlike" characteristics. Here, as among the Nupe, we find a correspondence among witch, prostitute, and market woman, a West African phenomenon.

The Yoruba playwright Wole Soyinka creates several of these mystically alluring prosit<ute/witch figures who represent the sexual power that women hold over men. Segi, the beautiful prostitute-owner of a nightclub in *Kongi's Harvest*, comes most quickly to mind. Around her the Executive Secretary's brain is addled and confused, afraid and weakened. Segi is able to come and go invisibly, and to Daodu, her lover, she is like a "silken thread wound deep down my throat," and a "python coiled in wait for rabbits" (1967:32). She is called "a right cannibal of the female species," and a "witch of night clubs" (1967:52). She is a powerful independent woman who organizes the country's prostitutes into an organization that protects Daodu during his Harvest speech, and that is instrumental in overthrowing Kongi. Her role is reminiscent of the prostitute Penda, in Sembene's *God's Bits of Wood*, who is often called witch, but who organizes an important woman's march from Thiès to Dakar during the last day of the general strike.

1.3. Yoruba Witches

The Yoruba of Nigeria provide an excellent example of an African society in which to explore in depth an image of woman as successful businesswoman, who at the same time has a strongly negative mirror image: She is a carnal witch who possesses incredible strength of psychic power with which she attacks male-controlled society.

Yoruba women have been able traditionally to obtain a great deal of economic independence from their husbands through their marketing roles. Money earned is their own, and with it women clothe themselves and their children and often defray their children's school expenses. The market woman who works 16-hour days to put her son through a university in Britain is proverbial. The Yoruba mother is idealized by her children and the relationship between mother and son is said to be often closer than that between husband and wife (Prince 1961:804). Although most Yoruba women are petty traders with only small monthly earnings, a successful trader may own a cloth shop in Ibadan's new commercial district. Such a business represents the highest aspirations of market women; shop owners may be wealthy enough to own cars, make pilgrimages to Mecca, and become influential patrons. There is no equivalent female-dominated profession in the West which combines the high status, regard, and cultural fulfillment associated with marketing among Yoruba women. (A friendship society formed by Yoruba market women is shown in Figure 1.)

Concomitant with feminine economic and personal independence observers have noted that Yoruba husband–wife relationships are strained and the divorce rate high. Lloyd claims that there are several reasons that account for the high rate of divorce among the Yoruba.* First, the Yoruba woman may herself initiate divorce, may repay her own bridewealth if she is a wealthy trader, and always has the prerogative of going to live in her lover's house, a prelude to divorce. Upon marriage her genetricial rights are transferred to her husband's descent group but her jural rights are not. She has a status separate from her husband's descent group and men often fear desertion and denial of their sons for the continuity of the patrilineage (Lloyd 1968:67–82).

In contrast to the strongly positive marketing role of Yoruba women stands the hideously negative role of the woman as witch. The Yoruba witch is thought to be a castrating, evil being who deals in flesh and lives on blood. Yoruba legend says that *Eshu*, the trickster-divinity, gave women their wicked power, the element of chance that he represents explaining the woman-as-witch's ability to malinger and malign the destiny of men. Witches are usually old women, but any woman can become a witch since all women are mystically linked together through their menstrual blood, and power is housed in their abdomens. Witchly power is transmitted invisibly like a breeze, and witches work at night when their souls pass out of their anuses while they are sleeping, and fly about as birds. The flesh of newborn babies is often said to be desired by them, both for consumption and for the construction of powerful

---

*Yoruba divorce rates correspond with those of many matrilineal Bantu people; Ijebu Yoruba divorce rates are higher than those of any peoples for which data are available except the Ndembu (Lloyd 1968:79). Levine (1970) has noted for other African societies the correlation among female economic independence, marital discord, and decline of a patrilineal ethos.

Figure 1. A Yoruba women's society in Ibadan meets on the morning of an *Egungun* (men's society) festival. The women wear identical cloth (aṣọ ẹgbẹ) which represents their mutual membership in the society.

charms. Witches may conspire to have a new woman join their midst; if so, it is believed that they prepare a stew in which infant flesh is used and serve it to the unwitting woman who will, when she partakes, thenceforth be a witch. The word for witch (*Aje*) may be a contraction of *Iya je,* meaning "mother eat," but it is so horrible to utter that witches are referred to as *Awon iya,* "mothers," or simply as *Aiye,* "the world."

Witches are commonly thought to interfere with reproduction. Prince says that impotence is common among Yoruba males and it is the prevalent idea that this is the work of witches (1961:798–799). A witch may steal the penis of a man and have intercourse with it, with herself or with another woman, or she may visit men at night and tamper with their testicles. Also, she can stop the flow of menstrual blood in a woman, since all women are interconnected, and she may obstruct the passage of a child from a womb or cause barrenness in a woman.

Men placate the witches by joining *Gelede,* a cult in which powerful old women are the ritual heads and men dressed in exaggerated female costumes dance to please their "mothers." Most men who belong to the cult have joined because of reproductive disorders, either their own or perhaps their wives'. In one *Gelede* dance that I saw in Ife, an elderly woman dressed in indigo-dyed cloth repeatedly switched the transvestite dancers with a wooden stick. Men who dance in *Gelede* say that "in the beginning God gave the world to the witches," giving them power to both create and kill. Impotent men, who have lost what regenerative power they had, imitate by dress and dance in *Gelede* the female image in which the regenerative and decadent aspects of the mystical life-force meet. Their transvestitism is a ritual intercession or mediation between their static male state and the active condition of the female life-force.

Today it is said that witches have powerful societies which male traditional doctors are not strong enough to defeat. Prince (1961, 1964) has documented their existence in Ibadan and nearly any Ibadan can relate stories about witches. It is felt that many wealthy men have gained their position by procuring charms from their "mothers" and that most important men have an "old woman" whom they listen to. Prince tells a story about a powerful political leader, killed in an automobile accident, who at one time kept an old woman in his house who told him what to do and where to go, and "when the time would be safe." Later he gave up taking her advice and was destroyed by the powerful "medicine" of his opponents (1961:799).

2. The Carnal Witch in Yoruba Contemporary Theater

It is perhaps in modern Yoruba drama, presented by predominantly male touring companies in the largest cities of western Nigeria, that the most contemporary folk interpretation of the carnal female can be found.* In these plays "accusations" of female sexuality abound and can be most clearly seen in five feminine dramatis personae: the prostitute, the co-wife, the witch, the half human/half animal, and the transvestite. We will look at these female characters in Yoruba plays and in the

*Research on the Yoruba theater was carried out by the author in Ibadan during 1971–1972. There are approximately ten performing groups in Ibadan. Plays are presented to large and enthusiastic audiences in an auditorium in Ibadan's new commercial district. Major theatrical companies also have weekly television shows on WNTV, Ibadan. Yoruba commercial theater dates from the late 1940s and early 1950s in both Lagos and Ibadan. Actors and directors have almost all been employed as carpenters, tailors, electricians, and the like before becoming actors. Major groups present about ten plays a year. Directors, audiences, and actors are all mostly male. Theater groups perform mainly to audiences composed of poor, wage-earning male workers whose fathers were rural farmers but whose own aspirations are directed toward the material life-style of the urban-educated elite, a life-style that they have no chance of obtaining due both to the now quasi-hereditary nature of the elite and to the almost stagnant economy in which there is little development in the rural sector and an expanding but very small industrial sector, which can provide only a minimum number of employment opportunities for the large numbers of urban migrants (Lloyd 1973:1).

conclusion will explore similarities between the characters and their relationship to the image of women in traditional Yoruba society.

2.1. The Prostitute

In the opening scene of a popular play entitled *Sixpence Owner of a Suitcase (Sisi Onigarawa)* by Ogunde Theater, a traditionally attired man, Mr. Alebiosu, is conversing with his poorly dressed male servant. Mr. Alebiosu,* who has been working for the government-run railroad for many years saving his money to get married, tells his servant that when he marries his new wife she will have to stay in the "bathroom" after the marriage for eight days, and wash with black soap. Alebiosu's statements reveal that he is a "bushman," a person without education, expecting his wife to conform to many traditional customs, such as staying inside his compound for several days after marriage, and washing with the traditional Yoruba black soap, which has magical as well as simple cleaning uses.

Alebiosu has sent money to his brother in the country to negotiate for a wife on his behalf, but Alebiosu's younger sister arrives and tells him that the money that was sent to his brother was not spent for the purpose of matrimony. The damask, handwoven cloth, lace, shoes, earrings, watches, and other goods that he sent as gifts for his potential wife were distributed among greedy relatives. Alebiosu's brother roofed his house with iron sheets, himself took a new wife, and with Alebiosu's money invested in his farm, produced cocoa pods as big as coconuts.

Alebiosu's houseboy chides him for acting as a rube in sending someone else the money for the wife, instead of choosing a woman himself. He claims that in a city like Ibadan, Alebiosu could have procured six wives for his money, rather than one wife from such a "remote" place. Alebiosu, much chastened, replies, "We who have come from remote villages still have not recovered from acting like bushmen. That's why this thing happens to us." The innocent Alebiosu, having attempted to marry in the customary fashion, resorts to finding a wife among modern women:

> ALEBIOSU: Now I will look for a modern girl who walks with her buttocks going from one side to another. There will be smoke coming out of her mouth [cigarettes]. She will wear trousers, shirt, blouses.
> HOUSEBOY: These girls will "shave your head and put paint there." [Literally: take all you have and leave nothing.] Let me see if your trousers are touching your toes now. Soon these girls will change it to knickers.

---

*The name Alebiosu, which means the "light of the moon," emphasizes the man's pure moral character.

These lines represent a typical Yoruba male description of modern women. Alebiosu is strangely captivated by this picture of the mulcting female and tells his houseboy to find him such a woman.

The houseboy says that he will negotiate on his master's behalf with a girl he sees in the morning at the market. She wears "good cloth" and "spectacles." The houseboy says he will sit down and smile, cross his legs, and whistle, and she will think he is the richest man in Ibadan. He says he will also carry a "plate" with him, so that she will know that they don't use "pots" to "chop" from in Alebiosu's household.*

In the next scene, the houseboy meets the girl and invites her to Alebiosu's house. Alebiosu informs the girl of his intentions:

> ALEBIOSU: I sent my boy for you because I have an important matter to tell you. I am a rich man so I am calling you to take your wealth from my property. My houseboy will tell you the same so you know it's true.
>
> GIRL: All right, I will stay. I will put my suitcase in the hallway.
>
> ALEBIOSU: Now we'll have a party. I've sent 100 invitations to Dahomey, 100 to Ghana, and to the Gold Coast, 275.†
>
> GIRL: What about the preparations for the celebration?
>
> ALEBIOSU: We will have three-pennies worth of meat for everyone. We will get vegetables from the roadside. There will be three-pennies for tomatoes, peppers, and onions. We can borrow salt from people in the compound.
>
> GIRL: We're rich, but you say we must look for food by the road, spend only three-pennies on meat, and beg for salt!! The market items will cost at least fifty pounds [150 dollars]!
>
> ALEBIOSU: Where will I get fifty pounds? Fifty pounds will buy all of Ibadan!
>
> GIRL: Now I see your secret: You haven't gotten married because you *economize*.

The modern woman criticizes Alebiosu for his financial conservatism and caution, demanding extensive expenditures for the wedding celebration.

The woman eventually agrees to the marriage, but just after the final arrangements take place Alebiosu receives a letter from his employer transferring him to Port Harcourt.‡ Before he departs Alebiosu leaves his new wife in the care of his best friend. His houseboy warns him that it is a mistake to leave his wife with a "wealthy well-known" friend.

---

*Crossing one's legs while sitting, whistling, eating from plates, and eyeglasses are all associated with European or high-status, educated behavior.
†Calling Ghana the Gold Coast is a "bushman" error.
‡A city in southeastern Nigeria.

After Alebiosu has departed, the friend talks to the new wife:

WIFE: What is a rich man like Alebiosu doing in a poor house, with poor clothes and poor food?

FRIEND: Why did you marry Alebiosu? He's full of "management."

WIFE: (Repeats all the instructions about buying the meager food supplies for the party.)

FRIEND: I've financed Alebiosu for fifteen days of every month after his small salary is gone.

WIFE: I've noticed the "color" of Alebiosu and there is no sign of richness there. But I can see you are rich.

FRIEND: We do not "manage" like Alebiosu. [Shows her a fistful of wadded bills and hands it to her.] Do what you like with this!

Before Alebiosu is gone more than a few minutes, his new wife agrees to an illicit relationship with his friend, after vehemently denouncing Alebiosu for his stinginess and backward ways.

After the wife's new "lover" leaves, a female visitor arrives—*Bisi*, the wife's best friend. The two women devise a mercenary scheme to procure more money from the wife's "two husbands," Alebiosu and his friend:

BISI: What are you doing here?

WIFE: I've gone on "transfer." The man I married before I came here is gone. I spent all his money and now he is bankrupt. He was educated but now all that remains is his "spoken English." Now I'm with another. I met his houseboy at a bus stop and we were like two cars colliding. All that is left is for me to have a baby for him. But I have no time for that.

BISI: I know a trick for fooling men and making them think you're pregnant. It's just arrived in our circle of "Sixpence Women." The new trick involves using a calabash as a sign of pregnancy. When will your husband arrive?

WIFE: In six months.

FRIEND: This calabash is just six months. When your husband comes you'll have to shiver and cry, "I'm suffering," and the like, to make him think you're pregnant.

Bisi ties a calabash under the wrapper of the wife's clothes, concealing it completely so that her stomach looks swollen as if in pregnancy. The wife then writes to her husband telling him that she is pregnant, demanding 50 pounds in order to pay for a doctor's care. She also asks for 150 pounds for a "new preparation" (drugs) for the baby.

In the next scene, approximately six months have passed and Alebiosu's friend is visiting the wife. The wife, wearing a large calabash, accuses Alebiosu's friend of being the "owner of the pregnant." He is not reluctant to accept the responsibility and cries, "Oh, I'm lucky my wife got pregnant!" Immediately his "wife" begins demanding money. The wife exploits the situation, demanding cash for medical care from

Alebiosu's false friend and thereby "doubling" her profit. She tells him the doctor's fee is 50 pounds and the treatment 200 pounds. But she continues doubling the sums of money until she reaches the incredible sum of 1,000 pounds. The duped friend says, "This is only the first child! The next six will cost me 7,000 pounds in all!" He leaves the stage and returns indulgently with the money and also powdered eggs, chocolate drink, and butter, telling her to eat such food every day.*

After the friend leaves, Alebiosu himself arrives. He too is elated by his wife's pregnancy and agrees to pay her expenses. Alas, his friend soon returns to brag of his conquest, and the identity of the genitor is hotly contested. Alebiosu's friend exclaims: "So! Your wife is pregnant. Did you mail it to her from Port Harcourt? I am the owner of tJ.e pregnancy!!" A fight ensues while the wife screams, "Please! The doctor has ordered that this pregnancy is not for shouting-o." Suddenly, as she screams and raises her arms, the calabash falls to the floor from under her wrapped skirt. She runs from the stage in horrified disbelief. The houseboy, stricken with laughter, imitates her pregnancy, which has "fallen off." Alebiosu moans: "I sent money to my country home and received no wife. When I go to hotel to find a wife, the women there change my long pants to knickers. And now my baby has changed to a calabash."

The wife soon reappears on the stage and with lowered head tells her husband that she is going away. The "innocent" Alebiosu pleads with her not to go, pointing out that she is not the only person to give birth to a "calabash." He explains that "some women even go to hospitals and give birth to monkeys and snakes." Alebiosu's naïveté contrasts sharply with his wife's worldliness. The sophisticated woman allows him to "comfort" her on the "loss" of her baby and she takes her suitcase back to the bedroom.

When she returns, Alebiosu tells her that he has been pensioned off by the railroad with 40,000 pounds. The wife is wild with glee. She immediately demands lace, woven cloth, damask, *bata* (manufactured) shoes, and jewelry so that no one can "abuse her" (speak boldly of her poverty). In an aside to the audience she thanks God "for helping me to bring my suitcase back to the house where money has arrived again."

In the next scene the wife and Bisi again devise a scheme to part the simple husband from his money. Later, the wife tells Alebiosu that she has thought of two ways with which they can increase his retirement pension. First, part of the money should be given to Bisi, who will

---

*These English food items are associated with prosperity and status, and with the modern woman who must be fed "modern" food.

purchase and trade imported cloth for them in all regions of Nigeria. Second, a "money doubler" should be summoned, a man who is endowed with the power to make "20,000 pounds become 40,000 pounds and 30,000 pounds become 60,000 pounds." Alebiosu innocently agrees to both plans, saying to the wife, "You are sensible." Both Bisi and her "friend," the "money doubler," quickly appear and take their respective share of the soon-to-be-poor man's pension.

In the final scene, Alebiosu is alone on the stage with a trunk in which he is to find his "doubled" money. When he opens it, it is full of scrap metal, the money doubler (who has left Ibadan) having retained the real cash. A messenger then arrives to inform Alebiosu that Bisi's truck, with all of Alebiosu's imported cloth in it, was involved in an accident in which everything was destroyed. While Alebiosu mourns his vanished pension, his wife quickly and silently packs her suitcase and departs.

The curtain closes. Hubert Ogunde, the eminent director of the company, appears on stage elegantly dressed and ends the show with the theme song from *Sixpence Owner of a Suitcase*, a song intensely derogatory of young women:

> One night I met a lively girl who couldn't bring water for a bath,
> She couldn't grind pepper for the soup,
> Will you please go out and pack out of my house.
> She doesn't want second wife, only herself,
> If she drinks she will beat her husband,
> If she goes out in the morning she will return in the midnight,
> Whether you do good, or do evil
> At life's end you will see what it has earned.

The Sixpence Woman (sixpence points to her cheapness of character) is a conniving, money-hungry female who repeatedly cheats her men, eventually destroying Alebiosu. She is witchlike in the sense that she wreaks destruction on males, is incapable of or not interested in giving birth, reserving her power for the creation of world havoc, is in league with other women, and mesmerizes her paramours. Yoruba male audience members repeatedly agreed that this is the way "women really are," and that "women only want money from men."

We will return to compare this Sixpence Wife to other female characters in the conclusion. But now let us briefly look at the other stage roles depicting Yoruba women.

2.2. The Co-Wife

Another typical female role in Yoruba theater is that of wife in a polygynous household. In the play *The Richman* (*Olowo Ojiji*), four wives who are petty traders are married to a man who has won the lottery and acquired a large amount of money. Although the Yoruba principle of seniority gives a wife status according to whether she is a first, second, third, or fourth wife, all wives being junior to the one first wedded, a husband should treat all equally. A wife can upset this balance through the utilization of "romantic charms." If the husband treats a wife deferentially chaos can reign in a polygynous household.*

In the first scene of *The Richman*, three wives are on stage making plans for the demise of the first married wife:

> SECOND WIFE: Our senior wife is like a hawk who swooped and took our husband.
> THIRD WIFE: Ever since our husband has gotten rich and bought a car he takes only her to ride in it.
> FOURTH WIFE: If he doesn't take her, she cries.

The wives invent false accusations, which they will take to their husband concerning the senior wife. The allegations include: that she was seen stealing their husband's teeth-cleaning stick, which she took to a "juju" house (a place where magic can be bought); that she has taken her junior wife's shoes; and that she has used black soap to win her husband's love.

When the husband and his senior wife return home, all three junior wives begin shouting these charges and others. One wife says that the part of her cleaning stick which touches her teeth was cut away and a photograph of her child stolen. She complains that she doesn't want to "get lean or get a headache, and doesn't want her child to die."† The accusations turn into a heated argument:

> SECOND WIFE: My sandals are missing.
> FIRST WIFE: Why would I steal sandals when I have superior shoes?
> THIRD WIFE: You cannot even prepare our husband's food.
> FOURTH WIFE: You don't even know yet if you're really married! I have many children. My first husband's children are in the U.K. and my second husband's are in secondary school.
> FIRST WIFE: Aha! So you've married so many husbands you haven't yet reached where you will stay!

The remarks of the fourth wife strike hard because they refer to the fact that the senior wife has no children, and thus no "real" marriage, a fact that becomes the crux of the argument. The first wife laments that her

---

*It is believed that a co-wife often procures magical "medicine" in order to win her husband's love and increase her own glamorous charms.
†These items could be used in sorcery and are "magically" identified with the victims.

co-wives abuse her for lack of children, and she begins to sing a popular song:

> Remind me O God to have children.
> Don't abuse me because I have no issue,
> Because what God will do nobody knows,
> If we could buy children,
> I would have bought one for myself,
> A person who is buried by his children,
> That indeed is the person who has children.

This lament, which emphasizes the role of caution in declaring the nature of a person's fate (the senior wife has no children but yet may bear some), catches the husband's sympathy and he quickly restores order. He commands the fourth wife to "leave his house" because she had not told him about her previous husbands, orders the others to be silent, and the childless senior wife unfairly prevails over both husband and co-wives.

We have seen two types of male–female relationships in Yoruba theater: one in which an older highly traditional man is ruined by an immoral prostitute, and one in which a traditional man is manipulated by his senior wife into giving her preferential treatment. What further themes are to be found?

2.3. Our Mothers

A third frequently enacted relationship between a man and a woman in Yoruba plays is that between a young man and an elderly witch. In the play Car Owner (Onimoto), Eluma, a poor male youth who wishes riches, befriends an expensively dressed young man from Lagos, called Bumbabumba. Eluma queries Bumbabumba about his source of wealth. Bumbabumba says that he's an importer/exporter whose customers give him money for things they desire. But once they have handed over their money, "They no longer remember where their money went," and don't return to claim it. He says that he can't talk about it in public but that "those who are responsible for my power create people as a blacksmith makes a hoe." Eluma begs Bumbabumba to take him to those powerful persons.

The next scene depicts Eluma's initiation into a secret society of young people—both male and female—who use the power of the "mother of the group," an old witch, in order to win success in their businesses. The witch does a commanding dance at stage front, a dance that is exciting, aggressive, fast-stepped, and very much in contrast to a woman's ordinarily subdued style of dancing. Her breasts are uncovered, her hair full of wild feathers,* and her chest and short wrapper covered with charms. She calls Eluma "my child" and tells him he must choose to eat the contents of a bag that she holds in her hand, contents that are "something from the *orisa* which will make you rich."† Eluma consumes the contents of the bag and visibly seems to grow more powerful, joining the society in a dance.

In the next scene Eluma has become a "purchaser" who conducts his business just as his friend Bumbabumba has described his own. Many people are seen bringing money to him in order to buy televisions, refrigerators, and imported cloth, but when they leave they remember nothing of where they have been. Eluma grows very rich and invites Bumbabumba to his house in order to thank him. Bumbabumba assesses Eluma's wealth during his visit and reports back to the witch and her secret society. The group then visits Eluma at home and while enticing him to smoke marijuana, they steal all of his money. Eluma consequently becomes addicted to the drug and goes mad both from the effects of the drug and from the dangerous power of the witch.

In the extremely popular play *With Their Backs to the Sea* (*K'ehin S'okun*), there is a similar relationship between a young man and a witch. In this play, which is based directly on the life of an armed robber who was executed in Nigeria in 1972, the central character is a young criminal who calls himself Dr. Danger and who obtains his power directly from a powerful witch. In the opening scene there are red lights flashing on the stage while a witch gives Dr. Danger a red bag, the contents of which he eats, and a black bag, the contents of which he washes down with gin, and ties a red sash around his waist. Both witch and criminal exit from the stage walking backward.

Later, just before a robbery is about to be committed, Dr. Danger summons the witch to his house in order to obtain more power. A clanging bell announces her entry and she appears on stage and sacrifices a goat. Then she gives Danger a cornucopia of magical methodology. She gives him a small clay oil lamp and instructs him that whenever he is going out the lamp should be lit and not put out until his return. Next she gives him a red belt studded with small calabashes covered with red cloth and tells him that when he's wearing it, wherever he is, if he places his back against a wall or if he jumps into a river he will return home. She also gives him a goat, which he is to treat as a human being, but if caught, he should eat the goat and he will turn into a "big stone."

*Birds are a symbol of witchcraft.
†*Orisa* are the divinities of the Yoruba pantheon.

As payment she says that Danger must build her a three-story house and give her an automobile as soon as he steals one.

Danger is eventually apprehended and his various charms fail to protect him. The light mysteriously goes out while he is away from home and the goat eats leaves when she is supposed to partake only of human food. Thus, Danger is duly executed while his witch remains alive to enjoy her earnings. His money and other goods are left to his wife, who also has some witchly power. She and her best friend in this play are child thieves who can change children into dogs, rats, or pigs, and change them back again. The friend has been in prison 30 times for her offenses. In addition, the wife's power is so great that she forced Danger to marry her in a "court ceremony" so that he could take no other legal wife. Thus, his second wife must live away from him and when his legal wife finds them together she beats the second wife with a stick and tells her that "I laugh like a white woman" on account of the court marriage. The second wife has some power too, for Danger says she has "long legs," the idiomatic expression for influence, and that she often has him released after he's arrested.

2.4. Half Human/Half Animal

Another variation on this theme of the "wild woman" beyond man's control, who has access to powers of life that may benefit or ruin those who come in contact with her, is that found in the play *Half Human/Half Animal*. In this play, which is based on a popular folk tale, the hero plays the part of a hunter and devotee of Ogun,* who happens upon an animal in the forest which is in the process of shedding its skin in order to expose a beautiful young woman underneath. The hunter swears to the young woman he will never reveal her secret if she promises to be his wife.

He takes her home where his first and second wives are arguing between themselves. They become suspicious at once of the beautiful girl, especially when they notice she eats with her mouth directly from her bowl not using her hands, that she cannot cook or clean, and that she slinks stealthily across a room rather than walking. The wives beat the girl often and finally decide upon a ruse that will allow them to discover the nature of her true origin. They ply their husband with palm wine and gin until he becomes incoherent and permits the wild girl's secret to slip out. When they confront her with it, she shows her enormous strength and flings the two gossipy co-wives across the room.

*Ogun is the god of iron, the votary of blacksmiths, hunters, and truck drivers.

Then she demands her animal skin from the hunter and departs for the forest to transform herself again into an animal.

Although in this drama the woman does not actually bring about the downfall of a man, she is depicted as existing outside the structured realm of patrilineal society and as being completely "unmanageable." She is irresistibly beautiful to the hunter, which causes him to withhold information from his two other wives, bringing more dissension to his household. Finally the hunter allows her to go free because she cannot adapt to life in civilized society.

2.5. The Transvestite

Another feminine persona dramatized in Yoruba plays is that of the transvestite male who dons the dress and habits of woman in order to manipulate men. This persona is similar to the ritual *Gelede* figure in appearance, but different in purpose. In *Gelede* the man dons the robes of the female in order to mediate or intercede with the life-giving and -taking forces of the universe. In the theater the male is motivated to wear the dress of woman as a means of gaining power. He imitates the image of the powerful woman, which assumes the recognition of power, but he may be seen to be a perversion of *Gelede,* for he is interested only in power and not in mediation. It is dangerous to play with the feminine image in such a manner, and as we might expect, the transvestite brings financial ruin to the men who have contact with her.

In the play *Husband and Wife (Tokotaya)* there is a good example of such a relationship. In this play a male disguises himself as a woman when he learns that there is a man living nearby who has had two child-less wives desert him, and who is therefore desperate to marry again and have children. It is suspected by the acquaintances of the man that he is impotent, a fact that explains for them his two previous divorces. The transvestite accosts the impotent man in the market, flirting with him in a very provocative way, and leads the man to eventually propose their marriage. The transvestite comes to live with the impotent man, promising that she will produce as many children as "rats" for him; but after moving into his house she finds a multitude of excuses not to share his bed. At first she accuses the pitiful man of not "kissing"* her cor-rectly; then she begins to continuously nag him, frightening him with her threats of leaving. She yells at him when he refuses to increase the amount of money he's given her for food: "You know, I've married forty husbands because not one of them could take care of me. If you don't

---

*"Kissing" is associated with European habits of love and is learned at the local cinema, where American films are shown.

give me money for meat, fish, oil, pepper, and chicken, I will leave you." Desperate for children, the impotent husband yields to the nag's demands; the transvestite is subsequently viewed in the next scene drinking up the husband's money at a palm wine bar.

The new wife's demands escalate until the poor husband has exhausted his resources completely on the irritable transvestite, never having had the opportunity to consummate the union. Finally, the husband demands to know why his wife never bathes, where his money has gone, and why she will not sleep with him. There is an onstage fight in which the transvestite is disrobed and his true sex revealed.

> HUSBAND: My God! What am I looking at in this room?
> TRANSVESTITE: Fool! Haven't you seen this thing in the world? I want to become a rich man of the world which is why I made myself a woman in order to get money.
> HUSBAND: I will call the police! Where is all my money?
> TRANSVESTITE: Your money is spent on anything that I wanted. Why call the police? Pray to God that I can still bear a child for you!

The final words of the transvestite ridicule the man by pointing out that he has as much chance of having a child by a man as by a woman, since he is impotent.

3. Conclusion

From the five examples of male–female relationships in Yoruba plays, we have seen that female personae are quite dynamic in their effects on males. Both the relationships between the sexes and the peculiarly disastrous consequences of these relationships for men can be related to the carnal image of women in Yoruba society.

The Sixpence Woman, who actually commands stage action for nearly the whole of the play, men only entering to hand over money to her, is childless and has no intention of having children for the patrilineage of her husbands. Indeed, she professes no allegiance to any man, mulcting the run of those who pass her way, having left one so ruined after contact with her that he had "only his spoken English left" when she departed. She preys on the witless men's desire for children, substituting the calabash for what her carnal appetites will not allow her to bear. She, like her traditional counterpart, the witch, contains power either to create man (by giving him children and self-continuity) or to destroy man, by financially draining him, thereby prohibiting him from contracting any further unions with women, "who marry men only for money and for children." Alebiosu is, in the end of *Sixpence Owner of a*

Suitcase, left with fewer prospects than the man mulcted by witches who can dance in *Gelede*. It is surely no accident of dramatic action, either, that in the end of this play and also in the end of *With Their Backs to the Sea* and *Car Owner* we find that main male characters have been completely destroyed, and that the female character who was the catalyst for that destruction is left, not alone, but in the company of feminine comrades in deceit, to enjoy the spoils of her victory. Women are, in the view of these male-dominated and -authored plays, and in that of traditional society, in league with one another. The mystical tie of menstrual blood which links one to another is symbolized by the ever-present conspiratorial girl friends in Yoruba plays. In *With Their Backs to the Sea*, the wife of Dr. Danger, who himself was created and destroyed through the power of a witch, was a child thief; her friend was a child thief and a witch of such power that she possessed the secret of the transmutation of matter; and her co-wife had mystical influence with the authorities.

In *Richman*, in which co-wives are depicted as backbiting, greedy, and suspicious nags, the senior wife is accused as a witch, on account of having an exclusive relationship with her husband, a relationship that must be bought at the price of childlessness, hence accumulated re-generative power and subsequent suspicion of bewitchment. In *Half Human/Half Animal* the nagging jealous co-wives discover by cunning the true nature of the uncivilized animal-creature, who symbolizes a woman who seeks to conceal her essence, "wild by nature," in the guise of wife in a polygynous household. The play's beginning showed the wild woman in a market before she returned to the forest where the hunter spotted her disrobing. There is a structural link set up between the wild forest and the marketplace, where in one there is found feminine power raw and unleashed, and in the other feminine power contained and structured.

The transvestite in *Husband and Wife* wears the symbol of femininity and thus imitates power, power that he hopes will make him a wealthy man of the world, the same status that the naïve Eluma of *Car Owner* had hoped to obtain by invoking the aid of a witch. The transvestite does manage to bankrupt the already sexually bankrupt impotent man, but himself only "eats" the profits for a short while, having spent most of his ill-gotten cash on the feminine accouterments necessary to defraud the trusting husband. The simple imitation of power, rather than the mediation of power as in *Gelede*, does the imitator little good, but strikes a desperate note as regards the plight of the impotent man.

Thus, women in Yoruba plays are wildly active characters who act as catalytic agents for the destinies of men, who themselves act only in regard to, and with the help of women. The money that women take from men signifies both their greed and their success, and their ability to render men completely and totally impotent, for one must possess either money or family to compete at all for status and prestige in Yoruba society. The female's repetitive mulcting of the male is both a demonstration and a prerogative of her power, just as a wealthy male demonstrates his power by mulcting his inferiors and his rivals. The mockery and fantasy that are focused in the figures of the transvestite, the prostitute, the witch, and the childless wife serve to both mesmerize and ridicule the masculine dramatis personae who play opposite them. The male stands transfixed and incapable of acting while the woman sets in motion the forces for his physical, social, and financial destruction. If a man succeeds it is because of a woman and if he fails it is also because of a woman, facts related to the ever-present paradox of woman's dual nature. The dual image of the Yoruba female is linked within her curious embodiment of both the regenerative and destructive aspects of the life-force. In its regenerative aspects, the life-force must flow through women and be materialized in children; in its decadent aspects it is conceptualized as accumulating in the storehouse of a woman's abdomen, where it is continuously converted into destructive power. In traditional society, the witch was blamed for accumulating a large account of such power and using it to decay the reproductive potential of others, thereby denying men children for the extension of their patrilineal families, which effectively cut them off from self-continuity and social status.

Without the concept of witchcraft, power would have flowed naturally through society, lodging only in socially structured positions, most of which were held by men in the traditional Yoruba patrilineage. However, the concept of witchcraft permitted great quantities of power to become lodged in women, who in turn were thought to use that power against the institutions of society. In this sense, witchcraft symbolizes the eternal struggle of the sexes in Yoruba society over control of the life-force, metaphorically alluded to by the *Gelede* initiate who claimed that "in the beginning God gave the world to the witches." Yoruba men, apparently, have been trying to get it back ever since! The female's dominance of the Yoruba marketplace further symbolizes the male's feeling of exclusion from power, particularly poor, urban wage-earning men such as those who attend Yoruba theater performances in Ibadan.

In the male-dominated world of the Yoruba, the position of women as socially and economically independent traders, in addition to their being powerful witches, throws a wedge into the patrilineal structure. As an independent trader who bears most of the financial support of her children, a woman often can exist without the aid of her husband and his patrilineage. Also, as we have noted above, the affectivity of the mother–son tie surpasses any other male–female link in Yoruba society and is threatening to the patrilineal structure. Both these factors contribute to the high rate of divorce among the Yoruba, and to the concern of men for their own potency.

Most ethnographers have written that a barren female is without purpose among the Yoruba, and that she may be despised as a witch, divorced by her husband, and returned to her own lineage. The facts, but not the emphasis, are true. Women also only marry men in order to have children, since the wife's desire for children is very strong. Thus, one could say that an impotent man is without purpose for the Yoruba woman, and that he is ridiculed and divorced by his wife, who returns home to her own lineage to seek another husband. Certainly both informants' accounts of women and the depictions of the pitiful impotent Yoruba male in dramatic performances bear this out.

Thus the carnal feminine image expressed through the sexual idiom of decadent reproductive power symbolizes the struggle between the sexes for power on many levels: sexual, social, and political, the derogatory female image being related to the normative ethos of the patrilineage. Society does violence to those whom it does not want to integrate, and thus witches have been scapegoated for many decades in Yoruba society, the last organized witch hunt, the famous *Atinga*, having taken place as recently as the early 1950s (Morton-Williams 1956:315–334).

In the Yoruba theater we have described several variations on the carnal image of woman: the prostitute, the childless co-wife, the half woman/half animal figure, the child thief, the transvestite. These figures have many structural similarities in common with the carnal witch, in that they describe the many faces of the scapegoated woman, whose guilt is symbolized less by her actual crimes than by the way she is made to embody the types of transgressions of prohibitions which endanger the social order of patrilineal society and its survival. As such, the Yoruba witch has much in common with her counterparts in many African societies, and with her sisters in both medieval Europe and contemporary Europe and America, where the image of the "castrating bitch" is often still applied to women who are seen as threatening men with their aggressive and "malelike" behavior. The phrase "she's trying to cut off his balls," used by American men to describe female behavior that is too "malelike," is reminiscent of the medieval fear of night-flying witches lusting to steal penises, of the Yoruba woman witch who purloined penises so she could have intercourse with men and women, of the

Sixpence Woman who rendered her husband impotent financially and socially, and of the Freudian female whose life was considered ruined because of her lack of a male organ.

References

Baroja, Julio. 1965. *The World of the Witches.* Chicago: University of Chicago Press.

Chesler, Phyllis. 1972. *Women and Madness.* New York: Doubleday.

Ehrenreich, Barbara and Deirdre English. 1973. *Witches, Midwives, and Nurses: A History of Women Healers.* New York: Feminist Press.

Ekwensi, Cyprian. 1969. *Jagua Nana.* Greenwich: Fawcett Publications.

Forde, Daryll. 1951. *The Yoruba Speaking Peoples of Southwest Nigeria.* London: International African Institute.

Gluckman, Max. 1965a. *Politics, Law, and Ritual in Tribal Societies.* Oxford: Basil Blackwell.

Gluckman, Max. 1965b. *Custom and Conflict in Tribal Society.* Oxford: Basil Blackwell.

Harner, Michael J. 1973. The role of hallucinogenic plants in European witchcraft. In M. J. Harner (ed.), *Hallucinogens and Shamanism.* New York: Oxford University Press. 125–150.

Harris, Marvin. 1974. *Cows, Pigs, Wars and Witches: The Riddles of Culture.* New York: Vintage Books.

Kramer, Heinrich and James Sprenger. 1971. *The Malleus Maleficarum.* New York: Dover Publications.

Levine, Robert. 1970. Sex roles and economic change in Africa. In J. Middleton (ed.), *Black Africa.* New York: MacMillan. 174–180.

Lloyd, Barbara. 1967. Indigenous Ibadan. In P. Lloyd, A. Mabogunje, and B. Awe (eds.), *The City of Ibadan.* London: Cambridge University Press. 59–83.

Lloyd, Peter. 1968. Divorce among the Yoruba. *American Anthropologist 70:67–82.*

Lloyd, Peter. 1973. Perceptions of class and social inequality among the Yoruba of western Nigeria. Paper given at the IX International Congress of Anthropological and Ethnological Sciences. Mimeo.

Morton-Williams, Peter. 1956. The Atinga cult among the southwestern Yoruba. *Bulletin de l'IFAN 18:*315–334.

Nadel, Siegfried. 1970. *Nupe Religion.* New York: Schocken Books.

Prince, Raymond. 1961. The Yoruba image of the witch. *Journal of Mental Science 107:*795–805.

Prince, Raymond. 1964. Indigenous Yoruba psychiatry. In Ari Kiev (ed.), *Magic, Faith, and Healing.* New York: Free Press.

Savramis, Demosthenes. 1974. *The Satanizing of Woman.* New York: Doubleday.

Sembene, Ousman. 1970. *God's Bits of Wood.* New York: Anchor Books, Doubleday.

Soyinka, Wole. 1967. *Kongi's Harvest.* London: Oxford University Press.

13

Patricia Cleckner

Jive Dope Fiend Whoes

In the Street and in Rehabilitation

> Sometimes I like to pretend I'm Wonder Woman.
> —An Addict Prostitute

1. The Psychological Stereotype

Until very recently the term *female drug user* conjured up an image of a shadowy emaciated black addict streetwalker: devious, dirty, and desperate for another fix. The woman behind this stereotype is not the norm, as drug researchers have been discovering. Middle-class prescription users by far outnumber their ghetto sisters. In the ghetto itself, the female users of narcotics often engage in property crimes, shoplifting and short con games. Yet the image of the "jive dope fiend whoe"* is a haunting one, since she represents, in some sense, the pariah of the pariahs, contradicting norms of both sobriety and sexual ownership, being a pleasure-seeker who rents her favors.

Among professionals the female addict is frequently regarded as an individual suffering from some sort of psychosexual dysfunction. A number of feminists have provided useful insights into this orientation. In speaking of the confusion of the women's movement with lesbianism, Ti-Grace Atkinson notes: "Now 'sex' for men is genital contact. So, if women rebel, it's clear to men, this rebellion would have to take the

---

*Whoe is a term used in black American dialect to designate "prostitute." It is derived from *whore*. There is considerable variation in spelling in existing literature. One alternate form is *ho* (Milner and Milner 1972).

Patricia Cleckner · Director of Research, Up Front, Inc., Miami, Florida.

form of 'woman.' A 'woman' is something to be screwed. Therefore . . . feminists . . . must be women who screw each other" (1974:84). Using the same logic, rehabilitation, as a male-dominated institution, operates on the premise that women are sexual objects. As such, any dynsfunction must be related to their sexuality.

Another insight is provided by Chesler in her analysis of women and madness (1972). She points out that therapists tend to treat problems of female patients by encouraging them to adjust to traditional sex roles, thus being guardians of social normalcy rather than of individual happiness, of cultural adjustments rather than psychodynamic harmony. Thus readjustment of the addict prostitute implies a realignment of sex role. While neither of these comments constitutes an anthropological analysis in the formal sense, both imply that there is a cultural factor that is generally ignored by drug rehabilitation professionals. The heroin addict community, especially as it exists in the ghetto street environment, is a genuine subculture that has its own values and world view (Weppner 1973; Agar 1973) in spite of the fact that it is responsive to and dependent on the dominant culture. As such, definitions of what constitutes normal behavior differ from those of the mainstream. Sexuality is no exception.

In a society as complex as the United States there is considerable intracultural variation in sex role definition. This is especially true today, as basic definitions of primary relationships and sexuality are undergoing rapid and profound transformations. According to the ethnoscientists the rules of these variations constitute the fabric of the culture itself (Tyler 1969). Economic exploitation of sexuality in the heroin subculture is a variation, elaboration, and distortion (in a technical rather than a moral sense) of dominant values regarding sexuality. As pimps and feminists alike have pointed out, it is possible to regard "selling pussy" as a norm rather than a deviation in sexual behavior: the dynamics of prostitution are a magnification of a more encompassing norm of manipulation of sexual desire for economic ends. The black addict subculture is shaped primarily by two essential features: the expense and the legal status of heroin. It is a black market item in an environment of economic scarcity. The addict life-style places a great deal of emphasis on acquiring money. Thus mainstream values related to this orientation are magnified. These include exploitation for material gain and emphasis on conspicuous consumption as a source of power and prestige. The dynamics of prostitution is shaped by these two factors.

In rehabilitation, and especially in the therapeutic community setting, treatment of males focuses on readjustment in terms of power and economic orientation. These factors are largely ignored in treating female addicts; rather, emphasis is placed on sexual adjustment. The idea that drug use is related to nontraditional sexuality in women, be it promiscuity, lesbianism, or prostitution, is an essential part of addict stereotypes. The ideal product of rehabilitation is a woman who is purified of these sexual aberrations and hence has no reason to resort to drug use. Thus attempts to "turn the addict whoe around" during treatment are focused on changes in sex role behavior rather than drug use. For women, adjustments in sexual identity are thought to play a more central role than changes in identity from addict to nonaddict. For example, at a recent conference on women and drugs, both male and female professionals surveyed regarded the principal contributing factors to substance abuse among women as family problems, sex role conflicts, and psychological instability. The same group regarded economic problems as the primary contributing factor to male substance abuse (Cleckner and Wells 1976). This interpretation of female addict problems, at least in the case of the prostitute, ignores important issues of economics and power. This attitude concerning the sexual role of the prostitute addict both in the street and in the therapeutic community is a reflection of the sexual and economic position of women in the larger culture.

2. Historical Perspective

The addict world today is dominated by males in a variety of ways. According to statistics based on appearance of users in institutional settings, the male addicts outnumber the female addicts. Within the subculture itself, strategies, values, and world view are more elaborate and complete in defining the male role than in defining the female role. Power relationships emphasize superiority of the male both as an addict and as a hustler. In addition, studies of addiction focus on the male addict far more frequently than on the female (Christenson and Swanson 1974). However, addiction has not always been a male-dominated phenomenon. During the nineteenth century there were more women than men addicted to opiates. Opium and derivatives were available over the counter and through mail orders. They were considered especially useful in alleviating pain resulting from "women's problems" and were known as "women's friends" (Brecher 1972). Some therapists today feel that more women than men continue to use opiates as self-medication.

With the passage of the Harrison Narcotics Act of 1914, the opiate user's profile shifted rapidly from a majority of white middle-class women to a predominance of ghetto-dwelling (not necessarily black) males engaging in criminal activities. This shift is commonly attributed to the fact that most women did not wish to engage in illegal activities to obtain their drugs. In fact, it is likely that many women continued their opiate use pattern for some time but did not come under the surveillance of officials who differentially enforced the narcotics law in areas where police efforts were already established (Lindesmith 1965). Eventually, however, a clear addict subculture emerged, especially in red-light districts, since these were places where residents were already familiar with the strategies for dealing with both police and customers. Thus the relationship between addiction and prostitution was established very early in the development of the subculture. During this period, women were often introduced to opiates through male associates, especially pimps (Dai 1937). This stereotyped pattern of women being "turned on" and "turned out" by males has persisted to the present, although it occurs much less frequently today.

Some early interpretations of the relationship between prostitutes and addiction were economic:

> It is quite true that many female addicts are prostitutes, and it is unfortunate that some who do not deserve it are given credit for sex immorality merely because they take drugs. Addiction produces prostitution by creating a necessity for drugs, the money for which cannot be secured in any other way (Kolb 1938:356).

At the same time, however, observers began to interpret addiction among women as a result of sexual and marital maladjustment (Dai 1937). As psychological and sociological theory regarding addiction grew, so did emphasis on sexual deviance among female addicts. This was reinforced by findings that the female addict was more socially maladjusted, coming from a more disorganized home environment than her male counterpart (see, for example, Chein et al. 1964; Waldorf 1973).

At the extreme end of this emphasis on sexuality is the psychoanalytical school. The following is illustrative of their perspective:

> Out of a need for rebellion against male authority, they often engage in precocious sexual activity in which they find no sexual gratification. Their association with addicts, who are inadequate males, fulfills their unconscious desire to reject the male partner; men are an object of competition, not sexual attraction. . . .
> The female addict likes to dress as a man. Her relationship with men is a castrating one: she has no desire for men to be potent, because sexual acceptance of the man will make her feel inferior to him, or rather make her aware of her basic feeling of inferiority (Kron and Brown 1965:146).

The clinical picture that has emerged from this psychological tradition is a view of the female addict as a passive–aggressive personality (Schultz 1974).

Recently some observers have claimed that addict women have begun to engage in more violent types of criminal activity. It has been argued that this shift is related to recent changes in sex roles, if not to the women's movement itself, although statistics are not clear and the relationship is tenuous at best. Directly related to feminist activities, however, is a movement to eliminate sexism in rehabilitation, which has previously been male-dominated. In the past two or three years there has been an attempt to create specialized and appropriate therapy for women who have long been neglected in the clinical setting. In spite of this reemphasis on aspects of sexual oppression, however, treatment of women remains focused on issues of psychology and sexuality.

3. So Low She Got to Look Up to Look Down

As was mentioned above, the essential features of the addict subculture center around the economic character of heroin as a black market drug. In the ghetto environment this commodity and its consumers have a special place in street life, addicts being considered the "greasiest" of the hustlers. If an addict is to maintain his or her habit in the ghetto environment of monetary scarcity, he or she must hustle. Hustling on the street is not only an economic fact but also a highly valued activity. "Gettin' over," meaning successfully hustling or "gaming on" somebody, is a respected skill, and the display of material wealth, in the form of cars or clothes, which results from this exploitation is a source of status. The management of the fast money of street finances is a complex distortion and elaboration of mainstream capitalist values. Since opportunity for gain is scarce, emphasis is placed on creating means of acquiring income and illusions of wealth to replace actual economic stability. The street environment is thus dominated by themes of manipulation and theatrical presentation, the elements of the latter being called "style." Subtle and exploitive use of power, prestige, and sexuality are the basis of the hustling activity. The street environment is male-dominated and the variety of games or hustles available to the male is both elaborate and sophisticated, ranging from brute force activities to subtle psychological manipulations. Women's repertoire is more limited; however, a female addict has a variety of means of supporting her habit and many women engage in a number of hustles during their addiction career. Traditionally, these have taken the form of variations on the domestic arts, such as shoplifting, check passing, credit card manipulation, and "whoein'," or prostitution. More recently the number of alternatives has increased as "women has gotten more bolder," engaging more frequently in robbery and other more aggressive property crimes. In the case of one lesbian woman addict I interviewed, pimping other women was a main source of income. While the achievement of status for women is treacherous and ambiguous at best, as will be described later, a woman may gain status, just as a man does, by demonstrating her skill at "gettin' over."

The hustle most often associated with women is prostitution. As the saying goes, "a woman is sittin' on a fortune." This activity offers a number of advantages suited to the addict life-style. It does not require consistent long-term commitment of regular hours. A whoe can turn a trick any time of the day. There is always opportunity and the penalties are slight. These simple economic advantages are reinforced by two related factors: the street ethic of sexual exploitation and the nature of street image.

As Eliot Liebow noted, sexual exploitation is highly valued in the street segment of ghetto society:

> Men and women talk of themselves and others as cynical, self-serving marauders, ceaselessly exploiting one another as use objects or objects of income. Sometimes, such motives are ascribed only to women: "them girls, they want FInance, not ROmance." But more often, the men prefer to see themselves as the exploiters, the women as the exploited, as in assessing a woman's desirability in terms of her wealth or earning power. Thus, for both men and women, the opposite sex is ideally regarded as a source of income (1967:137).

However, this ethic is not unequivocal and the human desire for affection, closeness, and sexual pleasure at times overrides the ability to manipulate from a superior position, or, as the pimps say, "keep your dick in your pocket." This ethic is, of course, the basis for the pimp–prostitute relationship, as well as the relationship between the whoe and her john or customer. There is a variety of arrangements on the street: "They got different sets of whoes. They got whoes that work for theyself. They got whoes that work for men. They got whoes that work for chicks." The ethical basis of these is always sexual exploitation but the dynamics are most complex in the pimp–prostitute relationship. As Milner and Milner point out, the pimp game is a dominance–dependency game that can be used to interpret all manner of sexual relationships. "Most pimps, however, believe they were raised by their mothers not to be pimps, but to be tricks. Trick marriage is seen by pimps as a man's servitude to a woman in exchange for her pussy" (1972:194).

The games played by both pimp and prostitute alike are psychological and often subtle in nature. A pimp may use a variety of means for obtaining the cooperation of a whoe, ranging from force and coercion to manipulation of feelings of attachment, as the two following examples illustrate:

> Its the IOU, blackmail but in a different way. Just like getting one of your people out of jail that's still part of the game and to get her out of jail to get her back on the street makin' money. They would have to pay more because they got theyself put in the position to go to jail but they couldn't get theyself out of it so they got to stick they hand out the bars and call they pimp and you got to come get em and the game you goin to run to them is how much that shit cost for em to get out for the lawyer's end.
>
> Its part of the game. She owe you because she got herself fucked up. She couldn't get herself out so she owe you for that day on and she really don't know how much it is cause you never tell her. It's always you pay this, have this, on such and such a day and she have it the next week the same thing and a lot of times she might come up with hey, I don't feel IOU this much. Then you just keep on.
>
> First you get the woman. You make love to her or whatever and if she dig you, you go about finding out to what extent. Like someone say, I do this for you, I do that for you, that mean they love you. Then I say, I've got to have some money for this and this and I don't have it and I don't know where I'm going to get it from and I've got to have it. And if they really care for you and they say something like well, hey, I don't have that money, I say, Damn baby, do you love me. You can get it. LOVE spell MONEY. Usually they get it.

The pimp–whoe relationship starts with honey and goes to vinegar.

In this sexual hierarchy the whoe is on the second rung of the hustling ladder. Most men feel that women are more naïve and less able to pull off the game, more susceptible to the pimp's "perfect conversation." However, a good whoe is one who knows how to hustle. She adds status to her man by knowing the game and yet being hustled by him. The following excerpt from a toast-type* poem illustrates this in describing Finger Poppin' Teddy's call girl Betty:

> Now Betty, it was said,
> could kill a grayboy in bed,
> and make the chumps submit.
> They would come before they came,
> then she would pick-pocket the lame,
> while telling him that he wasn't shit.
> —Lightnin' Rod (1973:45)

While this skill is highly regarded when a woman is using it to get

---

*A "toast" is an epic-type poem that is part of the oral tradition in the ghetto and in the prison environment. For a complete discussion of this genre see Abrahams (1964).

money for a pimp, it is a sign of greasiness and untrustworthiness when turned against a pimp. Nevertheless, many women take pride in their ability to get over and brag about their ability to survive on the street. Women who are independent brag most about never having had a pimp, and, from their personal accounts, appear to be the most subtle and sophisticated hookers. Many especially enjoy the power aspect of gaming on johns. It seems no accident that *hustling* may be used as a general term and may be applied specifically to prostitution. It is regarded by some as playing on people's "sex jones" just as a heroin dealer plays on the addict's "jones," or habit.

Getting over on johns is a source of pride to all prostitutes. One independent whoe describes some of her game as follows:

> The reason that I got me regular dates is that I run em games. I say, 'Hey, you got another date? Man, that other chick, she got a man. You go in that room and a man goin to kick that door in.' You know, drop a lug or something like that. Or, 'You've seen my date?' I say, 'You won't see her for a while but come on, I'll take her place. She told me it was all right.'

As Liebow pointed out in his street-corner study, the exploitation aspect of sexuality is not as cut-and-dried as street people would have one believe. Listening to reports without ever being in the street, one has the impression that each pimp has a stable or a number of whoes, and each whoe is an independent hooker. The reality is more complex. Every player strives to have a stable but few have the game or psychological prowess to control a number of women, let alone one. Every whoe strives for economic independence and invulnerability to men's games, but is constantly confronted with the temptations of male guidance, attention, protection, etc.

Among the addicts with whom I worked, the man–woman relationship often took the form of a couple who more or less live together. The woman often goes out and "whoes" since it is the easiest and least dangerous hustle. The male in the relationship is generally regarded as her "old man," not her "pimp." A long-term love relationship is often involved but may be one that is dominated generally by the desires of the man and one in which attachment is used for manipulative purposes by both parties. One ex-addict noted that addict couples are not different from nonaddict couples except that they must tolerate more pressure. Such couples exist mainly to get drugs as a team. The prognosis for these couples in treatment is not good, since the basis of the relationship is theoretically removed. These relationships are uniquely adapted to the addiction life-style, having a cohesiveness that is impossible between addict and nonaddict, and an economic design that is antithetical to the square life.

On the street, prestige is based not so much on the type of activity engaged in as on the way it is executed. This style element is accomplished through "image," which is a projection of appearance and behavior. For the male, the criteria for a good image are unambiguous but flexible. A good player is "cool," or psychologically detached, and "slick," or able to slide in and out of situations and manipulate them in such a way as to maintain the illusion he projects. He must do this without getting "slimey" or breaking certain basic codes such as the sanction against "dropping a dime on someone," or informing the police, and the prohibition against hustling a "crime partner," or hustling associate. Sliminess and "greasiness" (a term applied to both behavioral style and bad appearance) result from a lack of finesse at game and image.

The female addict's image is both more ambiguous and more difficult to maintain. She is more likely to be gamed on by her male crime partner. If she accepts his game she is regarded as stupid but loyal. If she does not, she is regarded as smart but treacherous. In general, women addicts are seen as "greasier" than their male counterparts. When male addicts are asked to characterize women on the street, they respond ambivalently. Some claim that women are more naïve, that they are more likely both to show their hand when gaming and to reveal their psychological weaknesses, making themselves more vulnerable to being gamed upon. Others claim that they are more treacherous, more likely to gain in situations where there is a sanction against doing so. In general, women just are not as good at hustling in the street. The cards are stacked against them. This might be interpreted as a function of their structural position. They are both the object of games and the gamers. In the situation of the whoe, for example, the male pimp is a player and the john is the person gamed on. They are two different people. The whoe, on the other hand, plays both roles.

In this context the female addict attempts to establish her image. Generally she does so by means of appearance and style, not in gaming so much as in dress and behavior. Respect for a person "as a man" or "as a woman" is an extremely important value in ghetto life, which is an essential component of the street whoe's image. In creating this image she must use the materials at hand. She does not have the value of unambiguous monogamy to fall back on, but she does have a variety of other items to work with, including her ability to survive on the street and her behavioral style and appearance.

Self-respect is manifested in proper grooming and bearing, "how a person keep herself." As Ladner noted in her study of ghetto women, appearance is an essential component in establishing female identity:

> . . . dressing is an outlet. In a minor way it might be viewed as a compensa-
> tion for all those things which she cannot obtain within the present state of
> her existence. It can be recognized as a positive approach to fantasy because
> it provides her with the strength in an important area to proclaim her worth
> and perhaps, too, raises her level of self-esteem (1971:123).

Ladner also points out that "lookin' clean and stylin' '" are merely exten-
sions of material values in the dominant culture. Street women manifest
this concern in the way they handle tracks: for example, by shooting
only in the hands and wearing gloves, or by boasting that they are so
careful that they never get tracks at all. Also, there is a concern over not
becoming "greasy," i.e., disheveled and dirty. In fact, most women
addicts dress quite well and tastefully most of the time, and it is only
when a drug run has been going for some time that a woman will stop
paying attention to her appearance.

While "struttin' your stuff" or display of sexual attributes is important in attracting johns, dress is not considered essential in getting tricks:

> No. One thing I learned about a man is that they buy a piece of ass, You can
> come out there lookin' like this here, you'll cop. You come out there all
> dressed up, you might not get nowhere. If you come out there and he want a
> piece of ass, he don't care who you look like. He won't care if sores all over
> your arms. Tricks is not choosey.

However, it does serve to differentiate the quality of whoe, from "flat
backer" to "call girl." In addition it serves to identify pure status. Stylin'
in the form of dress is a key means of establishing status and of
creating the illusions necessary to execute a variety of games effectively,
ranging from check passing to using males for exploitive purposes. But
even respect established through appearance is tenuous, since women
are subject to "rip-offs," or theft. While a man may always keep his
"rep," or reputation, a woman may easily lose the materials she has
acquired in creating her image. The power and prestige aspects of life are
very important to street women, although there is clearly a conflict
in many women's minds concerning the degradation involved in
"whoein' '" and many addict women claim that they did not "peddle
their asses." There is also compensatory pride in hustling ability and a
positive focus on the material rewards obtained as a result of the activity.

4. Turning Around

With a few exceptions, rehabilitation of women addicts has focused
on sexual aspects of personal identity. By emphasizing sexuality, such
efforts ignore economic skills developed in the street and conflicts over

status and prestige which result from women's position in the hustling hierarchy. Therapeutic communities are 24-hour facilities that rely on encounter groups, behavior modification, and isolation from the street environment as methods of rehabilitation. The first therapeutic community was Synanon. Others include Daytop and Phoenix House (for a complete discussion of therapeutic communities see Yablonsky 1965; Sugarman 1974). As in other mental health settings, the objective is the reintegration of the individual into mainstream society. The definition of mainstream values in such institutions has a unique quality, however, since most of the staffs are mainly ex-addicts. Expectations for behavior are a combination of reversed or transformed street values, middle-class mores, and rules oriented toward communal life. The basic goal of such programs is to "turn the addict around" or to rehabilitate him or her. In this process, many street values and behaviors are transformed or literally reversed.

One illustration of this is the management of sexual encounters at one therapeutic community where I conducted research a number of years ago. Sexuality is a particularly powerful force in therapeutic settings and each institution has its own unique way of handling it. In some therapeutic communities, no sexual contact is permitted. Many others have less rigid policies. In the therapeutic community in question, rooms called "guest rooms" were set aside for this purpose.

In order for a couple to spend a night in a guest room, permission must be given by the staff. In addition, each partner is subject to interrogation in encounter groups, in order to evaluate their level of commitment. The couple is also teased and harassed during and after the event. Other residents continually knock on the door and yell directions and encouragements throughout the proceedings. Between the couple there is ritualized division of labor. The male is responsible for the preparation of the room, borrowing colored lights, records and record player or radio, and flowers. The female borrows clothing and makeup and spends a considerable amount of time preparing herself for the evening. The entire event is structured and monitored by the staff and other residents according to the unique value orientation of the therapeutic community. Some elements, such as staff and resident participation and borrowing behavior, are a reflection of communal intimacy. Most personal property is taken away when a resident enters the house, so that resources are limited and often shared. Therapeutic monitoring and the intimacy of 24-hour proximity mean that there are no secrets in the house. Where sexual activity is limited, residents are permitted to participate vicariously through hazing and elicitation of details afterward.

The most striking thing about this event, however, is the exaggeration and stylization of middle-class monogamous norms. The structure of the event is an attempt to reverse street sexuality with its businesslike, uninvolved, and exploitive atmosphere. Residents must prove themselves to be "in love" and the entire event is romanticized in the extreme. Any indication of temporary involvement for sexual gratification only is discouraged, except in older residents who are given passes to go outside the house to "take care of business." This fairyland approach to sexuality is appealing to many new female residents as it recalls childhood fantasies of ideal adult life:

> In the early stages of treatment, female clients try to emulate their perception of "other women" in American society. The portrait emerges of women who want to be sexually alluring, experience romance (courtship and marriage), have babies, wear pink ribbons and be passive and submissive in relating to men (Levy and Broudy 1975:293).

In their search for identity, they are often met with a variety of mixed messages, unattainable and unsatisfying alternatives, and male-oriented demands.

Rehabilitation constitutes a purification process. For men this involves a turning away from drugs. For women it involves a double transformation of both drug use patterns and sexual behavior. As was mentioned above, women experience difficulty establishing their self-respect on the street, resulting in part from conflicts between the values they were raised with and "what they have to do to get over." In the street, this conflict is partially resolved by defining prostitution as an economic necessity and focusing on the power aspects of interaction with johns. In the therapeutic environment, the legitimacy of this perspective is denied and exploration of deep-level guilts is encouraged.

Hustling ability of male residents is honored and attempts are made to redirect skills toward an ethic of "positive manipulation." There is very little complimentary recognition of hustling skills developed by the whoe while she was in the street. Rather her relationship with the john is seen as a source of degradation. The whoe herself experiences considerable conflict over her hustling role and resolution of her guilt feelings is important to her readjustment. The atmosphere in which this is to be accomplished, however, often functions in such a way as to make it extremely difficult for her to readjust. In many instances her confessionals are performed in the context of groups, in the presence of male residents who have not "gotten down" since they entered the house. There is thus a voyeuristic overtone to these events. There is no complimentary confessional of shame on the part of male residents who may have sexually exploited women on the street. The reason for this is partially that men do not often engage in deviant or frequent sexual activity as a part of the hustle, as women are required to do in servicing johns. Male exploitation of sexual needs is more often psychological rather than physical. In addition some feminists might claim that the sadomasochistic orientation of the pimp game is more closely related to acceptable standards of sexual ownership and interaction than is the activity of turning tricks, and that therefore, male clients are not required to make major adjustments in their orientation.

A double standard is enforced in a variety of ways. The first demand placed on the whoe in the therapeutic community is that she change her image with regard to feminine appearance. Women are often accused of being openly seductive. Modesty of dress is a major concern in most houses. Attention is given to length of skirts and decolletage, as well as style of walk and stance. No parallel attention is given to seductiveness on the part of male clients. One of the reasons for this differential treatment is structural. Overall, women make up between one-fifth and one-third of treatment populations (Levy and Broudy 1975). This unequal distribution, in addition to tight controls on sexuality, contributes to a high level of frustration and tension in the house. Women are often scapegoated in this situation. The orientation tends to emphasize shameful aspects of dress and style, reversing street norms which define dress as a source of prestige. This reversal is reinforced by the scarcity of clothing in the communal setting. The one unambiguous source of status in the street is thus reinterpreted.

In addition to a predominance of male clients, the staffs of all but a few therapeutic communities are mainly male, and therapy for women has been male-dominated. One of the most blatant examples of the consequences of this was described by Schultz to Kaubin, who reported her colleague's experience:

> Since the program she was working in prohibited sexual relations among residents, the residents were encouraged to masturbate. At one point some of the female residents came to her complaining that a male therapist had explained how to masturbate: each woman should stick a finger up her vagina and wiggle it. For some reason this wasn't working (1974:477–478).

In encounters, women are outnumbered by men. They often serve a function of being used for projection of feelings about women by males in the group. The encounter itself is an extremely aggressive activity and much emphasis is placed on the expression of anger. As was noted above, street women have a great deal of repressed anger. They are encouraged to express it in groups and to assert themselves as independent beings. At the same time they are often the recipients of vitriolic attacks by the males in the group, who outnumber them. This is accompanied by expressions of contempt such as "whoe," "bitch," and "cunt," since vocabulary in groups is peppered with street expressions. As was mentioned, this is combined with voyeuristic discussion of sexual acts performed on the street, legitimized by the premise that women addicts suffer primarily from psychosexual dysfunction. The purpose of this activity is to bring the resident to a point where the ego structure that has developed in the street collapses. At this point alternative roles and behaviors are encouraged and the individual is expected to explore and develop these outside the encounter.

Alternatives offered to women generally take the form of traditional roles. Emphasis is placed on developing parenting skills and reorienting toward acceptable sexual conduct. Behaviors related to street survival are rarely encouraged or utilized in attempts to shape a new personality:

> Women were being taught a new set of behaviors to please males. They were told to give up their sleazy bitch street ways, and to stop using their cunts to attract men. If a woman happened to be naturally sexy and sensuous, she was accused of seducing the men, and chastised. If she was unfemininely aggressive and angry, she was told she was treacherous and that she was losing her sensitivity and humanity. If she was Lesbian, she was accused of being a man-hater and "sick." She was learning, again, to repress a part of herself which belonged to her and to become an "honest paper doll" cut out in man's image (Schultz 1974:19).

In short, while males are encouraged to use the skills and qualities they gained on the street in reforming their personalities, women are encouraged to deny those aspects of themselves which contributed to their street survival.

This differential approach expresses itself most clearly in the area of economic preparation, which includes job assignments in the house and vocational training. Males' natural hustling abilities are often turned to the acquisition of goods for the house by hustling donations of goods from business men. Men are assigned to traditional masculine activities such as repair and engineering while women are often assigned household and secretarial work. My own experience as participant observer is instructive in this regard. When given an opportunity to choose a job, I decided to test the system by requesting work on the "engineering crew," having observed that there were no women in that department. Curiously enough I was assigned a gardening job within the department. Like the men on the crew, I did not change my attire at dinner time. After one week, I was confronted in encounter for not being feminine and looking like a "bull dagger" (lesbian). I was reassigned to a waitress job, while the men on the crew continued to wear their work clothes to dinner. The message that women are ultimately destined to be men's helpmates is also reinforced by a practice described by Peak and Glankoff (1975) as acquisition of female patients as booty. It is not uncommon for women patients who are doing particularly well to develop relationships with male staff members. Such behavior, while sometimes a source of concern, generally means advancement for the client.

Overall, female clients are less likely to complete treatment successfully. At the conference on women and drug abuse cited above, therapists reported that although women are outnumbered by men in programs, their dropout rate is higher. A number of explanations have been used in explaining this phenomenon, ranging from sociological and psychological arguments that women, who have more problems, are more difficult to treat, to arguments that women have more outside commitments to lovers and children and are less likely to remain in isolated settings as a consequence, to interpretations based on the idea that it is easier for a woman to acquire money and maintain herself on the street. Feminist analysts, however, maintain that it is a consequence of discrimination in an environment of male ex-addicts who continue to unconsciously hold the street view of women while demanding that women assume roles matched to their ideals of womanhood. From an anthropological viewpoint, it would seem that there are two structural factors contributing to women's failure in treatment. First, the role definition set as an ideal in the therapeutic community is such that, although it appeals to childhood expectations of addicted women, it is very difficult to attain. The problem is compounded by the fact that female residents do not have access to role models because of all-male staffs. In addition, as Levy and Broudy (1975) point out, women who work on therapeutic community staffs are often career- rather than home- and family-oriented. Second, during the treatment process women are exposed to mixed messages that emphasize guilt and unworthiness while denying skills and strengths developed in the street.

5. Sex Role Definition as Cultural Variation

Sex role definitions in the street and in therapeutic communities are variations of mainstream values which are adapted to particular environmental demands. In both cases, the traditional position of woman as structural inferior is maintained, although in the latter case the women's movement has begun to have the effect of reversing this trend. In the street, economic scarcity is a prime feature that shapes variation. Sexuality is used as an exploitable resource. In the absence of economic stability, women rely on appearance and short-term conspicuous consumption as a source of prestige. Emphasis is placed on personal appearance rather than on home, husband, and children, and on gaming rather than on career skills acceptable in the mainstream. The addict prostitute finds it difficult to live up to the image of faithful wife in an economic environment that does not provide the resources necessary for the maintenance of a stable household. Thus, when she has a pimp, sexual ownership is replaced by "leasing agreements." Compensation often takes the form of power manipulation with regard to male clients and focuses on external manifestations of womanhood as a source of self-respect. In the therapeutic community, sources of status available on the street are denied and residents are asked to return to traditional sex roles. The criteria for conduct are limited by a number of structural features, which, in fact, do not correspond to environmental features typical of monogamous relationships. The distribution of material goods is mainly communal and sexuality is monitored and publicly evaluated.

In addition, three factors shape women's behavior in the house. First, the unequal ratio of men to women creates sexual tensions that are controlled by emphasis on modesty and suppression of overt sexual display. Second, male-dominated staffing has a tendency to encourage male-oriented standards of feminine identity. Third, the psychosexual theory of the etiology of female addiction places emphasis on pathological aspects of women's behavior on the street. This, in turn, often leads to denial of skills gained in the street environment.

As many feminists have argued, realignment of treatment by increasing female staff and encouraging more flexible sex role alternatives may in fact render treatment of women more effective. Such readjustments may lead to the elimination of ambiguities brought about by contrasts between negative definitions of street behavior and positive definitions of idealized traditional behavior. Also, expanded vocational opportunities would provide women with an opportunity to redirect skills gained in the street environment.

ACKNOWLEDGMENT

Research for this chapter, conducted in New York City in 1973 and in Miami in 1975, was supported by Public Health Service Research Grant # DA01073-02 of the National Institute on Drug Abuse at the Division of Addiction Sciences, Department of Psychiatry, University of Miami.

References

Abrahams, Roger D. 1964. *Deep Down in the Jungle*. Hatboro, Pa.: Folklore Associates.

Agar, Michael. 1973. *Ripping and Running: A Formal Ethnography of Urban Heroin Addicts*. New York: Academic Press.

Atkinson, Ti-Grace. 1974. *Amazon Odyssey*. New York: Links Books.

Brecher, Edward M. and the editors of *Consumer Reports*. 1972. *Licit and Illicit Drugs*. Mt. Vernon, N.Y.: Consumers Union.

Chein, Isidor, Donald L. Gerard, Robert S. Lee, and Eva Rosenfeld. 1964. *The Road to H: Narcotics, Delinquency and Social Policy*. New York: Basic Books.

Chesler, Phyllis. 1972. *Women and Madness*. New York: Avon Books.

Christenson, Susan J. and Alice Q. Swanson. 1974. Women and drug use: An annotated bibliography. *Journal of Psychedelic Drugs* 6(4):371–414.

Cleckner, Patricia J. and Karen S. Wells. 1976. Some results of the survey of participants in the National Forum on Women, Alcohol and Drugs. In *Drugs Alcohol and Women: A National Forum Source Book*. Washington, D.C.: National Research and Communications Associates. 250–268.

Dai, Bingham. 1937. *Opium Addiction in Chicago*. Montclair, N.J.: Patterson Smith.

Kaubin, Brenda J. 1974. Sexism shades the lives and treatment of female addicts. *Contemporary Drug Problems* 3(4):471–484.

Kolb, Lawrence. 1938. Drug addiction among women. *Proceedings of the American Prison Association*. New York. 349–357.

Kron, Yves J. and Edward M. Brown. 1965. *Mainline to Nowhere: The Making of a Heroin Addict*. Cleveland: World Publishing.

Ladner, Joyce A. 1971. *Tomorrow's Tomorrow: The Black Woman*. New York: Doubleday.

Levy, Stephen J. and Marie Broudy. 1975. Sex role differences in the therapeutic community: Moving from sexism to androgyny. *Journal of Psychedelic Drugs* 7(3):291–297.

Liebow, Elliot. 1967. *Tally's Corner: A Study of Negro Streetcorner Men*. Boston: Little, Brown.

Lightnin' Rod. 1973. *Hustler's Convention*. New York: Crown.

Lindesmith, Alfred. 1965. *The Addict and the Law*. New York: Random House.

Milner, Christina and Richard Milner. 1972. *Black Players*. Boston: Little, Brown.

Peak, Jeannie L. and Peter Glankoff. 1975. The female patient as booty. In E. Senay, V. Shorty, and H. Alksne (eds.), *Developments in the Field of Drug Abuse*. Cambridge, Mass.: Schenkman. 509–512.

Schultz, Ardelle M. 1974. Radical feminism: A treatment modality for addicted women. Paper presented at the National Drug Abuse Conference, Chicago. Xerox.

Sugarman, Barry. 1974. *Daytop Village: A Therapeutic Community*. New York: Holt, Rinehart & Winston.

Tyler, Stephen A. (ed.). 1969. *Cognitive Anthropology*. New York: Holt, Rinehart & Winston.

Waldorf, Dan. 1973. *Careers in Dope*. Englewood Cliffs, N.J.: Prentice-Hall.

Weppner, Robert S. 1973. An anthropological view of the street addict's world. *Human Organization* 32(2):111–121.

Yablonsky, Lewis. 1965. *Synanon: The Tunnel Back*. New York: Macmillan.

Index